Innovation and the Auto Industry

Innovation and the Auto Industry

Product, Process and Work Organization

Richard Whipp and Peter Clark

St Martin's Press   New York

First published in the United States of America in 1986

Printed in Great Britain

ISBN 0-312-41810-8

Library of Congress Cataloging-in-Publication Data
Whipp, Richard
    Innovation and the auto industry.
    Bibliography: p.
    Includes index.
    1. Automobile industry and trade—Great Britain—
Technological innovations.   2. Automobile industry
workers—Great Britain—Effect of technological
innovations on.   3. British Leyland Limited.
I. Clark, Peter A.   II. Title
HD9710.G72W45   1986   338.4 '56292 '0941   85-25200
ISBN 0-312-41810-8

Contents

List of Tables

List of Figures

Preface

This is the first book-length publication arising from the Economic and Social Research Council's intiative on work organization. The initiative, which established the Work Organization Research Centre (WORC), was devised to stimulate inter-disciplinary studies of innovation in Britain. The British automobile industry seemed a suitable place to begin such research. In spite of the social criticism and media attention which the industry has received there has been remarkably little research into design and innovation, nor sustained analysis of the changes in work organization during the last two notable decades. This book tries to remedy this neglect by exploring a key transitional period for the British auto industry via an examination of a major project situated within its appropriate national and international contexts.

The work of the late Bill Abernathy provided our analytical point of departure. Bill was a consultant to our research until his untimely death. He was especially keen to contribute his ideas on American industry towards an understanding of the European auto sector. In many respects he became a mentor to the project, influencing the formation of questions, giving advice freely and making provocative yet constructive criticism. Whilst the responsibility for the interpretation of these ideas remains our own, their development owes a great deal to his enthusiasm and inspiration.

In the course of our study we have received wide-ranging help which we are anxious to acknowledge. First and foremost we are indebted to those who work, or used to work, in the industry and who responded so generously to our questions. At their request they remain anonymous; their evidence is cited by reference to their function or title (sometimes abbreviated in order to preserve anonymity). The precise location of their interview evidence is indicated by the page number of interview transcripts or the tape indicator (TI) reading of tape-recorded testimony. Where unpublished documents are cited without an archival location, they have been supplied by individuals who do not wish to divulge their identities. During our research we were pleased to receive working papers and to benefit from discussions within the growing network of students of the international auto industry; citations are made below.

Among our colleagues in WORC, Dr Jennifer Tann alerted us to the existence of the Rover Archive (now in the possession of the British Motor Industry Heritage Trust, Studley, Warwickshire); Professor Ray Loveridge loaned his research notes on the industry and made useful suggestions; Dr Chris Smith provided thoughtful commentary. Pat Clark assisted with the initial examination of the archive and with many other tasks. The book could not have been completed without the patient and caring contributions of Beryl Marston and Caroline Jury. The production of a full-length first draft was made possible by Beryl, who accomplished the task with her customary good humour and while mastering our outgoing word processing technology. Caroline produced the final copy whilst decoding the incoming generation of new technology; her calmness and exemplary work standards in the final concentrated phase of corrections and revisions maintained both our spirits and our good relations with the publisher.

Finally, we would like to thank Peter Moulson of Frances Pinter, who handled the commissioning and delivery of our manuscript with a reassuring courtesy and a commendable firmness.

Richard Whipp
Peter Clark
Aston University
June 1985

1 Introduction

The processes of innovation in the automobile industry have, up to now, been dealt with in very fragmentary ways. The aspects of innovation related to cars, plant and factory operations or the organization of work have each been dealt with by specialist writers. Some excellent studies have emerged, yet they do not sufficiently highlight the inter-linkages between the main problem areas. This book tries to break new ground by examining the experience of a British auto manufacturer in mounting a major innovation project in the context of the changing world car industry of the 1970s and 1980s. Detailed empirical investigation is combined with an attempt to synthesize and qualify the range of orthodox perspectives on innovation in the auto sector.

The book is in three parts:

I. an analysis of models of innovation and their relevance to the auto industry; the models are assessed in respect of their understanding of the links between design and innovation as well as their treatment of the interrelations between product, production process and work organization changes;
II. an in-depth study of the problems involved in design and innovation for car manufacturers in the last fifteen years;
III. an examination of the implications of the study for the way social scientists understand the auto industry.

Recent examinations of the industry have implied a great deal, but leave untreated the area which is at the centre of this study—the process of design and innovation. The study interprets design and innovation as the ability of an enterprise to envisage and deliberately create a new product (including its components) which may involve, by intention or indirectly, changes in the production process and the form of work organization. It is the way in which design has connections with and implications for so many features of an organization that makes it worthy of study.

Part I will indicate that design and innovation has become increasingly important in the context of the intensely competitive markets of the late twentieth century. It will be argued that design and innovation in the car industry has to be examined as part of the attempt by companies to create an ordered collection or 'portfolio' of productive units. The notion of the productive unit was proposed by Abernathy. As a unit of analysis, it does two things. First, it enables the large enterprise to be disaggregated into relevant component parts for the purpose of study. Second, it is useful for the examination of design and innovation because the productive unit refers to both product and production. Abernathy stated that

a special unit of analysis is therefore needed to encompass both the product and the characteristics of the manufacturing unit that produced it. . . . A productive unit is defined as the integral production process that is located at one place under a common management to produce a particular product line. The unit's characteristics are determined by a variety of factors—whether mass production is involved, how the production process is organised, the cost and type of equipment, and work force skills . . . such a unit might be an automobile assembly plant for a given type of car, or an automobile engine plant for a particular type of engine, or a stamping plant and the intended body. . . . The important feature of the definition is that both product and process characteristics are considered jointly. Together they best represent constraints and opportunities for change.[1]

The productive unit deals with the characteristics of the product and production process in some detail, but work organization is dealt with very generally and rather indirectly. It is here that a major revision and extension to the concept will be introduced. Abernathy did not address the overall organization of the enterprise in which the portfolio of productive units was generated. Nor did his analysis deal with the processes and politics involved; thus, the capacity to undertake design and innovation was taken for granted. This book will make the unravelling and reconstruction of these phenomena a central feature. The capacity of a major British car manufacturer to attempt a radical design and innovation project in the turbulent market conditions of the 1970s will be explored and explained via a four-part framework. In broad terms, this involved a detailed examination of the company/corporation's inclinations, resources and pattern of experience related to design and innovation. Second, this profile will in turn be related to the dominant characteristics of the automobile sector. An assessment is made of the extent to which the company and project in question embodied those features or tried to transform and even confront them. Third, the analysis of the project is deepened by the use of the comparative dimension. The distinctive reasons for the company/corporation's design capacity are revealed by comparing their experience with that of other producers, here and abroad. The generation of that capacity over the company's life-course during the twentieth century is made clear by the fourth element of the framework, the use of an historical perspective.

The case study presented in Part II has been selected in order to highlight the complex nature of design and innovation. Part II is devoted to an exploration of the British Leyland SD1 project—a venture conceived in 1968, operational in 1976 and shut down in 1982. The contention is that by examining the Rover Company—which became part of British Leyland in 1968 and was chosen to house the project in 1971—over its seventy-year history, a crucial dimension is brought to the prevailing analyses of the auto industry. The integration of past and present offers a more insightful view of how and why design and innovation exhibits the long-term patterns and immediate forms that it does. The well established arrangement of the Rover Company's business strategy and design capacity, with their imbalanced attention to the product at the expense of production or work organization, is contrasted to the crisis-ridden attempts of BL to create a corporate strategy. The structural tensions which were set up by the incompatibility of the two strategies are traced through the SD1 project, the first major project undertaken by the corporation. The key phases of the project, from concept through to translation, commissioning and operation, are reconstructed using evidence and testimony relating to all levels of the enterprise, including corporation and division, company and plant, management and work-force. The facets of the SD1 exercise are aligned with its wider sectoral setting. The result is that the project becomes a first-rate prism through which one can view the changes involved in the re-structuring of the auto industry during the upheavals of the 1970s.

Part III presents the conclusions of the study. Automobile manufacture has so often been taken as the very emblem of twentieth-century industry, and its methods of operation regarded as the leading edge of work organization practices. We will suggest that this image of the car industry, portrayed by the social science community, was overdrawn for the industry in Britain in the past and given the changes of the 1970s and 1980s, that picture is now sorely outmoded.

Notes

1. W. J. Abernathy, *The Productivity Dilemma. Roadblock to Innovation in the Automobile Industry*, Baltimore, 1978, p. 49.

PART I

2 Innovation and industrial change

The retardation debate is the generic title given to the growing collection of essays and books which offer an interpretation of the relative economic decline of Britain since 1965 and earlier, possibly since 1890. Some analysts contend that Britain's position in the late twentieth century North Atlantic will parallel the decline experienced in the late sixteenth century by Spain in the context of the Mediterranean. There is widespread agreement among all analysts that if the tendencies of the seventies continue throughout the rest of the century, then the GNP per head for Britain will be amongst the lowest in Europe by the mid-1990s. Yet, as Mathias and Caves observe,[1] the actual rate of increase in GNP since 1965 is substantially above that obtaining through the whole period of great economic growth and influence in the nineteenth century. The comparison is that other countries have achieved a faster rate of growth. Central to the explanations of the comparative rates of growth has been the argument that industrial change in Britain is slower, more costly and less productive than that of major enterprises in other comparable societies.

The capacity to introduce major, strategic innovations on a periodic basis, and/or to maintain a steady amount of incremental innovation, is regarded as vital by many participants in the retardation debate. Strategic innovation is the name which is often variously used to describe such large-scale changes within enterprises. Strategic innovation refers to changes in technology and forms of work organization at all levels, which includes boards of directors or the various interfaces between a company and its suppliers or potential customers. Strategic innovation also embraces the technologies and forms of work organization adopted in the design and planning of an innovation and its execution, from the commissioning of new production facilities through to its operational form. While the capacity to develop and facilitate strategic innovation is regarded as a central requirement in contemporary capitalist competition, little attention has been given to the range of forces and components involved.[2]

Innovation has been approached by economists, yet it remains apparently very much of a 'black box'.[3] The bulk of their attention has been towards innovations in products or production processes; work organization has been largely ignored or its changing form seen largely as residual. Little progress has been made in unravelling the roles and relationships which appear within the process of innovation, most notably those relating to management and labour. Key features of innovation, such as design, have received only partial treatment from specialist interests.[4] The small number of existing studies in strategic innovation are insufficiently historical and comparative, and the field is marked by a continuing fragmentation of effort between disciplines. This book seeks to address these limitations. Perspectives and studies which have dealt with innovation in a fragmentary manner will be reorganized here around the theme of design and innovation. The study will contribute to the dissolution of certain, though by no means all, disciplinary boundaries.

The major theme of this chapter is the exploration of design and innovation as a totality. Writers have seldom attempted to grasp the total process of innovation; instead it has been approached via specialist concerns. Considerable efforts have been made by economists in the past to analyse patterns of innovation in products or production arrangements, while changes in work organzation have been dealt with separately by social scientists. In this book the intention is to encompass design and innovation as a totality by recognizing that changes in product, production and work organization are intimately related and cannot adequately be understood apart. This approach builds on the seminal work on innovation by Abernathy, who used engineering and economic analyses to understand the long-term changes in products and production processes.[5] By adding the insights offered by social scientists, and in particular their knowledge of work organization, one can offer an important extension of his work. Design and innovation of a productive unit—the combination of a product, its process of manufacture and the form of work organization involved—is the object of this study. A review of existing approaches to innovation follows in Section I; the following sections outline how the differing specialist concerns can be synthesized and used to form a new framework of enquiry.

Sections II–V of this chapter outline a four-part framework for examining design and innovation. The distinctiveness of the framework lies in its combination of four main elements. Innovation in productive units is examined along two major dimensions, the historical and the comparative; it is in turn analysed at two main levels, the sector and the enterprise. The historical and comparative study of innovation has not been strongly developed hitherto in the combined sense, while few studies have applied these two dimensions to innovative activity at the sectoral and enterprise levels. This chapter presents the framework in the following way. Section II demonstrates the relevance of the historical dimension. It is argued that processes of change can be conceptualized in both narrative and schematic ways. In addition, these processes require reconstruction according to the multiple time frames and trajectories involved. The ability to distinguish long-term trends from short-term shifts provides a vital means of assessing the degree of innovativeness in any given project, as well as differentiating apparent novelty from what may be cyclical phenomena. The way in which chosen alterations in productive units may seek to break with, yet at the same time embody the past, is also addressed. Section III is concerned with the comparative dimension. This part of the framework exposes the need to compare innovation (whether in a single enterprise or in aggregate terms across an industry) both within a country and between societies. It is hypothesized that there is a distinctive pattern of innovative activity across the British economy and that this pattern differs from those of other nations owing to the different societal cultures involved.

Sections IV and V deal with the sector and enterprise as key contexts for innovations. After constructing a working understanding of 'the sector', Section IV maintains that the evolution of sectors through their life cycle is critical to understanding the detailed form of innovation within productive units. Social, economic and political pressures meet at the level of the sector with the result that, over the long term, these forces condition the form which productive units may take at any given point. Sectors exhibit often unique bodies of thought and generic forms of technological or social development which inform the process of design and innovation. Section V begins by defining the different types of innovation related to the productive unit within an enterprise, and then indicates how they are connected to the sectoral level via a 'case-in-sector' approach. Insights from diverse specialist treatments of innovation will help to reveal the structural, cultural and political aspects of design and innovation. A simple processual model of design and innovation is constructed: this will provide a basic research tool to be developed in later chapters. How the four-part framework will be applied to the study of the SD1 project in the context of the British car industry is indicated in each of the sections in this chapter.

I Design and innovation

This book presents a framework which has been constructed to examine industrial change and innovation in general, and has been applied in a specific case-in-sector investigation of the automobile industry.[6] Design and innovation in the automobile industry has not hitherto been the subject of scholarly attention. During the period in question, a major restructuring of British-owned firms occurred, most notably between Leyland and the British Motor Corporation, yet also involving smaller, specialist firms like Rover and Jaguar. Shortly after the creation of British Leyland, its senior management began a process of strategic innovations, including the project for using Rover as the base for a 'European luxury car'. By the mid-1970s the parent company was in deep financial trouble, and the state intervened. Other major projects were started, including the Metro and the collaboration with Japanese firms. The events of the period from 1965 to the 1980s are often presented as though new tendencies occurred which were suddenly disruptive, but have now been overcome. This viewpoint implies that the historical causes have been understood, and the implications for the future adequately digested. In this research we attempt to construct a framework which will provide a detached yet focused assessment of the problems of design and innovation in that industry.

It is necessary to construct a framework because the existing analytical approaches to innovation are lacking. Whilst economists interested in innovation have concentrated on products and production processes,[7] writers on work organization have also shown preferences. It is exceptional for authors, from whatever background, to attempt to deal with the interrelationships of product, production and work organization. This point is developed in the next section, which is followed by a statement of the main components of an alternative framework. The second half of the chapter will outline the four elements of our framework for analysing design and innovation.

Engineers who have tackled the area of design and innovation have traditionally limited their attention to product development and project methodology. Although one authority in the area defines engineering design as 'a purposeful activity directed towards the goal of fulfilling human needs, particularly those which can be met by technological factors of our civilisation',[8] the concerns of engineers have been more pragmatic. The same author's handbook in effect limits engineering design 'to those areas where the logical application of scientific principles is an essential method of solution'. The bulk of his time is spent dealing with models of 'Design Procedure', 'Techniques of Problem Formulation' or 'Techniques for Creative Thinking'.[9] Clearly, these tell us a good deal about the practising design engineer, but this treatment of design by itself is of little value to those who seek to understand the processes of design and innovation set within their wider social contexts. Only recently have engineers such as Cooley addressed these issues by in fact challenging engineering conventions and asking 'who designs?' and 'for what purpose?'.[10] Chapter 4 will show how the accepted values and practices of Rover's and British Leyland's engineers help explain part of the course of the SD1 project. Yet the project also indicates how the actions of the engineers were only a small element in the more complex set of relationships involved.

The extent of research by social scientists on production techniques, work organization and management or worker behaviour would, at first sight, appear promising for the analysis of design and innovation. However, in common with other disciplines, their examinations have either been directed to very specific needs or noted for important blind spots. Organization theorists, management scientists and technology specialists have gravitated towards the problems of structure and the means of achieving efficient, rational design. Explorations of change, governance and the labour process are given less attention. Indeed, governance is treated as unproblematic in the mainstream management literature in relation to design.

The essential objective of the orthodox approaches has been to provide a general diagnostic theory which can be applied to any sort of work organization. The diagnostic theory can now be codified into a pedagogy of rules which can readily be taught in schools of business and which may become incorporated into the software of expert systems. There are a number of cogent statements of the diagnostic theory and extensive reviews of the relevant literature.[11] The diagnostic theory mainly provides legitimacy to the notion of a managerial dynamic as the visible guiding hand allocating resources, but the theory has only been used occasionally in direct interventions in enterprises.[12]

The theories of organization design contend that enterprises possess a structure of decision making which should contain a defined capacity to encode incoming information and translate this information into actions. The existing pedagogy assumes that it is possible to construct a design blueprint of the most appropriate form of work organization. The theory presents the possibility of designing a range of alternative forms of work organization for the same set of tasks.[13] Certainly the diagnostic theory is more subtle than the radical critiques suggest.[14] Yet appropriateness is judged implicitly,[15] and it is assumed that corporate executives have the power to shape work organization according to the blueprint. It is assumed that if the executives fail in this task, then an underlying Darwinian logic will eliminate the inappropriate forms in the competition between capitals. The details of the social selection process in organization design have been elaborated by Aldrich and McKelvey.[16]

The orthodox approach has adopted a well-established American practice of organizing knowledge in terms of those variables which are influential and are assumed to be open to the control of rational agents. It is notable that the earlier, post-war emphasis on leadership has been massively extended to the whole area of what Chandler termed the 'economies of co-ordination'. Consequently, the blueprints neglect the historical origins and capacities of the enterprise, and assume that its members are largely inert agents, bonded with a common, undisputed framework of legitimized authority.

Structure is the central notion and the objective of design here. The aim is to prescribe structure in the singular.[17] There are three dominant ways in which structure is conceptualized, though it is assumed that the three varieties of usage are essentially complementary. Structure may be defined as prescriptions and artifacts,[18] and/or as stable, enduring attitudes,[19] and/or as enduring configurations of differentiation and integration.[20] Structure is theorized as singular—the structure—and treated largely as though it were homogeneous through levels of the enterprise. This feature is sometimes moderated, especially in the distinctions of hierarchy introduced by Tannenbaum.[21] However, without exception, the structure is treated as homogenous through time.[22] This crucial assumption leads to the neglect of strategic innovation and to the omission of the analysis of the structural dynamics of its achievement.[23]

Research methodology in the structural approach tends to consist of certain basic features. A medium-sized sample, say fifty establishments, is selected and key informants are invited to provide answers to several hundred items, sets of which make up the basic variables in the analytic approach. Each variable, such as centralization, can therefore be tapped by using remote indicators which permit the research to produce a more impressive profile of the structure of the establishment than either its executives or other case-based research methodologies could have produced themselves. The methodology of the conventional structural approach requires only short, focused visits to the sites, and thus causes only slight disruption whilst sometimes providing management with feedback. In the case of attitude studies, the members of an enterprise are normally corralled into groups which are then instructed and receive questionnaires to complete. In any of the approaches to structure, the aim is to take a cross-sectional slice of an organization, because the total sample of slices provides the answers which are sought. The definition of a longitudinal study becomes that of making a second visit to the establishment at some later date to re-apply the same instruments and to probe for changes. The absence of change is often taken as verification of the ability of this approach towards structure to have abstracted the important features. Longitudinal research, therefore, is a simple extension of the basic methodology constructed to tap lagged effects between variables. There are impressive indications of what can be learnt from this dominant methodology, in spite of the way it ignores the problem of historical reconstruction.

The 'before' and 'after' research strategy is a major subvariant, and an important one. It has largely been used to examine changes in work organization thought to be associated with the introduction of new technology. This template of research enquiry was established and laid down in the early 1960s, and has been used frequently since. There is a problem arising from the tendency in orthodox studies to attribute the difference between the before-profit and the after-profit situation to changes in technology. As a result, technology is reified and theorized as an exogenous, abstract force to which changes can be attributed. No attention is given to the processes of strategic innovation, nor of incremental innovation within which the specific position in an establishment should be theorized. The limitations of this will be addressed below.

Orthodox approaches do have numerous positive features which are often neglected by their critics. The manifesto of the orthodox approach promulgated in the very early 1960s was centred on a critique of the then dominant case-work approach in which vast generalizations were hitched to single case studies juxtaposed beside abstracted frameworks. Gouldner's study of bureaucracy exemplified the case approach.[24] The manifesto of the now orthodox approach sought to ground empirical work in a more articulated and more precise specification of how concepts were operationalized and a more statistically shaped set of generalizations. Since then, the orthodox structure approach has challenged romantic case studies and exposed the covering law models hidden in their presentation. These are not small achievements. At the level of empirical findings, these studies seem to have uncovered a small number of immutable tendencies which occur irrespective of time or place. Size is the central variable around which other important features seem to configure in an almost universal manner.[25]

However, there has been too partial a theorization of the findings of these empirical investigations, and insufficient explicit attention has been given to the problems of politics and organizational governance. The entire area of the labour process has been avoided. Similarly, the problems of innovation and of the diffusion of innovations have been dealt with in a very unsatisfactory manner. The range of alternative forms of work organization revealed by the orthodox approach, whilst impressive, has not resulted in the imaginative examination of alternatives.[26]

The neglect of strategic innovation has been achieved by the once implicit, now increasingly explicit, reliance on a socio-evolutionary theory in organizational studies. Thus, attention is given to the institutional level, especially the relationships between top executives and their suppliers of resources: banks, other corporations and the state, for example. The influence of the transaction costs approach of Williamson has led to the increased recognition of organization failures. This recognition has been reinforced by the economic movements of the 1970s, particularly those emanating from increased market competition world-wide. Even so, there is a relatively complacent view of adaptation by enterprises in the literature, which rests mainly on American experience. The focus is on populations of establishments, and the claim is that the adaptation process is inevitable. In an influential piece of reasoning about organizational change, March[27] correctly draws attention to the slow yet persistent ways in which standard operating procedures are modified in daily practice, thereby facilitating adaptation. A similarly sanguine viewpoint pervades a seven-sector analysis of the adaptive potential of American enterprises in the twentieth century.[28] All these important explications of the orthodox structure approach fail to address the acute problems of industrial change faced in the British context.

Orthodox structural approaches have been vigorously challenged by the so-called 'radical' writers (sometimes referred to as 'radical structuralists'). Undoubtedly the most influential challenge to the hitherto dominant approach came from Braverman and the labour process debate which his work is said to have initiated in the mid-1970s.[29] The debate questioned that work should inevitably be run by 'bosses' or managers, and that this was necessarily the most 'efficient' means. Braverman and his followers argued that, far from taking the form of the modern enterprise as given, as in the orthodox literature, it had in fact to be explained. The distinctive features of business in the mature capitalist economy was its hierarchical ordering. The explanation for this hierarchy lay in its profitability. Greater control over the labour process enabled employers to increase their profits. As Edwards put it: 'To understand the reason for workplace hierarchy and to comprehend the twentieth century transformation of the labor [sic] process, we need to focus on the profit system— that is, on capitalism.'[30] Yet, the radical writers' concentration on the capitalist profit system led them to ascribe to managers an almost unfettered power to design and organize their chosen forms of the labour process. In 1974, in eg France, Aglietta argued that the even resourceful technocrats employed by capital had switched to teamwork and unilaterally defined it as the new model form of work organization.[31] The radical structuralists relied heavily in their early work on the experience of the American economy: understandably, their attention was drawn to the phenomenal growth of the American corporations and their industrial oligopoly. The consistent theme within most accounts of this growth has been the ability of employers to organize, re-organize and indeed revolutionize the labour process.[32]

British labour historians and some industrial sociologists have found the growth of capitalism in their country to be rather different. The distinctive feature of the British experience of industrialization has been its combined and yet uneven development.[33] Whilst capital accumulation may be 'the fundamental dynamic of capitalism', it has been played out with wide variations and in the context of numerous influences. The degree of competition and conflict, size of enterprises, extent of unionization, the nature of worker consciousness and the degree of state intervention, *inter alia*, may shape or constrain the process of accumulation at the level of the firm or sector.[34] Great emphasis has been placed on the 'peculiarity' of the British road to capitalism.[35]

Detailed studies carried out within this broad approach have not only challenged the Bravermanesque line, but have indirectly undermined the orthodox position.[36] Two examples, drawn from examinations of skill and managerial strategy, illustrate the point that management unquestionably designs, creates and controls the labour process.

Penn argues that Braverman's proposition that 'the de-skilling of labour is part of a general tendency for capitalist managements to use scientific knowledge to subdivide labour and increase their control over all parts of the profit-making process' is not sustained by evidence from Britain. Instead, he points out how skilled manual work is a general and deeply-embedded feature of traditional British industry; occupations are organized around the identity of skill, and a range of norms dedicated to the presentation of skill. Not only are occupations actively structured around skill identities, they are translated into formal and informal organization. Penn demonstrates how machinery, throughout industrialization, has required skilled workers for both maintenance and operation.[37]

In a similar vein, Kelly and Wood have questioned the imprecise use of the term 'managerial strategy' in both organizational theory and amongst radical writers. They conclude that 'we cannot assume all firms have strategies, and certainly not in all areas and in any integrated fashion'. Furthermore, they show how the thrust of 'modern' personnel management and industrial relations thinking has been to encourage formal policies, since they apparently do not exist in practice in any widespread way.[38]

The orthodox approach is therefore being questioned from several directions. Although there are signs that counter-perspectives are now reorganized and gaining ground, the current production of texts indicates that the standard notion of managerial prerogatives in designing organizational structure remains alive and influential. The need is for a new approach to design and innovation which can do two things. First, it must synthesize the insights offered by the specialist interests identified above. Second, it should go beyond their limitations by focusing on the interrelationships involved in the design of products, production processes and work organization by addressing the multiple structures within the enterprise and by locating design and innovation within the appropriate historical perspective and comparative contexts.

Design and innovation have not been studied previously from an historical point of view combined with inter-sectorial and international comparisons. It is necessary therefore to establish a broad framework as an organizing device for research and analysis. Figure 2.1 is a schematic

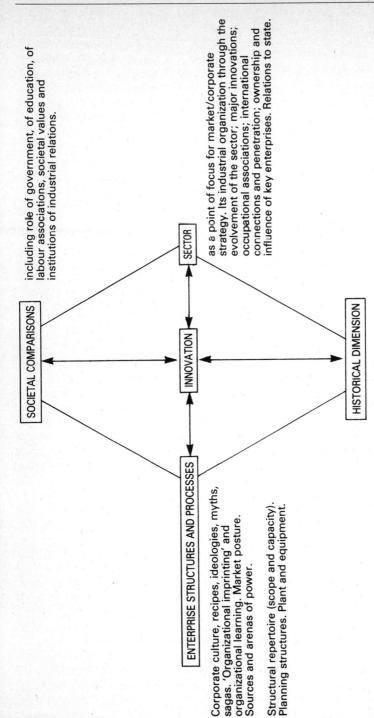

Figure 2.1 Framework of inquiry.

SOCIETAL COMPARISONS

including role of government, of education, of labour associations, societal values and institutions of industrial relations.

SECTOR

as a point of focus for market/corporate strategy. Its industrial organization through the evolvement of the sector; major innovations; occupational associations; international connections and penetration; ownership and influence of key enterprises. Relations to state.

INNOVATION

HISTORICAL DIMENSION

ENTERPRISE STRUCTURES AND PROCESSES

Corporate culture, recipes, ideologies, myths, sagas. 'Organizational imprinting' and organizational learning. Market posture. Sources and arenas of power.

Structural repertoire (scope and capacity). Planning structures. Plant and equipment.

summary of the four major pillars of analysis which have been selectively combined. These pillars are: the historical dimension, the comparative dimension, the sector, and the enterprise.

Figure 2.1 is based on the first case-in-sector investigation undertaken in the automobile industry. The case is a reconstruction of the SD1 project conceived by British Leyland in 1971. The SD1 (Special Development 1) car was to be manufactured under the Rover marque in a totally new production facility in Solihull in the West Midlands. The Rover Company, which originated in Coventry in 1896 and moved to Solihull in 1939, remained an independent manufacturer of luxury cars until 1967, when the company finally merged with Leyland. In 1969, Leyland and the British Motor Corporation merged. At first, the Rover Company continued as a largely autonomous unit within BL, and Rover designers began their own project to produce a new P8 car. In 1971 the BL board took the decision to make a major incursion into the European luxury car market and transform the production capacity of the Rover Company. The new factory was opened in June 1976. Six years later, the plant was closed and production of the SD1 transferred to the BL Cowley plant, Oxford. In 1982, Austin Rover—the division of BL responsible for car production (except for Jaguar)—announced that it was collaborating with Nissan, a Japanese manufacturer, in the development of a replacement for the SD1.

The SD1 project is an excellent example of an attempt at design and innovation. At the level of the enterprise, this was not only the first major project undertaken by BL, it was clearly meant to be a strategic innovation involving key changes in product, production and work organization (see Figure 2.2). When the SD1 venture is located within the British car sector, it will be shown to have taken place at a critical moment in the development of both the British and world markets. The use of an historical and comparative dimension enhances the relevance of the project for an understanding of innovation in the automobile industry. The SD1 project bears the imprint of its immediate historical circumstances, together with all the hallmarks of Rover's and the sector's life-course over the twentieth century. The comparative context is equally revealing. As the SD1 project is set against the experience of other car companies in Britain and elsewhere, the distinctive pattern of design and innovation in the British industry emerges.

The study is based on primary and secondary material derived from the Rover Company, from British Leyland and from the car industry in general. Strong emphasis has been placed on documentary and archival material covering the period 1896–1982 which has been barely used up until now. Board minutes, production records, design blueprints, process sheets and contemporary photographs of plants and products, for example, have been used in an attempt to reconstruct the evolution of design and innovation in the Rover Company and BL. Key respondents have been interviewed in depth, ranging from the senior management through to the track workers involved, as well as car industry experts. Primary evidence has been compared against published sources; archival material was used to confirm or confront oral testimony. This range of

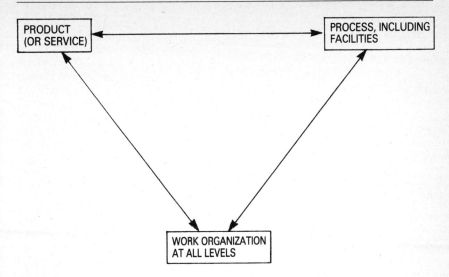

Figure 2.2 The triangle of dimensions.

evidence has been both assembled and interpreted by reference to our analytical framework which developed in parallel to the process of reconstruction. The framework is presented in the following four sections.

II Historical dimension

It is frequently stated that research on work organization should adopt a historical perspective.[39] Similar statements are made about design and business strategy.[40] Behind this agreement there seems to be remarkably little attention to the problematics of the directions which should be taken in order to achieve these objectives. How is the historical dimension made into a portable perspective? Any historical investigation must address four intimately connected issues: to what extent a narrative or schema provides the intellectual glue to a conceptualization of processes; the problematics of the time dimension, especially in accounting for events whose trajectories cannot adequately be understood in the single register of calendar and clock timing; detecting long-term tendencies and the issue of periodization, particularly the difficulty of identifying 'turning-points'; and determining the influence of the past on the present into the future.

First, there is a choice of whether to theorize processes within a narrative or within a generalizing, analytic schema. Many historians would dispute the claim that all their work is imbued with implicit models. There is little doubting that many historical studies are grounded in the objective of arranging events against the time-scale of the calendar in order to remove anachronisms.[41] Some historians have attempted to find a bridge between the choice of narrative as the 'thematic glue' for arranging events, and the construction of an analytic schema. The case for history as narrative has been put vigorously by Hexter[42] in his celebrated review of the work of the one historian who has led the attempt to bridge sociological and historical work, Braudel. The narrative approach presents history as a series of plots with an unfolding which is meaningful; there is a story to be told. Hexter cites the example of the 1951 baseball final in the United States in which there was a dramatic turnaround of events.

The exponents of the analytic approach have different intentions. They are trying to uncover patterns within diverse collections of events, possibly by detecting previously unseen mechanisms. The best and most influential example of this is in the dialectical analysis of capitalism by Marx, and its various elaborations: compare Mandel with Althusser and Thompson,[43] for example. The attempt to construct analytic schemas and to 'recover' immanent law-like propensities is equally contentious.

Today, the tendency is to stand between narrative and analytic schemas.[44] Arguably, one end of the bridge is occupied by the Annalists and the other by Gurvitch.[45] The debates between them (up to 1965) contain many points of agreement. We have chosen to situate the investigation of the British auto industry on the bridge between narrative and analytic schemas. Clearly, in the case of the Rover Company's seventy-year history there is a story to be told, with major episodes (such as the Land Rover, the P6 and the merger with Leyland) to be accounted for. Yet, by itself, such a narrative of events would be of limited use. It will be necessary therefore to situate the company's experience within the overall pattern of development in the British car industry, and to discover how far Rover conformed with or diverged from the larger mechanisms involved.

Second, there is the problem of 'time' in the historical study of work organization.[46] The problematic nature of time was hinted at in philosophy and history throughout the eighteenth and nineteenth centuries, yet these centuries were largely dominated by the Newtonian conception of a single, unitary, homogeneous time based around the movements of the earth and the mechanism of the clock. Between 1880 and 1914 this dominating idea was overthrown in the sciences, and especially in the humanities.[47] Leading thinkers promoted the theory of a plurality of time-reckoning systems, including sidereal time, and of the subjectivity of the experiences of time.[48] Although these paradigmatic shifts influenced some sociologists, historians and novelists, the striking feature is the degree to which their implications lie outside contemporary analyses. In sociology[49] and in history, the implications of these debates were partially carried forward, yet they have not sufficiently penetrated the study of innovation or work.

Marx correctly drew attention to the ways in which some capitalists were using the orderly framework of the calendar and the clock to commodify time, to reduce unproductive periods in the working day, and to schedule activities profitably. This tendency, only very slightly developed in the nineteenth century, became institutionalized in the twentieth century as 'best practice' in American enterprises.[50] Today, these temporal practices are spreading from capitalist enterprises into the public, non-market sector.[51] Modern social theorizing emphasizes a plurality of times and the relative, social construction of times, therefore, the analysis of the trajectories of events in which work organization is immersed requires attention to many different, parallel, possibly unconnected trajectories and to unintended consequences.[52] Braudel, and more recently Hareven, have argued that there are different time frames for the economy and for civil society and that the role of historical analysis is to reconstruct these diverse trajectories.

Third, the issue of long-term tendencies in industry should be related to the problem of periodization and of detecting turning-points, for example from extensive to intensive intensification of work, or from craft to mass production. Detecting discontinuities is problematic. Ramsay[53] has demonstrated that in Britain, since 1860, employers have adopted participative approaches most often when the economic conditions of trade have undermined the pressure of being a member of 'the reserve army of the unemployed'. There is an underlying tendency for the strategy of participation to be used cyclically, yet also for there to be a move towards gradually institutionalizing greater access by members of the work-force to areas of decision making. This has been restricted largely to the implementation of decisions rather than their strategic evolvement. Simmel[54] detected a similar pattern of 'structural dormancy' of a principle followed by its activation, with respect to the work organization of London tailors in the eighteenth and nineteenth centuries. During periods of anticipated warfare, the tailors were rigidly and hierarchically organized through the inns which were centres for contact with government agents. In times of peace, the tailors operated in a decentralized format. Similar principles of work organization underpinned the Birmingham arms industry in the nineteenth century.[55] In addition, Friedman[56] argues that employers in the Coventry auto industry adjusted their forms of work organization between direct control or responsible autonomy according to the strength of the market for cars. Each of these studies raises the issue: what has changed?

The problem has been addressed by Ladurie in his structure-event-structure perspective. This assumes that an existing structure contains a repertoire of interlocked behaviours and performances,[57] from which particular components can be activated according to the situation. An 'event' is a set of occurrences which alters some features of the repertoire. The alteration may be in the content of the repertoire (e.g. adding/dropping components) or in the relationship between situations and responses. Thus, an event is a turning-point in which novel elements are introduced and subsequently institutionalized in the new structure. Applying this mode of analysis to the research on Rover suggests that the history of the company can be periodized as follows: 1896–1924, Structure A; 1924–32, turning-point; 1932–63, Structure B; 1963–82, turning-point. After each transition point, the basic repertoire of the company was re-scripted. This theme is elaborated in Chapter 3.

Fourth, establishing the specific influence of the past upon the present and future is highly complex. The intention of historical sociology is to theorize from the past into the future. It is assumed that the past shapes and informs contemporary events, and hence the future to some degree. There are two variants of this assumption. One, associated with the

French Annales School and with Foucault, argues that there are hidden, 'silent', deeply sedimented rules which were laid down in the distant past, yet influence everyday life in the 1980s. This is the 'strong' case: the past shapes the future, strongly. According to this view, the individualism of the British postulated by some historians can be traced back to events occurring in the twelfth century. Exponents of the 'open' case combine a sensitivity to the ways in which the past might inform the future with a search for discontinuities and the emergence of novel elements. The open approach may be illustrated by Chandler's account of the emergence of a managerial stratum in the United States after 1870, and by Zeldin's analysis of new individualistic tendencies amongst the French.[58] The debate between the 'strong' and 'open' variants is fruitful, because it raises the issue of the degree to which the past may have an influence.[59] The problem is to identify the 'deep rules',[60] to uncover the ways in which they were laid down and the contexts in which this occurred,[61] and to assess the strength of their impact on present behaviour, if at all.

More,[62] for example, argues that in all the 'de-skilling debate', very little attention has been given to the systematic long-term development of training as the vehicle for the appropriation of skill during the development of the capitalist labour process. The close connection between training and the ownership of tasks remains unexplored: yet training is central. The introduction of training and its acceptance in the American setting in the nineteenth century constituted an important, novel development. The broad relevance of this has been explored by Parsons in his analysis of education as a means for maintaining the adaptive potential of American society. More concretely, Noble has sketched the linkages between corporate executives and higher education in the shaping of American managerial practices, but has not sufficiently explicated the training of operatives.[63] In the British context, the continuing absence of systematic operator training on an American scale has passed unnoticed. This omission is remarkable, especially when important aspects of the commissioning and operation of major projects—such as the SD1—rely on training to develop the necessary skills for new production methods, as will be seen in Chapter 5.

A significant yet unrecognized piece of structural differentiation in the automobile industry is that of the development of a separate design function and its transformation into a key adaptive mechanism within companies. There is clear evidence that, from 1906 to 1925, Ford developed the design of the car, the factory and the work organization around the explicit but rigid aim of optimizing productivity. In so doing, the company gained an initial advantage over its competitors, but also acquired a structural repertoire (see Section V) which became a 'roadblock to innovation'. In 1925, when General Motors developed a form of structural differentiation in which design was applied continuously to a range of cars, each of which was given annual styling through the work of Harley Earl,[64] this introduced a new adaptive requirement for survival in the automobile industry. It became necessary to develop a capacity to align decisions across three key areas in order to minimize costs and maximize the market-based requirements for innovation—or, more precisely—for styling (Figure 2.2). Subsequently, the complex and varied market and production cycles involved in 'total design' became routinized and reinforced by their own technology. In the case of Ford[65] there was a strong linking of 'total design' to the details of commissioning new car lines, including the detailed content of training. These examples illustrate key insertions of truly novel adaptive features by enterprises which set the pattern of their activities for decades. In the case of Rover's historical experience, it was the realization of an adaptive capacity in 1929–32 (and its confirmation in 1945) which influenced the company's actions throughout the turbulence of the 1960s and 1970s.

Research on these developments—from the past—needs to examine their emergence, their processes of abortion and, where applicable, their institutionalization. In the case of Chrysler in the 1970s, they fashioned their concept of 'total design' to encompass the following: a seven-to-ten-year cycle for establishing the continuing image of a complete range of cars; a five-to-seven-year cycle to develop the technology, to change customers' attitudes, to build up credibility, to educate legislators and to respond to government initiatives; a three-year cycle of the design and retooling of a new production line; an annual cycle for the styling of a new model.[66] In the Rover Company, the particular mix of cyclical activity in these areas was quite different; product design activities were spread over exceptionally long periods of up to twelve years, for instance. The rhythm of innovation within the company's productive units was therefore specific to Rover and requires separate reconstruction.

The use of an historical dimension in the study of innovation also has certain methodological implications. It is not simply that historical study can extend the range of circumstances against which insights generated in the present may be compared. Industrial forms in the present are rooted in the past, but in order to recover these antecedents, basic skills of historical enquiry must be used. Therefore, appropriate units of time must be employed which, as in Rover's case, do not neatly fit calendar time or the conventional periods used in economic history. Such periods are only ever artificial constructions which do not apply universally to all organizations or industries. The design process of the SD1 from 1968 to 1976 can only be fully understood in relation to the larger process of change across the whole company and sector, which has to be measured in decades. A critical approach to the use of historical evidence is also vital. This involves an awareness of the way in which sources are generated, their evidential context and the necessary limitations of material derived from the past. The relevance of language must be acknowledged. Contemporary usage must be reconstructed and changes in vocabulary monitored in order to understand the generation of new concepts which pre-date material innovation. Above all, those involved in the changes which are investigated here will be shown to have defined their positions in the present (of the 1970s) in relation to the past. An independent scrutiny of that past by the researcher enables him to assess those positions more critically.

III The comparative dimension

The retardation debate presumes that the patterns of industrial change in Britain possess an easily recognizable degree of commonality across the branches of industry. The debate assumes a common pattern of lateness in entering new sectors and/or an incapacity to make the periodic transitions from one stage in the sector life cycle to the next stage. The exponents of the retardation thesis have not, in general, disaggregated the different branches of industry. Pavitt,[67] in a recent review of industrial change, contends that there is a diversity across sectors in their degree of innovation. Case studies compare the coal industry, textiles, chemicals and others. Unfortunately, there are no chapters on retail, on the leisure and holiday industry or on personal services. Yet these are sectors in which there is some international evidence to sustain the notion of relatively good performance in industrial change. Pavitt's contention regarding diversity is weakened by chapters in the book which argue that British managements are generally uneducated, under-motivated and too class-conscious. Pavitt has therefore made an initial case for diversity. The case needs further exploration and refinement by making comparisons with and between countries.

The assumption of a commonality across sectors requires close scrutiny. The hypothetical notion of a distinctive British variety is proposed as an analytical device. This notion suggests that there is an identifiable range within Britain which typifies the form, pace and anticipation with which design and innovation are accomplished. Also, the idea of a distinctive variety implies that the British range will be identifiably different from that range found in other countries. The concept remains hypothetical not least because, as the car industry shows, there may be a range of different design and innovation capacities within any one sector. If industrial change in a society does possess an identifiable pattern, then how can that pattern be conceptualized, and what kinds of theoretical reasoning are required? At this stage we can give little more than a hint of the directions which should be taken. The very different approaches to inter-societal analyses suggested by Crozier and by Giddens provide complementary perspectives which may be incorporated into the basic framework of investigation.

Crozier, over a period of more than twenty-five years, has sought to demonstrate that there are theoretical and empirical contributions which, in combination with a societal and historically informed perspective, constitute the most fruitful approach to industrial change. The particular mark of Crozier's thinking is the attempt to incorporate the universalistic theorizing on organization crystallized—for example, by the Carnegie School—with the European style of societal analysis. Thus, Crozier argued that empirical studies of the French state tobacco monopoly and of the French state postal, telegraph and telephone (postal cheque and clearing division) were examples of bureaucracies which exhibited distinctly, unambiguously, identifiably French cultural predispositions. In *The Bureaucratic Phenomenon*,[68] the reader is led through the two case studies into a discussion of organization theory—especially the theory of power and uncertainty—to the climax where all the earlier features are explained in terms of the French institutions and their dynamics. Crozier overviews research on French culture, on the French family, on French education and on French businesses. The conclusion is that there is a distinctly French pattern; that is, a pattern in the singular. Later,[69] this argument was explicated in the statement that all industrial change was typified by long periods of inertia, during which the existing configuration of dominance inhibited almost all change. During these long periods, tensions accumulated but did not lead to the alteration of the existing structures. Then, suddenly and very quickly, there was a period of dramatic change followed by more long periods of inertia. Crozier described this pattern as typically French, implying that its pattern would be found very widely in the public and in the private sectors. However, there was little systematic comparison with other countries. Nor have other researchers attempted the complex task of using Crozier's work to make comparisons. Clark[70] provides some tentative support for Crozier's claims in a study of industrial change in the British-owned cigarette industry, a study which followed Crozier's attempt to identify social patterns in industrial change.

The problem with Crozier's reasoning is that there is evidence from major French enterprises of more diversity in the pattern of industrial change than one is led to expect. In the automobile industry, Bardou et al. report differences in the innovation patterns of Citroen and of Renault. Therefore, the singularity of pattern suggested in the earlier formulation of Crozier seems problematic. Yet, the thrust towards the theory of a societal propensity/propensities for industrial change has received considerable impetus from the revival of cross-societal investigations emanating from the work of Maurice and colleagues in Aix-en-Provence and of the Sociologie du Travail group in Paris.[71] Their researches point towards a societal structuring which constrains industrial change through the combination of tensions arising from a matrix of institutions: the family, the state, the educational system. It seems plausible therefore to prise open Crozier's reasoning and suggest that a society may possess a distinctive variety of design and innovation capacities and a unique pattern of industrial change. Any one industry, such as automobiles, can therefore be investigated with a view to discovering how far it is bound by such constraints and where it is located within the wider range of innovative ability.

Giddens's contribution has been more indirect, but of equal potential.[72] The dissolving of the boundaries between the social sciences—economics, sociology, geography, history—has been a central preoccupation and has an obvious relevance to the framework of this book. Equally important is his presentation of a perspective using concepts for the analysis of society as a configuration of institutions around the state, and the dynamics of the relations between these institutions in terms of the actions of individuals. According to Giddens, all individual subjects enter a social world which is littered with pre-existing structural arrangements: situated practices.

Subjects encounter these, and through the acquisition of a combination of habits and of a competence in reflective thought facilitated through the medium of language, subjects gain the potential to interpret situated practices in terms of their own projects. Giddens makes implicit use of Hagerstrand's[73] contention that subjects follow specific trajectories through space and through time. Giddens suggests that the subject constructs an individual project which tends to shape the unfolding of the trajectory. However, Gregory,[74] in one of the few pieces of empirical work based on Giddens's theorizing, demonstrates that the unseen 'invisible hand' of the economy also plays a part. This interpretation is somewhat closer to Hagerstrand's use of the notion of trajectory, whilst retaining Giddens's intention to leave the subject with a zone of manoeuvre. The state is a crucial component in the pre-existing structuration of situated practices. Giddens follows a familiar track in arguing that the state replaced the city as the key social unit in Western Europe after 1500.

Situated practices are recursive, iterative and contain the day-to-day operation of dominance. Power is therefore present in the unfolding of the practices, and does not exist as some disembodied additional force.[75] Situated practices normally consist of a set of episodes known to the particular subjects. Some situated practices are publicly known over a wide geographical area, and there will be a template which may be recorded. The wedding ceremonies are obvious examples and the variety of books of etiquette are extensions around the basic template. Attending a football match is made up of a set of diverse situated practices. Social settings contain a dynamic tension between individuals, groups and possibly strata, each of whom interpret the rules of disorder and face rules of order.

According to Giddens, all structuration consists of situated practices and a component of language. Subjects can interpret the practices. Consequently, the existence and re-accomplishment of situated practices tend to be local: that is, specific to a geographical area, possibly to one street, to a region, or to a society. Very few practices will be portable across nations, unless special arrangements of an inter-societal kind are consciously attempted. The emphasis is on 'attempted', because Giddens argues that outcomes are typically unintended, even when they lead to new situated practices. The state and its apparatus contains bundles of situated practices. In this case, many of the practices are articulated into rules which are written down and public. Yet even these crystallized rules are subject to interpretation by unformulated, unreflected, taken-for-granted practices which were sedimented in the past. Thus, Ministers of State for the British National Health Service initiate changes in the relationships between doctors, nurses and administrators, but the doctors and nurses already possess bundles of rules and situated practices which are known to them and which are used to interpret orders by the state.[76] In Giddens's formulation, a societal culture will contain a variety of deep rules, many of which are contradictory, yet the totality of which will promote some tendencies rather than others.

It might be thought that the qualitive approach to the study of organizations would provide some guidelines, but the treatment of ritual and culture still has as its object a universal theory rather than the formulation of a basis for comparison.[77] Parallel to Giddens, work by Thompson and Gregory on the British experience of industrialization is more instructive. These authors locate this major episode of industrial change in society, which is understood to be made of up very complex 'games'. These games are governed by visible rules (of law and constitution), but also by invisible rules which 'the players know so deeply that they are never spoken, and which must be inferred by the observer'. The whole of life goes forward within 'structures' of such visible and invisible rules. However, Thompson argues that the creative interactions between the players—conscious or otherwise—re-shape the structures within which they take place. This understanding of structures (plural) sees them not simply as barriers to or constraints on action, but instead as 'essentially involved in the production of life'.[78]

This approach can be usefully applied not only to industrial change in the general sense, but more particularly to an investigation of innovation. First, it leads one to ask, what were the structures of visible and invisible rules which govern the processes of design and innovation within enterprises? Second, the question arises as to what are the important levels at which these rules operate, and what is the impact of those rules generated and reproduced at the societal, regional, community or company level? Research on the car industry already maintains that management has developed such rules relating to decision making and strategy, but what are the codes connected to the design and commissioning of new products and production methods? Do workers possess their own rules and the capacity to re-shape the structures in which they work, associated with new projects? Third, an attempt to decode these structures and practices within the British car industry necessarily raises the question of how far they are peculiar, if not to the national industry, then to specific corporations and plants within their own regional or communal settings. This approach admits the possibility, therefore, that the differing abilities of national car industries or their corporations to sustain design and innovation can be partially explained by reference to the social structures in which they occur. We will seek to uncover the rules which operate at the sector level in Britain and elsewhere. Chapter 3 attempts to reassemble the practices which were produced within the Rover Company around design and innovation. In Chapters 4 and 5 the many different codes which structured the SD1 project and the way in which actors were either constrained by them or managed to change them are reconstructed. In each chapter, comparisons are made between the practices of British and foreign car manufacturers in order to estimate the distinctiveness or otherwise of Rover and BL.

IV The sector

The sector is a key analytic construct. The sectors, or branches, of the British economy vary in their market profiles and in their exposure to international penetration. This section offers a broad characterization of the sector, and then examines the relevance of the theory of the sector life-cycle models. Particular reference is made to the model constructed by Abernathy[79] to explain the American experience from 1896 to the 1970s. That model presumes that there are socio-evolutionary pressures operating and that these are the major channels through which economic resources are allocated between competing enterprises and competing regional zones. The intention here is to present a sector perspective.

The concept of sector has barely been used in the study of work organization, though it does have a position in the Marxian analysis of the uneven development of the different branches of industry and in different geographical zones. Also, the definition of sectors in government publications and in state policies (often relating to the standard industrial classification) is not necessarily the most useful definition for research.

Broadly speaking, the notion 'sector' applies to collections of enterprises which provide similar goods and services, possibly in competition with each other, though the degree of competition may well be regulated in practice. Sectors will vary in their homogeneity. The coal industry in Britain is organized by the state-owned National Coal Board. This sector represents a collection of collieries and centres of research and development which, in many respects, share practices and central institutions to a very high degree. Capital investment and manpower policies are applied to the sector as a whole, though they have differential consequences within the sector. By comparison with coal, the carpet-manufacturing sector is small, highly competitive and contains a diversity of firms. The tourist and hotel sector, which includes catering within those establishments, is unlike coal in its industrial organization. The tourist sector is equally large, in fact it is larger when judged in terms of employment and of contribution to the national economy. However, in its industrial organization, the tourist and hotel sector is loosely organized, contains a large variety of independent decision centres, and is somewaht amorphous. There are state-aided agencies within that sector which have some co-ordinating role.

Sectors vary in the degree to which they are drawn into the international division of labour and into competition/penetration from overseas enterprises. Some of the penetration is indirect, as in the health sector, where there is heavy purchasing of American capital goods. There is also indirect penetration by overseas pharmaceutical enterprises which supply drugs and similar products to the National Health Service.

In automobiles and electricals, the equivalent British sectors are currently facing very strong international competition. The British automobile sector is now heavily penetrated, and the British-owned parts now represent less than 20 per cent of the annual car sales. The survival of even this small part has required state support. Similarly, in the information technology sector, Britain has only a small, 6 per cent share of the world market, and its home market is heavily penetrated by American and Japanese enterprises.

According to the various theories and interpretations of long-term movements in the economy, it seems that sectors are founded at particular historical times and that, once founded, they evolve in identifiable ways. The sectors for automobiles, electricals and chemicals were all founded in the period 1890–1910. It has been hypothesized by Stinchcombe[80] that the founding conditions of a sector have long-term impacts on subsequent survival and development. There are important situated practices which evolve and connect enterprises to the infrastructure of institutions (e.g. to education or finance), with long-term consequences. It seems that founding contains an unintended crystallization of societal propensities with economic relationships. This crystallization is often fateful, because it sets enterprises along some learning paths which may turn out to be inoperable. Teulings,[81] in a reconstruction of the role of Philips at Eindhoven in the founding of the Netherlands electrical sector, suggests that such founding processes will be directly impacted by the international policies of other states and their major enterprises. Teulings contends that Philips's transformation from a small-scale producer of electric light bulbs was, in significant part, facilitated by German–American enterprises. If the founding of sectors is as important as suggested by Stinchcombe's more general thesis, then the policy consequences of this require direct attention.

The studies from the Science Policy Research Unit (SPRU) suggest that sectors have marked consequences for the profile of occupational employment and hence for manpower.[82] There seems to be a crucial linkage between the societal tendencies discussed in the previous section and the unfolding (or failure to unfold) of specific sectors. For example, the kinds of knowledge conceived by those involved in 'founding' a sector may be important. Saul, for instance, contends that the British automobile industry lacked the incorporation of certain areas of applied knowledge and certain situated practices in reflective knowledge which were required in the long-term evolvement of the sector.[83]

Sectors may be characterized by distinctive corporate languages, constructs and frameworks, all of which are pre-theoretical and local to the sector, yet all of which have an important influence on the evolvement of learning paths in the sector. The possibility is suggested in a number of studies: of the Lancashire cotton industry, the American automobile industry, and the British West Midlands forging sector.[84] Weick's concept of bodies of thought helps reveal some of the implicit assumptions within sectors. Bodies of thought are constructed by members of organizations on the basis of past experiences which are reassembled to produce a version of the past—sometimes expressed in 'sagas' or key stories. The past is used as the point of departure to create an initial framework of reference consisting of generalized rules which are intuitively appropriate when judged by those located in the same contexts. The frameworks are information-seeking structures which direct attention, control perception, filter experience and help to define the meaning of experiences in that sector. The bodies of thought, therefore, provide a language of constructs and the rules connecting the constructs, which interprets contemporary experience in terms of the specially constituted local version of history.

Such bodies of thought represent the discursive and reflective aspects of situated practices, though, as Argyris and Schon[85] demonstrate, they are not very open to enquiry, to reflection or to major transformations in the short run. Rather, they provide a vehicle for maintaining images of reality amongst connected subjects. If the notion of bodies of thought is relevant at the sector level, then it would be important to identify their consequences for industrial innovation in the automobile sector.

Sectors are usually the focus for various kinds of dependency on resources: finance, suppliers, labour. Finance may have certain sector features because loaning agencies make their calculations based on ratios derived from the sector. Suppliers of two kinds may or may not be closely connected. The retail sector, for example, has very diverse relationships with its suppliers. The North American retail sector treats the downstream suppliers of manufactured garments in a very distant manner, except in the local spot market of New York.[86] In contrast, the British retail sector developed closer linkages, especially in the case of Marks & Spencer. Technologies vary over time in the degree to which they are specific to a sector. Early American sawing machines were specific to the timber industry, but later the industry became a learning pool for equipment supply across a number of sectors. Kaplinsky[87] provides a general framework for the development of technology from:

1. machines transforming a raw material;
2. machines linking fixed machines transforming raw materials;
3. control machines connecting all equipment into a self-regulating operation.

This framework provides a means of exploring the uneven evolvement of technology across sectors, as well as implying that there is a high degree of autonomous development of technology. At some stages the technologies will have cross-sector consequences. The creation of automated warehouses and of machinery for packaging is an obvious example of where the technology supply industry is likely to be general. In phases where the cross-sectoral technological pace of development is high, then it seems likely that capital will try to minimize the costs of specialist technocratic staff (e.g. maintenance engineers, research and development experts). This criss-cross of technological developments creates the uncertain interface between technology dependence and the sector. The uncertainty has largely been ignored in organization studies, although the preoccupation of top corporate managements with the mysteries of technological forecasting illustrates the problems which can be generated.

State actions and policies are often directed towards the sector, though the degree of direct involvement by states differs. In Britain the state has a deep involvement in military capital goods, and this affects various sectors which interface with military projects (e.g. aerospace, electronics). Kaldor[88] contends that military expenditures absorb a very high proportion of the supply of scientific manpower in Britain. Noble[89] suggests that the United States military is a major source of inventions which spill through for commercial development in various civilian sectors, most notably high technology.

State involvement in the automobile industry is common. In the United States, the Reagan Government confirmed the massive support given to Chrysler in 1980; in France the major firm Renault is state-owned and the French Government has become progressively involved in that sector; the same is true for German state and land state governments (e.g. BMW). At the general level, the state's policies have consequences for sectors and vice versa. Dunnett[90] claims that the British automobile sector was used by successive governments as a means of regulating the economy.

The sector is the meeting-point between the producer and the consumer, so sectors are likely to reflect the national tastes, thereby giving indigenous enterprises a potential advantage. Jones[91] argues that a 'world car' is unlikely, simply because of national differences in taste for the size and styling of cars.

The notion of sectors having identifiable patterns of transformation through various states has preoccupied academics for a long time. One of the most sophisticated presentations of a sector life-cycle model is that by Abernathy, which is constructed for the automobile sector in particular and for complex products in general.

The theory of the sector life-cycle is an attempt to discover patterns within the dynamics of the events of industrial organization over periods of several decades. Life-cycle theories for the sector make use of two implicit assumptions: the population-ecology model of competition and survival, and the design hierarchy thesis.[92] It is assumed that a natural selection process is operating within industrial sectors, through which the allocation of economic returns leads to the demise of some enterprises and the growth of others. The general theory of a socio-evolutionary selective process has been elaborated—with a number of cautionary pointers— by Campbell.[93] Later, Weick[94] elaborated the kinds of internal, organizational mechanisms which Campbell's reasoning had implied. Aldrich[95] demonstrated the possibility of examining populations of enterprises and examining their capacity to grow and survive in terms of their capacity to obtain resources. More recently, Aldrich and McKelvey have argued that the actual 'design' of work organization is the product of a competitive process for scarce resources between enterprises. 'Natural' selection differentiates enterprises so that some are eliminated. Organization learning is the process, it is argued, through which enterprises should acquire those practices which are necessary for survival. Jelinek[96] suggests how Texas Instruments institutionalized the process of organization learning, and even managed to gain a degree of corporate control embodied in the standard operating procedures. Also, it seems likely that the repertoire of standard operating procedures is quite strongly, though not wholly, shaped in the founding period. Organizational learning occurs here, but it is doubtful if the members are reflectively aware of this learning.

The concept of a design hierarchy provides a bridge between the selection criteria operating in the environments and the relative success of different enterprises. The idea is taken from the early work of Alexander, an architectural theorist.[97] In a somewhat mechanistic manner, which he later recanted, Alexander argued that any piece of architecture contained

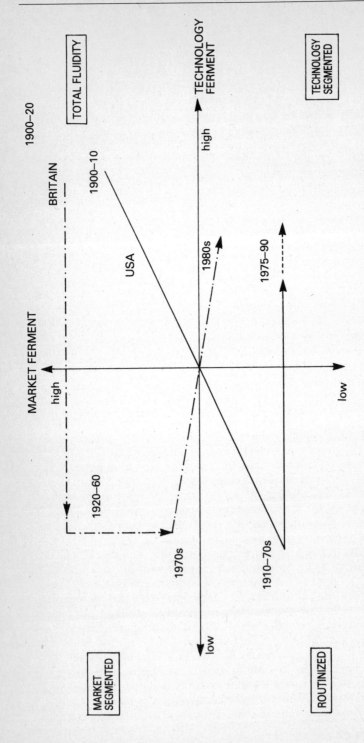

Figure 2.3   An Anglo-American comparison of the auto industry: market and technology profile, 1900–1980s.

a wide variety of dimensions, each facing a distinct environment: the weather, ground strength, customer preferences, patterns of behaviour. In principle, dimensions could be grouped and arranged in a decision tree. Alexander suggested pieces of architecture must seek for designed, deliberate acceptance across all the dimensions, and he conceptualized the process of reaching acceptability as an hierarchical process. The point may be transferred to the automobile. In 1900 the car was essentially the combination of a portable power source and a coach-built body. World-wide, thousands of small suppliers produced small numbers of custom-built cars. In this period the design hierarchy was unformed. Then, in the United States, Henry Ford combined a new variety of parts into a design which soon took more than 50 per cent of the American market and 30 per cent of the British market. At this point, a design hierarchy had emerged but, as becomes clear, the hierarchy changes. Abernathy explicitly adopts and refines the notion of a design hierarchy, and implicitly incorporates evolutionary perspectives into his theory of a sector life-cycle. The theory is advanced on the basis of a detailed collation of basic data available from the archives of the Ford Motor Company in the United States.[98]

The basic unit of analysis for Abernathy is the productive unit: a combination of the product and the production facilities. Normally, an enterprise possesses a portfolio which minimally includes productive units for engines, for car bodies and car assembly. The idea of a portfolio helps express Abernathy's observation that different productive units will be in different stages of development. Further, it is evident that the 'technology evolvement' model of Kaplinsky also fits rather neatly into this schema. In the American auto industry, the engine-making side has evolved quite differently to final assembly; the former was subjected to long production runs in the early part of this century, whilst the latter was always kept sufficiently flexible to allow for the annual styling changes which characterized General Motors and later the whole American industry.

Looking at the American industry as a totality, Abernathy contends that some seven decades can be shown to contain a broad movement along two dimensions: market and technology. Each dimension can be scaled from rapid change to slow change. Figure 2.3 combines the dimensions, traces the American case and suggests the British route from 1900 to the early 1980s. In the architectural stage, neither the customer nor the supplier had a clear idea of what the car might do, or how it might be constructed. However, by 1908, as indicated, Ford had discovered an initial design hierarchy. Later, in the mid-1920s, GM introduced styling and the market concept of a range of cars, one for each segment. Even so, many of the components, especially the engine, were manufactured on a mass basis. In fact, the Americans achieved massive economies of scale in engine production at an earlier stage than in the rest of the world. It was in engine manufacture and assembly that the three stages of the Kaplinsky framework were first completed. Transfer machines, for example, were in operation in the 1940s, and they were part of the technology exported under Marshall Aid (1945–51) to France and installed at Renault, and it was the sight of these machines which led Touraine to recognize that

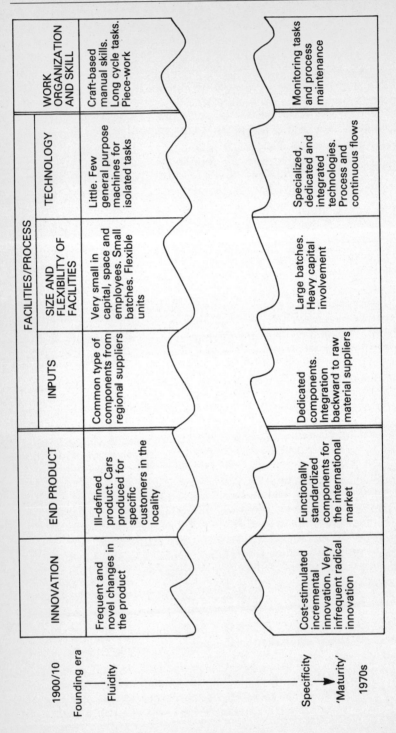

Figure 2.4 Innovation tendencies in productive units. Source: derived from Abernathy, *The Productivity Dilemma*, 1978, pp. 148–9.

there was much more diversity in the work organization of the automobile industry than his mentor, Georges Friedmann, had supposed.[99]

Figure 2.4 is based on Abernathy.[100] On the left-hand side, the direction of the arrow downward expresses the unfolding of the productive unit life-cycle. The central tendency is for productive units to combine the three main dimensions—product, process and work organization—differently as the life-cycle develops from innovatory production to incremental innovation to styling innovation. There are seven columns in the figure, of which the first two express aspects of the product:

— its main line characteristics;
— the mode of change from radical to incremental.

The next four columns refer to aspects of the production process through which the product is manufactured:
— the sourcing of inputs of components;
— the capacity of the factory from small to large;
— the process equipment from general purpose to specialist;
— the configuration of process equipment.

The final column covers aspects of work organization in terms of the characteristics of tasks and the kinds of labour employed. The figure is both based on a collation of empirical materials, and is also a prescriptive conception intended to be a framework which executives should use to anticipate future developments and to guide their own planning of change. In the United States automobile industry, the engine productive unit has travelled down the path of the central tendency, and was firmly in the fifth stage of fundamentally standardized products by the 1970s. By comparison, the final assembly as a productive unit was around the mid-stages, because final assembly was where the styling and annual modifications were introduced.

Writing in 1978, Abernathy identified a basic tendency in the corporate management of the American auto industry towards achieving high productivity yet at the increasing expense of technological innovation. Arguably, that strategy had been well suited to the American market, though it should be remembered that foreign penetration was inhibited by the Second World War and its aftermath. Abernathy correctly identified a dilemma: the productivity dilemma. There was a choice in the 1970s between a continuing tendency towards mass production/low innovation, towards a more fragmentary innovation as in European car markets, or mass production/high innovation, as in Japan. The life-cycle of the sector articulates with the life-cycle of the productive unit. In the sectors where the design hierarchy throws up a dominant design, a high proportion of the portfolio of production units should become settled and fixed. In the United States that was the case after the creation of the 'roadster', and this lasted into the 1970s. The dominant design was retained with minimal alterations based on styling and in the combination of components put together at the stage of final assembly.[101] However, the European auto industry evolved from the same architectural stage as that of the American industry, but it moved less towards a specific pattern and more towards the searching for market segments. This pattern became evident in the 1930s, for example, when Rover shifted from being orientated towards a range of segments and concentrated more on the luxury British car market, or at least a segment of that market. Markets were more fragmented in the European case; they remained divided by national taste and the degree of purchasing power between social groups. In Europe, more generally, there were fewer instances of the tendency towards a dominant design. Consequently, few European enterprises gained the market power of the two big American companies. Indeed, the latter were both able to enter and survive in the European market as part of its rich variety and greater volatility compared to America. This situation began to change in the 1970s.

In 1980, Abernathy and colleagues[102] produced a comparison of the productivity of American and Japanese methods of manufacturing cars. In a short seminal article, they concluded that the Japanese could, for example, achieve considerable savings simply by minimizing the levels of inventory—the 'just-in-time' system. It was estimated that the Japanese costs of inventory were about 10 per cent of their American competitors. It now seemed that the dilemma was being resolved in favour of foreign exporters of small cars to the United States. These changes in the American dominance of their own markets coincided with a high degree of technological ferment as the impacts of the microelectronic revolution began to alter the nature of production, especially the batch size. Abernathy sought to explain the situation in the late 1970s and 1980s by arguing that the American auto industry had moved into de-maturity.

Abernathy and colleagues re-examined the notion of a sector life-cycle in *The Industrial Renaissance*,[103] where they argued that life-cycle models are not analogous to biological life-cycles. They go further in their critique of the teaching of the American business schools, and maintain that there has been too strong a tendency for academics to proclaim mechanistic models of complex processes. The point was negative, because it would be possible to re-examine the life-cycle model through the perspective of organizations and environments, as proposed by Aldrich.[104] The socio-evolutionary perspective, for example, focuses attention on the degree to which the American and European environments are similar, yet there were important dissimilarities in tastes.

The theory linking product and process to the variability in customer demand is one which has an established basis in production engineering and in organization studies since the work of Woodward.[105] However, in Woodward's thinking, the unit of analysis was always given as the establishment rather than the total enterprise. Until Abernathy, there was no systematic attempt to theorize enterprises as possessing portfolios of productive units. Indeed, this area was also neglected in business policy thinking where the treatment of diversification is very largely in terms of unrelated product markets. Abernathy also extended Woodward by locating the product/process aspect in the context of industrial organization at the level of the sector. These are important extensions.

In the following chapters the British auto sector is examined in its own right and in comparison to the American and European profiles. These chapters will focus on the founding experience of the British sector and the long-term importance of the learning paths and practices which were initiated in the first decades of this century. The main 'bodies of thought' which were produced, especially in the inter-war years, will be mapped and the Rover Company's version of the sector's languages, frameworks and strategies will be reconstructed. A preliminary review of the sector's history indicates how the pattern of technological development in Britain both embodies certain features of American models, yet also diverges from them in crucial respects. The sector life-cycle in Britain was far less straightforward than its American counterpart. The dominant design was slower to emerge, while market and technological changes were more erratic. Above all, the fact that the mass market for cars did not appear as quickly nor as completely as in the American case had many ramifications for the type of product, production arrangements and modes of work organization which resulted, and the pace and direction of their changes.

In the study of the SD1 project, the product/process interface has been doubly extended. First, as indicated in Figure 2.2, the whole area of work organization has been considerably enlarged from the brief but insightful treatment by Abernathy. Second, the product/process interface proposed by Abernathy requires reconsideration when applied to analyse and explain events within the European automobile industry. Here the structure of demand and the strategies of competition were very different to the United States case, though these strategies were certainly impacted by the presence of Ford and GM in Europe. In addition, the conceptualization of technology by Abernathy was very much influenced by the theories of American production engineering, with their bias towards technological solutions.

Part II will indicate the relevance, in the British context, not only of the social processes involved in innovation, but also of the way sectors and enterprises develop their own long-term problems of management/labour relations and how they connect with changes in productive units.

V Enterprises

The fourth area of the framework deals with the level of the enterprise, and requires the outline of those analytical requirements for the 'case-in-sector' perspective. The first tasks are to define strategic innovation and to summarize briefly the reasons for an additional perspective to those already contributed from business policy and from business histories. The main temporal features of the processual analysis at the enterprise level require specifying and linking to the sector. This will involve the examination of structural repertoires, organization culture and organization learning. Finally, there are several issues which require attention: the competitiveness of an innovation and its design repertoire, the question of who has access to the key decision arenas, the cognitizing of the innovation by 'work organizers', and the social relations of the design process. Innovation is a concept which is occasionally used in a very loose way, and therefore it is important to define strategic innovation, and other concepts such as systemic innovation and incremental innovation, which are closely related.

The implications of the theory of long-wave fluctuations in the cautious form of its usage by Freeman and colleagues[106] is that some swarming of inventions occurs from time to time, and that this swarming often indicates the founding of a new sector. If so, then the Abernathy sector life-cycle model would suggest that within a sector there are periods of low and high intensity in the degree to which existing productive units (i.e. product, process and work organization) are transformed. In the case of engine plants in the United States, it seems that since 1920, and possibly earlier, there has been a steady, rather even, incremental process through which manufacturing was progressively built into a technology. Indeed, the engine manufacturing productive unit in the United States seems to be a good example of travelling down the three stages in Kaplinsky's model. This movement has involved innovation, but it has been a steady move in a particular direction.

Clearly, the shape of sector innovations is the cumulation of the innovations in particular enterprises in that sector. The concept of strategic innovation is usually applied to the period after the founding of the sector. There is a general implicit use of a set of distinctions from major to minor with the concepts running from 'strategic innovation', 'radical innovation', 'incremental innovation', 'cosmetic/styling innovation'.

If the productive unit is taken as part of the frame of definition, then a strategic innovation for the enterprise may be defined as one or more of the following:

1. a total change in the portfolio of productive units of the enterprise, either by moving away from original product markets and/or by diversifying into new product markets which are only loosely related;
2. a shift in the position of a productive unit in terms of two or more of the trinity of dimensions along the fluidity/specificity scale;
3. major structural changes in work organization at all levels, whilst leaving the product and process aspects largely unchanged. This type of strategic innovation is often suggested in the literature on organization development, and is implied in the widely read book by Peters and Waterman.[107]

These three are categories of strategic change for the enterprise. For each of them there is a sense in which the enterprise is designated as having a new project—though this designation may be confined to a relatively small group of corporate executives with their hand on some of the mechanisms for change (e.g. corporate budgets).

Radical change is therefore, by implication, simply less extensive than strategic innovation, but is nevertheless substantial. However, the term radical is used very freely in trade journals and in the press. Caution is required, since a large enterprise might undertake a radical innovation in only one of the many productive units in its portfolio. Whitaker and

Shimmin,[108] for example, describe the establishment of a new food pro-cessing plant in Chirk in Wales for the multinational food company Cad-bury Schweppes. It is evident that this factory both introduced a new technology and also anticipated a new principle of corporate organization in terms of geographically diversified, small productive units, rather than large units concentrated at the Bournville site in Birmingham. There was a radical alteration in that productive unit, but at the stage of its designing, translation into facilities and work organization and its commissioning, the radical area was highly focused in a relatively small part of the total multinational. Clearly, radical innovations are important: as Whipp and Smith argue,[109] the Chirk concept, once successful, became something of a template for other more strategic innovations. Returning to the defini-tion of strategic innovation, there is a clear distinction between the example just given of radical innovation, and the immense changes experienced by British Leyland during the 1970s, and for the Rover Company once it was incorporated after 1967.

Strategic and radical innovation has attracted so much attention in the media—which has also influenced the focus of research—that some have argued that incremental innovation has been under-recognized. The argu-ment is put very clearly by Rosenberg[110] when he draws attention to 'learning by doing' and 'learning by using', both of which might, in the absence of other sources of change, lead to annual improvements in the steady modification to equipment and to work organization which follow radical innovations in most leading enterprises. Any brake on incremental innovation would have dramatic effects on competitive costs within just a few years, and over a decade would almost certainly be fateful. Incre-mental innovation is part of the daily working life of the technocrats in industrial engineering, in R & D, in maintenance and in similar occu-pations. Cosmetic or styling innovation may be defined as a process whereby the enterprise is able to retain an orientation towards pro-ductivity rather than innovation by focusing the area of change where it is highly visible, yet readily achievable. The auto industry in the United States established a high competence in this form of change, especially after the roadster model became the dominant design.

Using these concepts with the Rover and SD1 case study means that strategic innovation may be applied to the periods 1928–32 and 1969–75, and that the concept of radical innovation might be more appropriate for describing major model changes (e.g. in the later P series) because these left the process and work organization aspects largely unchanged.

The design of strategic and radical innovations is an occasion when corporate choices are exercised across a series of dimensions. This process is recognized to be highly complex, yet structured; to be iterative, and yet to involve abortions, recycling, rejected trajectories;[111] often to take many years; to be a political process involving competition and struggle within corporate managements;[112] to involve competition and struggles between capital, corporate managements and labour; and to have fateful consequences. There is considerable uncertainty, especially about the actual capacities of new technologies. Exponents of the socio-evolutionary approach to the designing of the structure of enterprises contend that choices are constrained by their consequences, but it is clear that choices are exercised. The fact that consequences are perceived does not remove the exercising of choice by some grouping or strata.

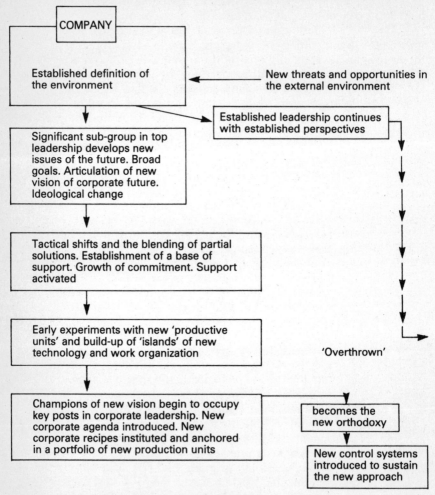

Figure 2.5 Implementing strategic change: the successful pattern. *Source*: derived from Quinn, *Strategy for Change: Logical Incrementalism*, 1980, p. 104.

Existing studies of strategic and radical innovation are both useful and limited. The business policy field is littered with prescriptive frameworks and our study is certainly interested in the extent to which prescriptive frameworks from the business schools are used by executives in corporate decision making. There are also important themes which are relevant, as well as in-depth case studies which are instructive about the unfolding of processes. However, the processual dynamics of strategic and radical innovation are dealt with in a manner which suggests that some modifications are required. One useful attempt to articulate a general perspective by grounding the concepts and the accounts of the processes in case study details does provide some suggestive ideas. This is the perspective of Quinn,[113] from which Figure 2.5 is derived to illustrate one conception of the many 'stages' and episodes which can occur. The fact that this is based on interviews with executives does suggest some caution, and there are other problems arising from his attempt to pour empirical illustrations into an essentially prescriptive framework. Yet Quinn's approach does have the virtue of highlighting some of the areas of political process which are involved.

The literature from business history contains discrete histories of particular firms which sometimes include attention to strategic/radical innovation. There are also more synoptic accounts of economies.[114] Amongst the specific business histories, those which follow the same themes and scope as Barker's reconstruction of the development of the float glass technique are exceptional.[115] By definition, that study became one of the sector as well as Pilkington's, simply because the float glass method revolutionized glass production for that sector in all parts of the world. Many of the studies from business policy and from business history are useful, yet they require location and extensions to satisfy the requirements of our framework of inquiry. In particular, they do not normally address the problems of design and innovation and their relation to structural repertoires, corporate cultures and capital/labour dynamics. For these reasons, additional features are needed.

The experience of the Ford Motor Company in the 1920s is instructive, because its corporate executives had managed to create the dominant design for the whole American industry, involving strategic, radical, incremental, and styling innovation, all around a single model, the Ford T. The original concept was elaborated rather than stretched; it remained the same basic car. Then, in the mid-1920s, the new General Motors introduced the strategic innovation of the market range, coupled with regular, deliberate, consumer-orientated modifications to the car and consequent changes in some of the productive units in its portfolio. In short, the GM management institutionalized the process of design and innovation, turning this into an anticipation of customer preferences through market research on activatable needs and on advertising to shape consumer behaviour.

Until the evolvement of design and innovation into a regular occurrence within large-scale enterprises, their main structural features in the early twentieth century had consisted of a number of productive units serving particular product markets and a central office/headquarters in the form of a quasi bank.[116] Once innovation-design became a requirement, then a further stage in the elaboration of the structuring of enterprises was required. Structural differentiation in the firm was becoming much more complex, because the adaptive sub-systems (of planners, engineers and financial specialists) had to be accommodated. These specialized techno-structures have been described by J. K. Galbraith while Noble and

Braverman attribute to them a key role in the design of work organization and choosing technologies.[117]

However, before examining the structural, cultural and learning aspects which are involved, it is useful to examine a simple schematization of design and innovation. The scheme is based on the case study[118] of a large cigarette manufacturer, John Players & Sons of Nottingham, England, and their approach to the planning and commissioning of a new factory which was to be the 'most technologically advanced in the world'. Their experience shows both the separation of the ongoing factories from the planning of the future, and also suggests that this planning goes through several major phases, each of which may be the province of specific sets of actors, but from most of which labour is excluded. The process covered five years before the full commissioning of the new operating system. What were the main activities in each phase?

The first phases of designing came when the small design group produced their concept of the new factory as an air-controlled, two-storey box with half the ground floor allocated to preparation of the tobacco leaf, the first floor devoted to making and packaging cigarettes and the remainder of the ground floor being used for final cartoning and despatch. This new flow was based on an ideal time-span of four hours. The concept of the new factory meant a reduction in throughput time from more than one hundred hours and a dramatic alteration in the temporal buffers between departments. Even in this early stage, long before the appointment of architects, the basic data from work study had been used to calculate potential savings in space, time and labour which the new factory would offer, especially if a shift system were introduced. The manpower planning showed considerable savings, including alterations to the role of the supervisor and the introduction of new occupations, the 'tobacco technician', as well as major changes to existing group structures on packing. It was clear from the changing balance of temporal buffers between the new departments that the detailed hour-by-hour deployment of labour was likely to be more centrally managed. This whole concept was based on projections about the availability of new equipment, particularly of equipment which would increase the flow and integration of the work-flow. The development of these broad concepts continued over the next three years, with various iterations and abortions, very much in the manner suggested by Mintzberg's analysis of decision making. Within a few months of the start of designing, various specialist advisers were appointed and the second major process—translating the concepts into the building, the equipment and into specific forms of work organization—had commenced and another collateral structure was created. The translation work included large-scale, carefully planned 'mock-ups' of the new layouts, comparing the performance of competing pieces of equipment. Machine complexes were simulated on paper and on the ground. Also, the process of anticipating the new factory work organization was anticipated by:

- the gradual elimination of certain strata and occupations in the existing factories;
- the introduction of new criteria for the selection and promotion of all categories of staff;
- the subordination of departmental-level decisions to a more centralized decisions structure;
- extensive preparation of the work-force through various internal media exercises and through a form of consultation on the work environment (e.g. colour choices);
- extensive use of external advisers.

The third stage, commissioning the factory, lasted around two years, after which the new operating system had taken over the production from much of the old system. It may be noted that, even now, the projected technological linkages between all segments of the workflow have not yet fully achieved the concept of integration which was being mooted more than fifteen years previously.[119]

This is a crude schematization of these processes but it does indicate the extent to which the enterprise possessed a 'design capacity' and was able to create and integrate a collection of collateral groups into a structure which guided the design and innovation processes. The Players example is also useful because it is derived from British experience. It is at least rooted in practice, in contrast to the abstract and prescriptive models of 'planning and design' developed by Nadler from American blueprints.[120] It may be as an example of a design process with a strong sense of direction and a highly rational pattern of activity that the Players experience sits uneasily with design and innovation in 'traditional' British sectors. However, it can provide a starting-point for research into the design process. The Players case appears to have a number of similarities to the models of design which are attributed to the auto industry. This four-part process will therefore provide, first, a means of comparing the practices of designing in the car sector and, second, a simple map to begin an investigation of the design process in Rover and BL in Part II.

Players, like many other enterprises, possessed a repertoire of structures which were part of the corporate culture. There is a general problem of developing a processual perspective which can handle the notion of a structural repertoire in such a way that events occurring infrequently lead to the transformation of the repertoire into a new structuration, as noted in the 'structure/event/structure' approach outlined earlier.

The analogy with the theatrical repertoire suggests that the various structures are only partially activated at any one time, but that dormant structures, containing situated practices, can be activated. The problem is one of finding units of analysis. March and Simon[121] theorized structure as a repertoire of performance programmes which can be activated when certain communication signals appear. In this case the performance programme is built into the role of specific actors as a defined script. The analogy might be made with the American football team, where the choice of a field play will influence which players from the large pool will actually take part in the next fifteen-second move. However, from the perspective of large enterprises employing thousands of employees, the notion of performance programmes is very general. The difficulty remains of finding approaches to structuration which can be used to analyse processes and which are also appropriate to the case-in-sector perspective.

At the level of the enterprise, the process perspective is problematic because as yet the concepts necessary for examining the unfolding of processes 'in time' have been only partially developed. The central problem relates to the unravelling of the dimensions of time appropriate to the economy, the sector and the social systems of the enterprise. As indicated earlier, the product markets of businesses are located in several time frames. These include the pulsations of the business cycle(s) and the highly subjective constructions of time related to all levels of the enterprise, including its operating system. These multiple time frames and their interrelations require careful identification. The example of Chrysler's design cycle, with some design and innovation projects taking up to twelve years, will be shown to have been in direct contrast to the four-year period envisaged by British Leyland. The structural difficulties which the new corporate design intentions posed were therefore immense for the SD1 project. In addition, the synchronization of the multiple time frames which strategic innovations involve becomes a major task for designers and project managers. The uncertainty, for example, of car sales, both within and between years, makes this objective extremely difficult to meet. Turner's study[122] of industrial relations in the British auto industry shows how workplace conflict revolves around these contingent time frames and the Rover Company was no exception. Yet these temporal aspects of the economic and social processes and their implications for design and innovation are only hinted at by Rogers, and largely neglected by exponents of the various process schools.

Corporate cultures, in the plural, require examination. Particular attention should be given to various organizational languages. Karpik[123] rightly states that executives from different functions tend to develop different 'logics of action', and that enterprises may be typified both by hierarchy of logics and by their configuration. However, the logics of action amongst executives represent only a part of organizational culture. Recent theorizing about organizational decision making has emphasized the micropolitics and the politicking of intra-managerial decision making. Even popular texts for the executive present themselves as adopting an evolutionary and political perspective.[124] Today, the politics of organizational decision making is taken for granted, but little attention is given to those outside management—either the owners of capital or labour. The relocation of the enterprise within the stratification and class features of societies has only recently returned as an area of focus.[125] Yet the recognition of these interactions extends the interpretation which is given to corporate cultures by a very long way. If language is as important as exponents of the process perspectives believe, and if also incremental innovation is important to long-term survival, then the languages and cultures of non-managerial groups are just as fateful for 'organizational efficiency' and 'organizational governance'. How these 'logics of action' and languages can influence the design process will be revealed by exploring their interplay in the SD1 project.

If design projects have become increasingly concerned with the commitment of huge resources and the direction of an enterprise, then such ventures have, it would seem, profound implications for relationships between employer and employed. Detailed studies of the capital/labour dynamic and its effect on design and innovation, and in particular the role of labour in the design process, are few. Noble concludes that, in America, unions have adopted a defensive posture: when confronted with changing technology, labour has generally limited its action to '*post-hoc* resistance'. This has meant that: 'labor's [*sic*] choices have not been registered in the actual design and deployment stages and that, therefore, the technology does not reflect its interest.'[126]

How far is this true for Britain, or at least the British auto industry? The contrasting unfolding of design capacities within the American and British sectors, together with their separate profiles of organized labour, lead one to hypothesize that considerable differences exist.

Marxist writers argue that conflict is central to the modern enterprise as the 'interests of workers and those of employers collide'. Moreover, conflict arises over how work shall be organized, what pace shall be established, under what conditions producers must labour, and what rights workers shall enjoy.[127] As we have suggested, the design process is where key managerial decisions over such questions are made. Surely the design process requires investigation, if only to understand the source of the collisions of interest between management and work-force. In the SD1 project it is (contrary to the American experience) the involvement of labour, both directly and indirectly, during the design process, which helps to explain the content and timing of workplace conflict over a ten-year period. The SD1 experience indicates that the design process, especially regarding strategic innovations, can become a possible arena for a range of interests within an enterprise to exert their power or establish the conditions upon which control of production can be erected.

The process perspectives also give considerable attention, though few detailed expositions, to organization learning. Returning to the analogy of the structural repertoire and the American football team, the players in the professional teams have to learn both a complex set of behaviours and a series of three-digit code words for activation. In a similar way, though less consciously, enterprises acquire repertoires of practices which are institutionalized. On the general level, it may be theorized that organizational learning is strongly shaped by the founding conditions of the enterprise, by the cumulative impacts over time, and by major crises. If so, this learning is buried deeply, is hard to describe and, according to Argyris and Schon,[128] is extremely resistant to rational articulation and reflective examination. Such learning is system-wide, and management's roles in this learning and their reliance on it cannot be satisfactorily treated in isolation. Various theorists have argued that there are deeply buried rules, sedimented in the past, encrusted in myths and sagas, and brought into display in organizational rituals, which are pervasive. One of the few systematic attempts to reconstruct such rules is by Hall[129] in his use of systems dynamics to examine the interrelationship between different sub-systems in the now defunct American weekend journal, the *Saturday Evening Post*. Hall shows that there is a network of rules for each sub-system and a set of rules which arose from the interaction of the sub-systems. The rules are embedded in situated practices, in the reward systems, and in the relative power of departments.

Four aspects of strategic innovation require specific attention. First, there is the extent to which the unfolding of specific examples of strategic innovation is along lines and through mechanisms which are institutionalized components of the structural repertoire of the enterprise. There is the additional issue of the extent to which these practices of design and innovation are competitive relative to rivals in the same sector. For example, in the case of British Leyland in the years immediately following the mergers of 1968–9, it is necessary to examine very closely the extent to which British Leyland possessed a structural repertoire for coping with strategic innovation. In the case of the companies which were merged (e.g. Rover), it is important to examine the extent to which their existing repertoire, was suited to the new requirements which BL's corporate policies introduced in the 1970s. This is especially so where Rover were charged with the task of designing and launching a high-volume, luxury car for the European market from a brand-new production facility in Solihull. Rover's previous strategic innovation process had been orientated towards craft-based, low-volume production for the British and Commonwealth markets.

Second, at which stages in the process of strategic innovation do particular members of the enterprise gain access to decision arenas: in short, who occupies the design space? Which members are absent, and does their absence also mean that their position is ignored? The degree of representation of labour is of interest, particularly with respect to the earlier stages of concept and translation. Some countries require enterprises to make information publicly available to labour representatives, but neither this requirement nor the need for technological agreements have been officially recognized in Britain.[130] Labour is usually approached at the commissioning stage, and offers of participation by management are usually highly qualified.[131] The American auto industry has negotiated a high degree of managerial prerogative in these areas, and these practices have been introduced in the large American sector of the British auto industry.[132] During the mid-1970s there was a brief period of 'participation' for BL, but this was unevenly spread through the firm. Yet the translation stage of selecting specific technologies (e.g. paint plants, assembly lines) is one in which equipment suppliers, internal engineers and external advisers may have the most direct impact on choices. A related issue concerns the ways in which those choices are legitimated and the explanations offered for choices which were ignored. The zones of manoeuvre available to decision makers in Britain may reflect the influence of machinery suppliers, especially their ability to supply new technologies. The auto industry in the 1970s is interesting because Volvo provided a clear template of an alternative form of technology and of work organization to the assembly line.

Third, there is the issue of the ways in which those who did have access to the design and translation stages conceived the range of possible technologies and forms of work organization which were available. Tanner and Lupton[133] have probed into the constructs which engineers may use and have made a useful start on the process of discovering how industrial engineers in different enterprises (and countries) cognitize the zones of manoeuvre. To what extent can they generate a range of alternatives? Two areas require investigation:

1. the extent to which there are identifiable 'templates', such as team work, measured day work, job ladders;
2. the degree to which the cultures of those involved in the design and translation process restrict the choices to certain variants already developed within the enterprise.

Fourth, particular attention should be given to certain aspects of the manpower policy. Manpower decisions operate at two levels: aggregates and structures. At the aggregate level, large enterprises usually attempt to calculate the normal amount of human work to be required in a new situation. This may be done from MTM. This calculation is made increasingly awkward because an increasing number of tasks are thinly and unevenly spread through space and time. The supermarket is a classic example where the flows of supplies and outflows of customers operate to definable patterns which result in fluctuating requirements for manpower. Here the focus of research should be on the degree to which time and space is commodified, and the rules used to deploy labour. At the structural level, there is the issue of translation of tasks into occupational roles within the internal and external labour markets. Touraine's[134] analysis of technical change and skill suggests that re-skilling is as important as de-skilling. The key point is the degree to which job knowledge is appropriated by the enterprise from labour, and is the prerogative of a training function. Where job knowledge is systematically appropriated and there is a strong training function, then strategic innovation is likely to be a highly designed process, possibly incorporating organization development practices, as in the petrochemical industries. In the SD1 project, the appropriation of job knowledge and the creation of skill was far more indeterminate.

Notes

1. R. E. Caves, 'Productivity Differences Amongst Industries', in R. E. Caves and L. B. Krause (eds), *Britain's Economic Performance*, Washington, 1980; P. Mathias, *The First Industrial Nation: An Economic History of Britain 1700–1914*, 2nd edn. 1983; D. H. Aldcroft (ed.), *The Development of British Industry and Foreign Competition 1875–1914*, 1968.
2. For an appreciation of the range of forces and components, see C. Freeman, *The Economics of Industrial Innovation*, 2nd edn, 1982.

3. N. Rosenberg, *Inside the Black Box: Technology and Economics*, 1982.
4. E. T. Penrose, *The Theory of the Growth of the Firm*, 1959.
5. See the special review conducted on behalf of the Economic and Social Research Council, England, by R. K. Brown and Associates, *Research Needs in Work Organization*, 1978.
6. P. A. Clark and R. Whipp, 'Industrial Change in Britain: A Comparative, Historical Enquiry into Innovation', ESRC Work Organization Research Centre, *Working Paper No. 5*, 1985.
7. G. Bannock, R. E. Baxter and R. Rees, *The Penguin Dictionary of Economics*, 3rd edn, 1984, p. 226.
8. N. L. Stevenson, *Introduction to Engineering Design*, New South Wales, 1976, p. 10; E. Dickerson and J. Robertson, *Planning and Design: The System Approach*, Lexington, 1975.
9. Svensson, op. cit., pp. 10 ff., 20–2, 28 ff.
10. M. Cooley, Counsel's address to the Young Blood Conference, Enquiry 2, 'The Future of Design Professions', Barbican Centre, 30 November 1983.
11. J. R. Galbraith, *Organization Design*, 1977; J. R. Galbraith and D. A. Nathanson, *Strategy Implementation*, St. Paul, 1978; P. C. Nystrom and W. H. Starbuck, *Handbook of Organizational Design*, 1981.
12. For example, P. A. Clark, *Organizational Design: Theory and Practice*, 1972.
13. Galbraith, op. cit.
14. M. Aglietta, *The Theory of Capitalist Regulation: the US Experience*, New York, 1964; H. Braverman, *Labor and Monopoly Capital: The Degradation of Work in the Twentieth Century*, 1974.
15. Galbraith, op. cit.
16. H. Aldrich, W. McKelvey and D. Ulrich, 'Design Strategy from the Population Perspective', *Journal of Management*, **10**, 1, 1984, pp. 67–86; H. Aldrich, *Organizations and Environments*, 1979.
17. P. A. Clark, 'Organization Design: Key Problems', *Administration and Society*, **7**, 2, 1975, pp. 213–56; P. A. Clark, 'Some Analytic Requirements of an Applied Organization Science', in R. H. Kilmann, L. R. Pondy and L. P. Slevin, *The Management of Organization Design: Strategies and Implementation*, 1976.
18. D. S. Pugh and D. J. Hickson, *The Aston Programme: Volume One*, 1976.
19. J. Hage and M. Aiken, *Social Change in Complex Organizations*, New York, 1970; A. S. Tannenbaum (ed.), *Control in Organizations*, New York, 1968.
20. P. R. Lawrence and J. Lorsch, *Organization and Environment*, Boston, 1967; P. R. Lawrence and D. Dyer, *Renewing American Industry*, 1983.
21. Tannenbaum, op. cit.
22. P. A. Clark, 'A Review of Theories of Time and Structure for Organizational Sociology', in S. Mitchell and S. Bachrach (eds), *Research in Sociology of Organizations*, 1985, pp. 35–79.
23. Clark and Whipp, op. cit.
24. A. W. Gouldner, *Patterns of Industrial Bureaucracy*, 1954.
25. Pugh and Hickson, op. cit.
26. C. Argyris, *The Applicability of Organizational Sociology*, 1972.
27. J. G. March, 'Footnotes to Organizational Change', mimeo., Stanford University, 1980.
28. Lawrence and Dyer, op. cit.
29. For an overview of the labour process literature, see P. Thompson, *The Nature of Work: An Introduction to Debates on the Labour Process*, 1983.
30. R. Edwards, *Contested Terrain: The Transformation of the Workplace in the Twentieth Century*, 1979, viii.

31. Aglietta, op. cit.
32. Edwards, op. cit., p. 16; D. Noble, *America by Design: Science, Technology and the Rise of Corporate Capitalism*, New York, 1977.
33. M. Dobb, *Studies in the Development of Capitalism*, 1946, rev. edn, 1963.
34. Edwards, op. cit., pp. 14–16.
35. T. Nairn, 'The English Working Class', in R. Blackburn (ed.), *Ideology in Social Science*, 1972, pp. 187–206.
36. See the collection of papers in H. F. Gospel and C. R. Littler, *Managerial Strategies and Industrial Relations*, 1983.
37. R. Penn, 'Technological Change, Skilled Manual Work and the Division of Labour', mimeo., Lancaster University, March 1984.
38. J. Kelly and S. Wood, 'Taylorism and the Recession', mimeo., London School of Economics, January 1983.
39. Brown, op. cit.; M. Zey-Ferrell and Michael Aiken, *Complex Organizations: Critical Perspectives*, 1981.
40. A. D. Chandler, *Strategy and Structure: Chapters in the History of the Industrial Enterprise*, 1962; A. D. Chandler, *The Invisible Hand: The Managerial Revolution in American Business*, 1977.
41. S. Toulmin and J. Goodfield, *The Discovery of Time*, 1965; F. Braudel, *On History*, Chicago, 1980; E. Le Roy Ladurie, *The Mind and the Method of the Historian*, 1981.
42. H. J. Hexter, 'Fernand Braudel and Mode Braudellian', *Journal of Modern History*, **XI**, 3, 1972, pp. 1–23.
43. See E. Mandel, *Late Capitalism*, 1978; L. Althusser and E. Balibar, *Reading Capital*, 2nd edn, 1970; E. P. Thompson, *The Making of the English Working Class*, 1963.
44. See P. Abrams, 'History, sociology and historical sociology', *Past and Present*, **87**, 2, 1980, pp. 3–16.
45. G. Gurvitch, *The Spectrum of Social Times*, 1964.
46. E. P. Thompson, 'Time, Work Discipline and Industrial Capitalism', *Past and Present*, **38**, 1967, pp. 56–97; A. Giddens, *Central Problems in Sociological Theory*, 1979; A. Giddens, *A Contemporary Critique of Historical Materialism*, 1981; A. Giddens, *Constitution of Society*, 1984; Abrams, op. cit.
47. S. Kern, *The Culture of Time and Space: 1880–1913*, 1984.
48. H. Bergson, *Time and Freewill*, 1910.
49. See, for example, P. A. Sorokin, *Sociocultural Causality, Space and Time*, 1943; Gurvitch, op. cit.; E. A. Tiryakian, 'Structural Sociology', in J. C. McKinney and E. A. Tiryakian, *Theoretical Sociology: Perspectives and Development*, 1970; W. E. Moore, *Man, Time and Society*, New York, 1963.
50. Rosenberg, op. cit.
51. P. A. Clark, *et al.*, 'The Porous Day. An enquiry into the Appropriation of Time with Reference to the State Sector', mimeo., ESRC Work Organization Research Centre, Aston University, 1984.
52. Giddens, op. cit.; T. Hareven, *Family Time and Industrial Time: The Relationship between the Family and Work in a New England Community*, 1982.
53. H. Ramsay, 'Cycle of control: worker participation in sociological and historical perspective', *Sociology*, **11**, No. 3, September 1977; 'Phantom participation: patterns of power and conflict', *Industrial Relations Journal*, **1**, No. 3, 1980.
54. G. Simmel, *Conflict*, 1955, pp. 58 ff.
55. N. Rosenberg, *The American System of Manufacture*, 1969.

56. A. L. Friedman, 'Management Strategies, Market Conditions and the Labour Process', mimeo., Bristol University, 1981.
57. E. Le Roy Ladurie, 'The "Event" and the "Long Term" in Social History: the Case of the Chouan Uprising', in his *The Territory of the Historian*, 1979, pp. 111–31.
58. T. Zeldin, *The French*, 1982.
59. S. Clegg and D. Dunkerley, *Organization, Class and Control*, 1979.
60. M. Foucault, *Discipline and Punish: The Birth of the Prison*, 1977.
61. Giddens, op. cit.
62. C. More, 'Skill and the survival of apprenticeship', in S. Wood, *The Degradation of Work? Skill, Deskilling and the Labour Process*, 1982, pp. 110–21.
63. Noble, op. cit.
64. S. Bayley, *Harley Earl and the Dream Machine*, 1983.
65. Abernathy, op. cit.
66. J. B. Quinn, *Strategies for Change, Logical Incrementalism*, Illinois, 1980.
67. K. Pavitt, *Technical Change and Britain's Economic Performance*, 1980.
68. M. Crozier, *The Bureaucratic Phenomenon*, 1964.
69. M. Crozier, *The Stalled Society*, New York, 1974.
70. P. A. Clark, 'Cultural context as a determinant of organizational rationality: a comparison of the tobacco industries in Britain and France', in C. J. Lammers and D. J. Hickson, *Organizations Alike and Unlike: International and Inter-institutional Studies in the Sociology of Organizations*, 1979.
71. M. Rose, *Servants of Post-Industrial Power?: 'sociologie du travail' in modern France*, 1979.
72. Giddens, op. cit.
73. T. Hagerstrand, *Propagation of Innovation Waves*, 1983.
74. D. Gregory, *Regional Transformation and the Industrial Revolution: A Geography of the Yorkshire Woollen Industry*, 1982.
75. Giddens, op. cit.
76. Department of Health and Social Security, *Steering Group on Health Services Information: First Report to the Secretary of State*, 1982.
77. See the special issue of the *Administrative Science Quarterly*, December 1979, on qualitative research methods and theories.
78. See E. P. Thompson, *The Making of the English Working Class*, 1968 edn, first published 1963; Gregory, op. cit., pp. 13–17.
79. Abernathy, op. cit.
80. A. L. Stinchcombe, 'Social Structure and Organization', in J. G. March (ed.), *Handbook of Organizations*, Chicago, 1965.
81. A. Teulings, 'The Power of Corporate Management: Powerlessness of the Manager', mimeo., University of Amsterdam, 1984.
82. R. Rothwell and W. Zegveld, *Technical Change and Employment*, 1979.
83. S. B. Saul, 'The Mechanical Engineering Industries in Britain, 1860–1914', in B. Supple, *Essays in British Business History*, 1977, pp. 31–48.
84. H. A. Turner, *Trade Union Growth, Structure and Policy: A Comparative Study of the Cotton Unions*, 1962; W. Lazonick and W. Mass, 'The Performance of the British Cotton Industry, 1870–1913', mimeo., Harvard University 1983; P. H. Grinyer and J-C. Spender, *Turnaround: Management Recipes for Strategies of Success*, 1979.
85. C. Argyris and D. A. Schon, *Organizational Learning: A Theory of Action Perspective*, 1978.
86. R. Woldinger, 'Immigrant entrepreneurs in the garment industry', *Social Problems*, **32**, 1, 1984, pp. 60–71.
87. R. Kaplinsky, *Automation: The Technology and Society*, 1984; 'The New

International Division of Labour in Manufacturing', mimeo., Institute of Development Studies, University of Sussex, 1984.

88. M. Kaldor, 'Technical Change in the Defence Industry', in Pavitt, op. cit., pp. 100–24.

89. Noble, op. cit.

90. P. J. S. Dunnett, *The Decline of the British Motor Industry: The Effects of Government Policy 1945–1979*, 1980.

91. D. T. Jones, *Maturity and Crisis in the European Car Industry*, 1981; 'Technology and the UK Automobile Industry', *Lloyds Bank Review*, April 1984, pp. 14–27.

92. Aldrich, McKelvey and Ulrich, op. cit.

93. D. T. Campbell, 'Variation and Selective Retention in Socio-cultural Evolution', in H. R. Baringer, G. I. Blanksten and R. Mack, *Social Change in Developing Areas*, Cambridge, Mass., 1965.

94. K. Weick, *Social Psychology of Organizing*, 1969.

95. Aldrich, op. cit.

96. M. Jelinek, *Institutionalizing Innovation. A Study of Organizational Learning Systems*, 1979.

97. C. Alexander, *Notes on the Synthesis of Form*, 1971.

98. Abernathy, op. cit.

99. G. Friedman, *Industrial Society: The Emergence of the Human Problems of Automation*, New York, 1955; A. Touraine, *l'Evolution du Travail Ouvrier aux Usines Renault*, Paris, 1955.

100. Abernathy, op. cit.

101. Abernathy, op. cit.

102. See C. Hayes and W. J. Abernathy, 'Managing Our Way to Economic Decline', *Harvard Business Review*, July/August 1980, pp. 69–77; W. J. Abernathy, K. B. Clark and A. M. Kantrow, 'The New Industrial Competition', *Harvard Business Review*, September/October 1981, pp. 68–81.

103. W. J. Abernathy and K. B. Clark, *Industrial Renaissance: Producing a Competitive Future for America*, Boston, 1983.

104. Aldrich, op. cit.

105. J. Woodward, *Industrial Organization: Theory and Practice*, 1965; *Industrial Organization: Behaviour and Control*, 1970.

106. C. Freeman, *Long Waves in the World Economy*, 1983; C. Freeman, J. Clark and L. Soete, *Unemployment and Technical Innovation: A Study of Long Waves and Economy*, 1982; J. Clark and C. Freeman, 'Long Waves, Inventions and Innovations', *Futures*, **13**, 1981, pp. 239–45.

107. T. J. Peters and R. H. Waterman, *In Search of Excellence: Lessons from America's Best Run Companies*, 1982.

108. A. Whitaker, *People, Tasks and Technology: A Study in Consensus*, 1982.

109. R. Whipp and C. Smith, 'Managerial Strategy and Capital Labour Dynamics: Participation in Context', ESRC Work Organization Research Centre, Working Paper No. 4, 1984.

110. Rosenberg, op. cit.

111. H. Mintzberg, D. Raisinghani and A. Theoret, 'The Structure of "Unstructured" Decision Processes', *Administrative Science Quarterly*, **21**, 1976, pp. 246–75.

112. P. Armstrong, 'Competition between the Organizational Professions and the Evolution of Management Control Strategies', in K. Thompson, *Work, Employment and Unemployment: Perspectives on Work and Society*, 1984, pp. 97–120.

113. Quinn, op. cit.; see also E. J. Miller and A. K. Rice, *Systems of Organization:*

The Control of Task and Sentient Boundaries, 1967, pp. 138 ff., for useful insights into the processes associated with 'Organizational Design and Building Systems'.

114. See, for example, F. Crouzet, *The Victorian Economy*, 1982.
115. T. C. Barker, *The Glassmakers: Pilkington: The Rise of an International Company, 1820–1962*, 1977.
116. O. E. Williamson, *Markets and Hierarchies: Analysis and Antitrust Implications*, New York, 1975.
117. J. K. Galbraith, *The New Industrial Estate*, Boston, 1967; see also Noble, op. cit., and Braverman, op. cit.
118. P. A. Clark, *Organizational Design: Theory and Practice*, 1972.
119. The Technology Policy Unit at Aston University undertakes studies of the degree to which trade unions are involved in technology agreements. See the reports by R. Williams and R. Moseley, 'Consensus, Control and Technical Change in the Work Place', 1982; H. Levie and R. Williams, 'User Involvement and Industrial Democracy', 1983; R. Williams and B. Pearce, 'Design, New Technology and Trade Unions', in *Design Policy, Vol. 1: Design and Society*, 1984.
120. G. Nadler, *The Planning and Design Approach*, 1981.
121. J. G. March and H. A. Simon, *Organization*, Boston, 1958.
122. H. A. Turner, G. G. Clack and G. Roberts, *Industrial Relations in the Motor Industry: A Study of Industrial Unrest and International Comparison*, 1967.
123. L. Karpik, *Organization and Environment: Theory, Issues and Reality*, 1978.
124. Peters and Waterman, op. cit.
125. For example, S. Hill, *Competition and Control at Work*, 1979.
126. D. Noble, 'Social Choice in Machine Design: The Case of Automatically Controlled Machine Tools', in A. Zimbalist (ed.), *Case Studies in the Labour Process*, New York, 1979, p. 45.
127. Hill, op. cit.
128. Argyris and Schon, op. cit.
129. R. I. Hall, 'A System Pathology of Organization: The Rise and Fall of the Saturday Evening Post', *Administrative Science Quarterly*, **2**, 1, 1976, pp. 165–211.
130. British employers have consistently opposed the legislation of employee participation and have been reluctant to engage in extensive technological agreements; see Note 119 *supra*.
131. Whipp and Smith, 'Managerial Strategy and Capital Labour Dynamics', pp. 70–3.
132. H. Beynon, *Working for Ford*, 2nd edn, 1984.
133. T. Lupton and I. Tanner, 'Work Organization Design in Europe', in K. D. Duncan, M. M. Gruneberg and D. Wallis, *Changes in Working Life*, 1980, pp. 217–36.
134. Touraine, op. cit.

PART II

3 The Rover Company, 1896–1968

Introduction

This is the first of three chapters presenting an analytically structured narrative of a speciality car firm in the British auto industry: Rover. Chapter 3 reconstructs the dynamics involved in the creation of the company's design hierarchy and its structural repertoire over a period of seven decades, from the 1890s into the 1960s. Unlike the previous chapters, this one will be a synthesis of concepts and narrative in which the model of design and innovation which is the central focus of the book becomes embedded in the events. It is appropriate to highlight certain features in the introduction.

First, the Rover Company is examined to discover how and when its members managed to develop a competence in design as a total process embracing the car, the facilities and the work organization. From the sector life-cycle model proposed by Abernathy, it would be expected that the British industry would have a founding period in which a great variety of manufacturers attempted to satisfy the uncertain demands of their customers. Then this founding period is likely to be followed by a 'shakeout' in which the basis of competition becomes price leadership. A dominant design begins to emerge. Thus, individual firms would be faced by the requirement to adapt their design hierarchies to the changing possibilities created by new materials and by new modes of manufacture. We would anticipate that each corporation would develop a repertoire of forms of work organization which would be likely to become crystalized and possibily fossilized as past practices based on successful problem solving being wrongly applied to new and different problems. It is likely that some corporate leaders could not recognize the external changes in the shape of the market and in the uses to which the consumers were putting cars. Also, it is likely that some corporations would be unable to adjust their repertoires because of the conflicting demands of external and internal events. Rover is a particularly good example of the stresses created for the structural repertoire by changes in the design hierarchies of firms which intend to survive.

Second, the chapter anchors the points made in Chapter 2 about the differences between the European markets compared with North America. The case of Rover in Britain should be seen in a general European perspective in which other similar firms (e.g. Volvo and BMW) sought to grapple with the opportunities and constraints of national markets whilst opening up other continental and overseas markets, especially in North America: of equal interest is the fate of North American firms in the European context, especially Ford after 1912 and General Motors after 1924. Each of these was influential as a representation of American 'best practice' in design skills, technology, work organization and marketing.

Third, the chapter provides an important opportunity to explore the extent to which the future is shaped by thinking and practices which are heavily embedded in the past. This claim, noted in Chapter 2, places a heavy stress on the reproduction of past practices and suggests that there are overpowering constraining institutions and relationships. However, as the Rover case study shows, key individuals occupying structurally important roles can have a strong influence in corporate turnarounds. The chapter shows that the individuals who buy cars and those who work in car factories are themselves situated on trajectories whose unfolding is shaped to some degree by their conceptions of future life styles. The paradox for the auto industry is to reconcile its dual reliance on individuals as consumers and as employees in the industry. The chapter illustrates how the importation to Rover in the 1960s of workers with life styles orientated to consumption rather than to service severely challenged the core values created over the previous three decades.

Fourth, the perspective of structure-event-structure provides a highly insightful means of analysing the learning capabilities of enterprises.[1] In the case of Rover, the initial structural repertoire was used with only slight elaboration and little modification for almost four decades, at the close of which the firm was faced by exit from the industry. Then came a relatively short period in which attempts were introduced to tighten up the existing structure, followed by the gradual introduction of a new structure based on a distinctive design recipe in the early 1930s. That new structure was carried forward into the sixties, when a new set of contextual crises surfaced. Each structure is a multi-layered social template[2] containing implicit practices used in the routines of daily working; introducing changes is therefore a slow process.

Fifth, designing as a total process can be conceived of as a one-shot event or as the establishment of capacities which can be re-configured. The former has been described by Gardiner[3] as lean designing, and the latter as robust designing. A capacity to engage in robust designing has crucial beneficial consequences. For example, in the United States, after the mid-1920s, General Motors developed a design hierarchy in which robust potentials were accentuated by using annual styling of the body and the interior whilst standardizing the production of components and engines. Robust designing requires an exceptional vision and a skill in linking together the car shape, the factory and the forms of work organization. In the case of Rover, it was the transition to robust designing—the P series—after 1932-4 which provided the cash flow necessary for corporate survival. The key figure was Wilks, who produced robust designs capable of considerable stretching. This approach was successfully applied to the selling of speciality saloon cars. However, the greatest success was in the four wheel drive Land Rover introduced in 1947. Over the next four decades, that basic model was stretched in a variety of ways to meet the needs of a variety of market sectors.

Sixth, the application of the comparative historical framework introduced in Chapter 2 reveals important differences between the British (and European) contexts and those found in North America. For these reasons, the sector life-cycle model of Abernathy requires revisions to accommodate changes in market capacity and in forms of production, including work organization. Previous interpretations and researches have tended to conflate the experiences of the British and the Americans into a single mode. Whilst there are important areas of similarity, it is the dissimilarities which are significant in explaining the role of North American enterprises in Europe and the lack of penetration of European firms in North America. One of the most important areas of dissimilarity is in the attention given to formal training as a way of retaining best practices and as the means of altering previous best practices. In the United States and Canada there is the parallel and complementary development of education in universities and of training within corporations. In practice, the numbers of people and the amounts of money invested in human capital through higher education and corporate training are similar. By comparison, in the United Kingdom the higher education sector is much slighter as a proportion of the adult population, and corporate training is smaller and more informal. This difference explains the dependence of British managements on skills developed by the employee, and has considerable consequences for the occupational consciousness of British workers, particularly in the auto industry which was situated in a region with a long tradition of small workshops, family trades and self-determination within a market nexus.

The chapter commences by presenting a periodization in which seven decades at Rover are broken down into four major periods, each typified by a distinctive set of problems. Each of these periods is examined in a very selective manner to show how the structural repertoire and the design hierarchy interacted. In the founding period of the British auto industry, Rover entered via the assembly of bicycles, yet found itself able to gain a substantial segment of the market. In the first decades Rover was diversified in its product range, both in types of car and in other products. The company entered the 1920s with an established repertoire and then found itself facing the cost-cutting mass production approaches of Austin and of Morris, who were attempting to adapt American concepts of production and work organization to the British market. Rover tended to persist with the established design hierarchy, but found that low financial returns were transformed into losses. In the late 1920s, under Searle, who was recruited as a general executive from outside the industry, there were attempts to improve the cost effectiveness, but this was mistakenly conceived in engineering rather than economic terms. Hence there was little grasp of the balance between batch size, market share and profits. Then came the period of S. B. Wilks in the 1930s, who re-aligned Rover with the market by focusing on the expensive speciality car sector which could afford the 'hand-built' methods of assembly. Wilks introduced robust designs with the P series of speciality saloons after 1932. This approach to designing optimized commonalities and some standardization whilst permitting considerable stretching of designs. In some cases a particular model came into production—with stretching—for a decade. This meant that Rover achieved a balance between the costs of design and re-tooling with the inflows of finance for the next model. By the early 1960s, the implicit design strategy of stretching robust designs had been recognized and articulated into a formal recipe for survival. So Rover's corporate management entered the 1960s with a sense of having developed a successful recipe.

This chapter forms a crucial background for understanding the events and turmoil which surrounded the SD1 project. Rover were the chosen focus for the Specialist Cars Division, created within British Leyland after the mergers of 1967–9. However, the designers in Rover—who were already heavily committed to the creation of the new P8 and P10 range— were then required to recommence the whole design process and to do so in collaboration with other groups within British Leyland with whom they had never previously undertaken joint activities. The ways in which the SD1 project unfolded were heavily shaped by the established approaches of Rover.

The examination of Rover can be broken into four distinct periods, each characterized by a specific set of problems. First, there was the period of founding, from 1896 to about 1920. The Rover Cycle Company was established by J. K. Starley in 1889 to manufacture and distribute the Rover Safety Cycle. After seven years, the company became public through the London Stock Exchange. In the next two decades, the company diversified into motor bicycles and automobiles, becoming in 1912 the world's largest manufacturer of these three items. The peak years were probably 1913–14, when Rover was producing good profits and their rivals, apart from Ford, were all relatively small. Yet there were unrealized problems, the appearance of which was delayed by the government's contracts for war work (e.g. ambulances), followed by two relatively calm years after 1918 when there was a heavy demand for cars.

Second, the period 1920–34 seemed to begin in a promising way. The Board paid out high dividends and Rover avoided the debacle which beset Austin, but the strategy of trying to grow by buying up a nearby firm proved doubly awkward. It absorbed a great deal of finance which might have been used to buy in components, as the highly entreprenurial Morris Company was doing in the same period. The new plant in Tyseley was also a source of problems of co-ordination and production control which were new to Rover's board and top management. The 1920s were a decade when the British market moved out of the architectural phase[4] into one in which companies obtained market niches of varying sizes. There was a slight trend towards the American pattern of a dominant design hierarchy, but this became attenuated. Price leadership became important, though not as decisive as in the United States and Canada. The 1920s soon brought Rover a period of losses and no dividends, culminating in 1928 in the financial restructuring of the share capital downward to 40 per cent of its capitalization. After a momentary burst of profitability came more financial difficulties. At this stage Rover might well have exited from the auto industry. However, the joint intervention of Lucas (the largest British component supplier and a major creditor) and the Lloyds Bank provided the financial breathing space which permitted the appointed financial

adviser to clear the debts and to create solvency. In this period an alteration occurred in the product market segment which the company was
targeting. Even so, the company retained its work organization of small to
medium batch production and matched this to a car design for a prosperous sector of the market which could pay the requisite price.

Third, after 1932, Wilks led Rover for three decades in which the
company concentrated upon supplying its new distinctive segment with
speciality saloon cars. Wilks's skill included the ability to create robust
designs which could be stretched sufficiently for the company to locate
market niches which provided favourable profits over long enough
periods to recoup the costs of investment and to build reserves for the new
cycle of major design and innovation. There was a successful period of
wartime production, including advanced work on engines, when the
company was around the forefront of leading design developments. Many
of these were incorporated into the cars. As is well known, the top
management discovered a notable solution to the post-1945 shortage of
steel when the Land Rover was developed as a four wheel drive utility
vehicle using aluminium. Its design and method of assembly were
strongly based on the craft and semi-skilled type of work organization
which had characterized the company for most of its history. After the
Land Rover—which sold initially to farmers and the military—came the
Range Rover as a more up-market stretching of the original concept. In
this way Rover developed two major product areas: the saloon car and the
four wheel drive models with subsidiary units producing engines and
other power train components. The 1950s were profitable and the
company established a rhythm of producing new model ranges. The P6
range of saloons was introduced after 1963.

Fourth, after 1963 the Rover Company had begun to adjust the factory
and work organization, but within existing concepts from small to
medium batch production. This continued from 1968 to 1972, when £4
million was expended designing the new P8/P10 saloons and the additional facilities adjacent to existing production in Solihull.

I Founding: diversification and growth

The period of the founding of the Rover Company intersected with two
different trajectories of economic development which must be treated as
the key contextual features. These were the 'cycle boom' and the founding
of the auto industry.

The cycle boom in Britain was facilitated by the urban character of work
and life, coupled to the increasing problems posed by horse-drawn transport. The latter occupied considerable space at home and on the roadways
as well as generating an immense problem when disposing of the two
kilos per day of excrement which were deposited. A Parliamentary
Committee of 1873 proposed the bicycle as a solution, but the implementation of this solution was limited by the simple fact that the pennyfarth-
ing cycle could only be ridden by the young and fit, and under certain
road conditions. In 1885 J. K. Starley totally redesigned the cycle to create

the modern form: an example of radical innovation. His cycle was known as the Rover Safety Cycle. This new design immediately extended the range of the population who could use the bicycle, and therefore created a massive demand.

J. K. Starley founded his own company, and apart from losses sustained in an American venture, the demand rose rapidly and trade expanded. Consequently, new monies were needed to finance expanded production facilities, and so Starley went public in 1896 with a capitalization of £150,000, most of which was represented by patents and goodwill. At this stage of the cycle industry's evolvement, the capital investments were mainly in inventory—at all stages—and in some buildings. Relatively small investments were made in equipment, and much of this was general purpose machinery rather than specialized machine tools. An even smaller proportion was invested in power machines.[5] The 'Cycle' was dropped from the company's name after Starley's death in 1902, and three years later a designer was hired for one year to produce an automobile for assembly alongside the cycle workshops. The nervous shareholders were reassured to learn that his new venture was undertaken 'reluctantly'. Even so, a six horsepower car was launched in 1906 and sold so well in the expanding British auto market that plans were constructed to double production.

From 1907 to 1924 the British market expanded more than tenfold, which is considerable except when compared with the United States, which began at three times the size of the British market and increased seventyfold in the same period. In that expanding market Rover soon acquired a 10 per cent share, then fell back to approximately 4 per cent. Even so, by 1909, almost 90 per cent of the profits came from cars, and a small number of motor cycles, whilst only 12 per cent came from bicycles as such. It has been argued that the origin of many British car firms in the bicycle industry was unfortunate because that industry was based on simple forms of assembly.[6] Hence there was little requirement for science or science-led engineering, nor was there any requirement to develop linkages into higher education, as was the case in chemicals.

The first period may be described as one of growth and of diversification. Starley was Managing Director until his death in 1902, at which time the Rover Cycle Company was assembling and selling 17,500 cycles per annum. The Minutes of the Directors for these first five years were preoccupied with financial matters and with the erection of sheds and stores in Coventry at the Meteor Works. Despite problems with suppliers of materials, the company continued to develop its sales force into Europe and into Australasia, as well as establishing seven major depots throughout the United Kingdom from which salesmen contacted the retailers.

The factory consisted of sheds with areas for storage placed at one end, separated by a wall. Within the sheds it seems that the sub-assembly work was organized into sections and there were indications that the movement of work was hindered by congestion.[7] Also, although bicycles were relatively similar, it is evident that each manufacturer introduced specific variations; hence an attempt by the War Office to purchase cycles which contained standardized, interchangeable parts was opposed by the Board.[8]

The Managing Director was responsible for the daily running of the factory. There was a collection of sections, each of which was headed by a supervisor who had the responsibility for controlling costs within that section. The costing system did not use standard costs, but there was an attempt to specify a budget for each section and this was recorded 'in green ink'. When supervisors kept the costs of the section below the green ink figures, they were paid a bonus. There was therefore a form of delegated control. The Managing Director was responsible to the Board for the running of the company. He had a Works Manager reporting to him who was responsible for internal co-ordination. There was little paperwork and few white-collar employees. At Board meetings the Secretary presented a summary of the trading position.

In the first five years the company faced two new problems: first, a temporary decline in the demand for cycles, and second, the raising of a cash flow to finance the new factory. Capital accumulation was principally in the form of buildings rather than plant and equipment. During this period, the shareholders received regular dividends and were relatively quiescent.[9] Early in 1902 the Board considered and rejected the decision to manufacture motor cycles, but after the death of Starley the decision was reversed. Starley's death coincided with the rise to influence of the Works Manager and his becoming Managing Director. The reformed Board decided to produce motor cycles and bought various licences for the manufacture of components. One year later, the Board were considering the production of a small car. The process of diversification was under way.

At this stage the cycle industry had reached a plateau of growth and a rationalization of firms was commencing. However, the British auto industry which was much later in establishing itself than in France or Germany, was just beginning. The extraordinary attempt by Lawson and associates to dominate the British industry by buying patents had just failed. Only Daimler (also in Coventry) were making cars on a regular basis.

In 1904 the Board allocated £1,000 to Mr Lewis for the designing and building of a small car. The Board prepared for future car production by purchasing licences for components and by buying a foundry and constructing an erecting shop. It is evident that the Managing Director also used his discretion to recruit new staff, including clerical workers and draughtsmen. In 1905 the company was ready to order one hundred sets of components for assembling. By 1907 they were achieving annual sales of 1,200 cars, and held about 10 per cent of the small British market. This was in fact a small peak, though it was unknown to the owners and employees of Rover.

The diversification into cars introduced further novel organizational problems. The shareholders were hesitant and had to be reassured. New types of staff were recruited, especially white-collar workers. There was a shortage of space on the existing site for both cycles and cars, and it therefore became necessary to transfer cycle production to a new site so that cars could be erected on the Meteor site. New purchases of equipment were necessary, and these were regarded with concern.[10] The existing approach to costing proved inadequate and so attempts were made in 1908 to compare production costs against the selling price and to design categories of expenditure.[11] This was followed by a determined attempt to reduce expenses by sacking staff and cutting the budgets. Unlike Henry Ford, the Rover company entered 1908 with the aim of producing a range of five sizes of car in small batches. Diversification was established and seemed to be working rather well.

Total sales of cars had hardly increased by 1912-13, yet the company still managed to achieve a profit of £130,000. Most of this came from cars, and Rover's position in the cycle industry—now dominated by Raleigh—was becoming marginalized. The opportunity to merge with Raleigh was rejected; the future appeared to be in cars. In practice, the immediate future was in war production on government contracts, from 1914 to 1918. Just prior to the outbreak of war, Rover's Board ensured that its financial position was secure, and this feature sustained the company through the immediate years after 1918. However, they were not able to obtain large new premises as a result of their war work in the manner successfully exploited by Austin at the Longbridge works in Birmingham.[12]

By 1920 the capitalization of Rover had been increased to just over £1 million. Yet, as Foreman-Peck[13] observes, these figures obscured certain general features. Except in the unusual years of 1912-13, the profit range/revenue ratio was rather poor, whilst the pay-out ratio ranged from 98 per cent (1900) to 40 per cent with the passing of the dividend in three years. At the end of this period the sharp increase in capitalization of the company was necessary to finance the manufacture of the cars, but its size required a high absorption of profits in dividends. Foreman-Peck concludes therefore that Rover was internally inefficient.

The changing pattern of the Directors' Minutes seems to belie the thesis of inefficiency. For example, there was a clear shift in the content of the agendas from matters of corporate ownership, of finance and the details of stock transfers, to increased attention to matters of production. Also, over the period of a quarter of a century it is possible to follow the increasing influence of the partnership of the Managing Director and the Works Manager. They brought a focus on plant and equipment as well as the elements of cost control. There was little attention to marketing as a specialist function.

These elaborations of the work organization amongst management need to be compared with international developments in management organization. In Rover it is important to note that, first, the corporate leadership was equally concerned with control and social order as with either the market situation or with the flows of work. Second, with respect to the market, sales responsibilities were devolved to travelling salesmen and to the depots in the early period, and then to the dealerships once car production commenced. In this period the sales statistics were collated by the Secretary, who reported the position and forecasts of the next three months. There is little attention to the systematic examination of work organization and to the searching for sources of costs which arise from bottlenecks. The economies of co-ordination[14] are barely mentioned. Rover established the design function through the employment of an external specialist on a short contract followed by the registration of all developments in the forms of patents.[15] It is clear that Rover produced a range of designs which were sold to the public in small batches.

The British market lacked the dominant design potential of the American market. The attempt by Ford to dominate the British market was of the first importance because their 25 per cent share of the market in 1912 set a cost dimension which became more important in the 1920s. However, the impact of American best practices on British firms did not appear until the 1920s. Rover achieved their successes when the market was in a very fluid state.

In this period, the board of Rover did not provide for design as a specialist function. Instead, the designing was part of the area of responsibility of the Works Manager, who considered new cars in terms of annual revisions to the assembly of components which could be arranged into a car. This was an adaptive process which created annual styling changes as an outcome rather than as a deliberate policy. The seasonal character of car sales is vitally important. The selling season was quite short, and its duration permitted a period of reflection and editing of performance. In the case of Rover there was a pattern in which the approach of the selling season was apprehended with nervousness followed by the very definite interpretation of successes and failures, coupled to highly optimistic statements about the next season. These were often reinforced by the experience of the annual motor show. Little direct attention was given to the analysis of competitors, nor to the examination of the American approaches.

The Rover experience of the problems of design conceived as a total process had been relatively simple. In effect, a design capacity had been acquired through proxies rather than through the institutionalization of the required structuration. The initial entry into cars had been achieved by hiring Lewis for less than two years and receiving from his directions an 8hp design which, although over-complex, was the basis for the 6hp model, for the short-lived 10/12 and the tourist class 16/20. Lewis succeeded in establishing the design of a family of engines which effectively powered the cars from 1905 to about 1910, after which there was a search for a new, more advanced and powerful engine. Because Rover bought in many components and enjoyed a close relationship with Daimler nearby, the Board, senior management and the work-force were able to acquire sufficient learning skills to undertake the remaining tasks of assembly based on the principles of cycle manufacture. In 1910 the acquisition of Clegg for eighteen months provided a further impetus to the design of cars which carried the company up to about 1920 in general terms and to 1924 in the case of the 14hp. Clegg further rationalized the design and assembly of engines, improved the reliability of the cars and set down the basic principles of 'tooling up', that is, matching the car to the requirements for plant, dies and jigs.[16] His design of the 12 provided the framework of design for the 14 and 18 models as a basic range. Their internal layout was conventional and created few problems of assembly. Before his departure, Rover had left the small car market and focused on the up-market 12 and 18 hp cars. Thus, when the Rover Board appointed Wild to handle both works management and design, they seemed not to have realized that they were living dangerously. Indeed, the intervention of war work obscured the underlying gaps.

The design of the factory was limited to the designation of major areas of space and the buying of new facilities. The arrangement of the space was the responsibility of the Works Manager. Overall, the growth and diversification of the Company had not been accompanied by the generation of a comprehensive model of design and of innovation.

II Facing exit: 1920–1932

In the 1920s there was a sharp transformation in the overall size and the composition of the United Kingdom market. Annual sales increased from under 100,000 new units to more than 400,000. Also, the recession which affected sales in the United States, Canada and France did not affect the British market, which remained relatively buoyant. The change in the composition of the market affected all segments by altering the type of expensive car, whilst opening a new market for the cheap lightweight car such as the Austin 7. The type of car which dominated the market changed radically to the small, cheap car at the inexpensive end of the tax range and with greater fuel economy.

By 1930 the market was dominated by two British firms—Morris and Austin—who held almost 80 per cent of total sales. These two were distinguished by the attempts of their owners and managements to discover forms of production and work organization which matched the smaller British market to the technological innovations and modes of organization already established in the United States and in Canada. Austin benefited from having new facilities as a consequence of wartime contracts for the government. These new buildings were paid for by the state. Morris, at Cowley in Oxford, was the leader in price reductions through the selective application of American production methods. He constantly reduced the manpower needed to assemble a car. In practice, Morris modified the methods of mass production on an American scale to the design hierarchy appropriate to the British market.

The American-owned Ford Company found the British context difficult to decode. Its corporate controllers in Detroit tended to impose designs which were too large for the consumer. Their market share fell dramatically. Early in the 1930s the American parent company took the unusual step of permitting its British subsidiary to develop its own products for the British and continental markets. However, the effects of this policy did not become apparent until later. General Motors entered the British—and hence the European—scene through the purchase of Vauxhall at Luton in 1924. Lewchuk[17] contends that Vauxhall attempted to initiate American technology: but they certainly failed to achieve the market share necessary for mass production. Rover entered this period after the successful financial experience of producing contract work (e.g. ambulances) for the Ministry of Defence. At first the demand for Rover cars rose steadily and the Board were encouraged; then, after 1924, a variety of new problems surfaced and substantial losses occurred in 1925. From then until the early 1930s, the company faced exit through liquidation.

Car design in this period continued to be by proxy. As previously, Rover bought a design from outside by spending £400,000 to acquire the 8 hp design of Sangster and a former government property as a production facility at Tyseley, some twenty miles from Coventry. The Tyseley plant constructed the chassis and wheels, after which the body was added in Coventry. This arrangement introduced novel problems of supervision at a distance. The new car was sturdy, unless driven at speeds of more than 35 m.p.h. About 17,000 were produced and sold between 1921 and 1924, but the entry of Austin in 1922 with the '7' forced the Sangster car off the market. Rover's decision to enter the cheap end of the car market in 1920 had brought them up against the more effective total design approaches of Austin and Morris; meanwhile, Sangster left the company.

Rover tended to be out of touch with changing design requirements. The first serious attempt to establish internal design structures were connected with the unsuccessful 14/15. This financial failure was followed by the unsuccessful attempt to design a 3.5 which only sold three cars. The solution to a weak product range was resolved by recruiting Poppe, a design expert, in 1924. He had been designing a new engine for several years, and brought this untested concept to Rover, where it was eventually installed in the 14/15. This car had many attendant problems. Poppe was more successful, however, with the design of a 'straight six' in 1927.

The growing financial crisis of 1928 was approached by recruiting Searle. His residency as Managing Director coincided with a brief upward spurt in demand, giving Rover 4 per cent of the market. However, Searle tended to focus only on car production through quantity and the attempt to create a cheap 10/25 in 1930 led to a car with poor appearance and performance. Searle may be credited with making one key appointment, that of Spencer Wilks, who became the first successful internal design leader linking the car, the plant and the work organization. Under his direction the 10/25 was transformed into the 'Family 10' and the 'Special 10', both successful. By 1932 Wilks was establishing new concepts of design based on standardization of components and the stretching of one basic design into several models for a range. His creation of the 'P' series is the subject of the following section.

The signs of impending problems were appearing by 1920, but did not become distinct for several years. In 1920 Rover sold all its production at a profit, but soon had to absorb a heavy loss on the newly purchased factory at Tyseley. This plant had been established as an additional base for the production of new cars. Despite this setback the shareholders were encouraged by the continuity of generous dividends. The top management re-examined the price of their cars, thus revealing an awareness of future tendencies, but decided to hold the existing prices. The Board sanctioned extra production of the 8 hp model, but later had to reduce the prices of the established models. Trade fell away, and this was attributed to the general atmosphere of industrial unrest.[18]

By 1923 Rover were facing the problems of their economies of scale and efficiency of production relative to the growing strength of Austin and of Morris in the cheap car market. The nature of the new problem went unrecognized by the Board and top management, who continued with established accountancy practices which laid great stress on historical rather than forward costing techniques. At Rover the selling price of the car was calculated by adding an allowance for profit on top of the production costs estimated by the Works Manager.[19] This process may be compared with American strategies of setting a price to be beaten by effective production and economies of scale. It seems unlikely that Rover had any accurate estimate of the economies of scale. The company gradually became involved in a vicious circle by which the relatively high price of its car adversely affected sales by slowing down their rate of demand. This had the consequence of accelerating the decay in the value of unsold stocks whilst also reducing the size of the cash flows.[20]

The year 1923 was another year of loss, with the Board paying the shareholders a dividend from past profits. The company was therefore in an increasingly weakened position to finance the total design of a new car, of new production facilities and new forms of work organization, including the retraining of staff. At this point the design process had nestled in amongst other functions, being the responsibility of one of the assistants to the Works Manager. So, when the Board recorded the following Minute they barely appreciated the extent of the task which needed to be undertaken: 'To design an 11 HP 4 cylinder car and a 14 HP 4 cylinder car on latest lines, in accordance with popular demand. To discontinue the manufacture of the 21 HP 6 cylinder car'.[21]

By early 1924 more difficulties were emerging. First, the drawings were delayed and so the Board called P. A. Poppe for an interview at which they 'impressed on him the urgent need for speed in the matter of new cars'.[22] The Board were right to be nervous since their existing product range was too expensive for the market. Their overseas agent in South Africa sent proposed selling prices which were below the costs of production. Further, it was discovered that the 14 hp model was costing more to produce than had been estimated. When Poppe was called to the Board he was asked to estimate the relationship between the size of a production run and the average costs of the new car then being designed. His suggestion for the production of one hundred units per week satisfied the Board, and he agreed to press on with getting the car into production.[23] The Board noted with anxiety that if the McKenna Duty were removed then continental car manufacturers would flood the British market with 'cheap models produced under unfair conditions'.[24] It is not surprising that in these circumstances it was decided that new demands for wage increases could not be met. In an unusual reference, the Sales Manager—for the first time—reported that delays in production were holding up sales. The action of the Sales Manager was a clear sign that the production engineering orientation of Rover was losing touch with the demands of the marketplace.

The shift in the psychological agenda of the Board was accompanied by other changes. For the first time there was an extended examination of the profit margins on each model in the six-car range. This revealed wide variations, from under 1 per cent on one car to a satisfactory margin on two others. However, this analysis was based on the assumption that costs for Rover would remain stable, and the discussion did not anticipate the possibility that rivals might force prices downward through volume production. After a more detailed examination of two models—the 8 hp and the 9 hp—the Managing Director

> raised the point as to the cost of these models compared with what the public were prepared to pay for them, and stated that, having consulted a number of the agents, he thought it would be impossible to list these cars at the suggested price of £200 and £160 respectively ... if the ... output of our works were to be sold, and he expressed the opinion that the manufacturing costs must be reduced.[25]

These statements lend some credence to the rumours which began to circulate in the press suggesting that Rover was bankrupt. The rumour disturbed the Board, and may have influenced their decision to distribute some of the small profits.

The year 1925 revealed the top management attempting to come to grips with the financial and organizational problems of simultaneously producing an on-going range of cars profitably whilst designing a new range of cars and being able to purchase the new plant and machinery. There was increased attention to the problems of future production. Plans for 1926 were discussed early in 1925. The new 14/45 car was still the source of problems. Plans were made to build up production over three months to 400 a month, ready for the seasonal demand. However, the agents were disturbed by various features of the car, especially the noisy valve gear; Poppe, now promoted to Chief Engineer with responsibility for the design of new cars, assured the Board that the problem was being resolved.

Meanwhile, the cash flow problem were increased by the 'grave lack of orders' for the new car. Once again the Sales Manager spoke out. Consequently, there were difficulties in paying suppliers, the overdraft at the bank spiralled upward, and Rover were pressed for mortgages on the plant to secure the increasing debt. The financial year closed with a record loss of £127,543, which was explained to shareholders as an exceptional situation arising from the development costs of the new car.[26]

The year 1926 was also a year of bad financial performance. The new 14/45 was not selling, and though the price was reduced in search of buyers, the Board were coming to the conclusion that the car was pitched at a segment of the market which was in fact very thin.[27] They decided to introduce more new designs. As previously, the approach to the design of cars was dictated by engineering rather than market considerations. The market was explored in only the sketchiest manner. Similarly, the design of the new factory facilities was only seriously begun when the design of the new car was almost complete. The 1926–7 season proved another serious financial loss. The following season began equally badly.

Early in 1928 it was clear that the Board had become uncertain about the market, and that this uncertainty was affecting their choices for the designs of new cars for the next season. That uncertainty was reflected in the renewed discussion of the role of the Works Manager as chief designer, and in the Board's decision to examine the book which recorded the alterations to designs. In the midst of that indecision the largest shareholders intervened and gained representation on the Board. By mid-year, the search for outside expertise had led to the approach to Col. Searle, to become joint Managing Director. The decision was taken whilst the existing Managing Director was abroad.

The four-year Searle era began and ended with unsold cars. There were two successful years, followed by two further years of heavy losses. Financially, the 1927–8 season was the cumulative point of a disastrous period. The directors revalued the stock and the plant and wrote down the value of ageing machinery and unsold stock. The result was an enormous loss of £600,000, which was absorbed by writing down the share capital from £1.05 million to £0.42 million.

Searle arrived in the middle of the 1928 selling season and prior to the production of the annual report. His arrival coincided with changes in the Board as a whole, which probably facilitated his extensive changes in many areas of operation. First, he secured approval to rearrange the sales force to create twelve regions, each of which contained many potential agents for the cars. The objective was to use the small garage as an agency. A new Sales Manager was appointed to manage the areas, but his functions were separate from the advertising effort, which was guided by Searle. Second, the time horizon of forward planning was slightly extended and there was a stronger focus on long-term thinking, but this was rather abstract and seems to have been in the form of the imposition of structured intentions rather than the careful weighting of factors. The plans were subject to unforeseen change. Also, the promised targets on profits were never achieved, even in the two profitable years. Searle retained Poppe as the joint designer and Works Manager, whilst giving considerable attention to controlling the flow of work through the factories. A system of progress control was installed and the Bedeaux consultants were employed to improve the efficiency of the plant, particularly at Tyseley; also, an additional consulting engineer was appointed. Several approaches were initiated towards potential partners, like Standard and Lanchester.

For the next two seasons its seemed that Rover was improving its performance, but then the years 1930–2 produced disastrous losses, arising from unsold cars. In this period there were further managerial changes, one of which brought Spencer Wilks into the position of Works Manager. Yet again, in 1932, Rover faced bankruptcy and Searle departed.

III Wilks and the P series

In the three decades following the crisis of 1930–2 the company moved from facing exit to establishing and holding a market niche in specialist luxury cars as well as establishing an international reputation for the four wheel drive Land Rover series. In 1932 the Lloyds Bank and the Lucas Company collaborated to provide Rover with the time to pay off their debts and to become re-established. This is a clear example of what institutional economists call loyalty.[28]

Two executives played a central role in the restructuring of Rover in the early 1930s: Graham and S. B. Wilks. The former was a nominee of the Bank. His role was to establish financial controls throughout the company and to centralize financial information where it was accessible to forward planning. His influence established a financial grid for decision making. The strength of this system was that it permitted top management to make financial assessments, but its limitation—hardly the fault of Graham—was that too little attention was directed towards the detailed reconstruction of the future financial prospects. However, the basic systems which Graham introduced were an important part of Rover's development of management controls.

It is evident from the Minutes of the Directors' Meetings and other sources in the archives that Rover's management did establish standardized practices for many activities. From Searle onward, these practices were increasingly regularized in formal, written format. So, for example, the practice of recording alterations to designs in a standard book was extended to other areas. These sources constituted 'bibles' which described past practice.[29] Once established, they tended to remain in their initial format.

S. B. Wilks is rightly credited with establishing the design recipe which lifted Rover and established its reputation. Wilks formalized two themes and coupled them to strategic decision making. One theme was to envisage the design of the car as a periodic affair in which a robust design was used as the basis for considerable stretching over a number of years. This became known as the P series. Thus, annual seasonal variations were given a direction. The other—and related—theme was to standardize the chassis and the engine as basic components which would remain stable over long periods, with only slight incremental modifications. At the same time Wilks put a premium on engineering refinement and incremental design.

In market terms, Wilks shifted Rover from the small car market into the speciality cars segment, and mainly in Britain. This market segment, reported to include a high proportion of professionals, was large enough to permit survival until the mid-1960s. Under Wilks a design hierarchy emerged which matched the market segment demand to periodic radical, robust designs of cars and these were skilfully translated into the requirements of production. Wilks developed the division of labour amongst top management and the growing staff roles (in engineering and design) so that its architecture balanced the requirements for specialization with largely informal mechanisms for integration. He was authoritative in a manner which was both consistent with the established sense of paternalism, yet was sufficiently in tune with wider changes to provide the basis for incorporating most parts of the work-force—at all levels—with a sense of direction and belonging. Unlike some of the previous leadership, whose competences were outside car production, Wilks was highly competent. For example, under his leadership Rover learned the complex methods of translating car designs into appropriate production requirements. It is important to note that many features of the established forms of work organization were carried forward through the next three decades. Thus, Rover employees were able to find recognizable outlets for their self-images as skilled craftsmen.

In Britain the effects of the international recession were less severe than in the United States. The market for cars remained satisfactory in total, though the costs of entry for new firms seeking to obtain niches began to grow. Rover progressed through the 1930s with a growing reputation for producing speciality cars. They also received recognition for their evident skills in product development. In this period the highly successful P2 series became a familiar sight.

After 1936 Rover began to collaborate with the Government in the creation of shadow factories to manufacture armaments for the anticipated conflict with Germany. They were unable to find a suitable site in Coventry and so made the very significant decision to construct a new shadow factory in Solihull, a residential suburb with the motto 'Urbs in rure', some twenty miles away and very close to the Tyseley factory. When the War came, Rover expanded its work-force dramatically and engaged in an array of major design and development projects, including the design of the jet engine.[30] Consequently, at the close of hostilities in 1945, they had extended their reputation as designers. After 1945 the Board decided to leave the blitzed site in Coventry and move the centre of operations to Solihull.

After 1946 Rover moved forward on three fronts. First, in saloon cars, the pre-war P2 series was replaced by the P3 in 1948 and then the highly successful P4 in 1949. The latter sold for fifteen years until 1964, with stretching into nine sub-variants. Overall, more than 130,000 were sold, with a peak year of 1955–6 when 15,000 were manufactured. Second, in product innovation, the designers continued their wartime activities. These developments included a gas turbine auto engine, but unfortunately this and some other ventures were never truly commercial.[31] Third, faced by wartime restrictions on the supply of steel for cars, Wilks and colleagues searched for alternatives. As is well-known, the Wilks brothers 're-invented' the wartime jeep and created a four wheel drive vehicle initially designed for farm work as a multi-use vehicle. This product was constructed from aluminium and was therefore not restricted by the steel shortage. The market in Britain was soon extended to the rest of the world. Within six years, Rover were selling more Land Rovers than saloon cars. Also, the vehicle was sold on a customized basis which fitted very neatly with the established experience of small batch production and with the forms of work organization based round craft assembly. Since the Land Rover was a high value added vehicle, it was not difficult to adapt the break-even point to the market. Later, this basic model was stretched into the up-market Range Rover. The market was extended from a rough, simple farm vehicle to a vehicle for the police, for the military and even for the rich to drive to social occasions. The image was soon linked with royalty.

IV P4 and P5: the 1950s

The 1950s were highly successful for the saloon cars and the Land Rovers. In the mid-1950s Rover received the first warning sign of the future. It became clear from the designing and planning of the P5 series that the costs of launching a new series had increased fourfold. The increase in costs arose in all areas: raw materials, new dies, changes to the body supplier, the purchase of new equipment for machining and for the movement of vehicles around the plant. These impending problems required the company to build up its reserves over a long period, ready for the new series. This requirement was made more difficult by the favourable dividends paid to shareholders; yet, if the shareholders were dissatisfied, then the company could be taken over.

In Britain the 1950s were a decade when the auto industry seemed to be doing well relative to other countries, the United States and Canada excepted. Although the era began with food rationing still in operation, there was an underlying upward trend in general living standards which reached its peak in the 1960s. The period was accompanied by the political transformation of the immediate post-war Socialist Governments, which had created several major public corporations, followed by the acceptance by the two major political parties of a mixed form of capitalism. The auto industry and all its elements—suppliers, manufacturers and dealers—were firmly in the private sector, except for the iron and steel industry which was periodically nationalized and privatized. In the 1950s the size and economic importance of the auto industry led the Government to take a strong interest, albeit at arm's length.

Throughout the 1950s Rover enjoyed successes. On the saloon car side, the basic P4, introduced in 1949, was in production right through until 1964. The P5 was designed in the mid-1950s and provided an insight into the future costs of production. Essentially, the P4 proved capable of stretching. On the four wheel side, the 1950s provided a steady growth in markets throughout the world, with annual sales averaging around 40,000 units. The move from Coventry to Solihull after 1946 seemed to have been very successful: certainly the work-force and the new local community considered 'the Rover' to be the epitome of the best British standards in manufacture. During the 1950s the flagship of Rover's innovative engineering was the gas turbine engine which, although unsuccessful in a strict commercial sense, did provide an important arena for the new generation of designers who came to the international forefront in the 1960s and 1970s.

By world standards Rover was a small independent producer like Volvo and many other European firms (e.g. BMW, Jaguar). It produced about 35,000 units annually, of which up to two-thirds were the four wheel drives. Rover's most profitable side was in the four wheel drive vehicles. However, the saloon side formed an integral and complementary part which, although only one-third of the total business, was highly compatible within the company's structural repertoire. In terms of organization learning, Rover's various geographically spread productive units (for gears, axles and engines) were moving in a similar rhythm and with common organizational languages.

By British standards Rover was a well-known, prestigious[32] car firm employing thousands in the West Midlands area and having small plants elsewhere. It was a large employer, even though its work-force was split into small sections and workshops. These were created by the top management as an essential corollory to small batch production. Thus, the highly acclaimed introduction of new assembly methods in 1946[33] failed to mention that the line was very slow and was a simple linking mechanism rather than a mode for the increasing pace of work and increasing managerial control. The new shadow factory contained many small sections and only a few large production areas. Further, when the company commissioned the architects to add new areas, these were typically designed to provide small spaces feeding into long corridors which could be used for final assembly. To the visitor and the work-force, the factories would have appeared to be honeycombed in an orderly collection of small spaces bounded by walls. This feature was not uncommon in Britain, even in the large batch production methods of cigarette making. At Rover the additions of space in the 1950s were focused on the creation of work bays rather than large, flexible areas. Only the final assembly area would have seemed large, yet even this area was subdivided into zones. The work-force at Rover experienced the 1950s as a decade of gentle increases in demand, with its major pulsations being contingent upon the specific character of each season's consumer spending.[34]

Rover exhibited three important features in the 1950s: a long-established corporate team, control systems which were simple (delegated and heavily shaped by paternalism), and extensive internal sectionalism, both hierarchical and departmental. Each of these features requires further elaboration because they all came under strain after the introduction of the P6 in 1963.

The corporate leadership was an experienced and cohesive team typified by longevity and family connections through blood relations and marriage. In these respects they were not unlike the British managements of medium and even large companies.[35] The management had entered the firm or the industry typically through personal, family contacts and had learned their skills through direct experience as assistants to established bosses. There were several families: Wilks, Poppes, Searles, Jackmans and others. Observers agree that 'adherence to the marque' typified the sense of teamness. An inside designer said, 'people at the top of the company were desperately interested; they were interested in engineering and they were interested in really making the product work in the customer's hands.'[36] Like most of British management in this and the following decade, their educational experience was most likely to have combined public school with short courses in the non-university sector of higher education. Whilst competence was clearly the basis for advancement under Wilks, this was not equated with higher educational qualifications, even in areas like engineering.

The overall approach to corporate control was simple, delegated and essentially paternal. The simplicity expressed itself in many ways. A report of 1964 noted that 'its policy has been to minimize the complexity of management'. Top management kept in touch with events—the 'hot news'[37]—by touring the plants on a daily basis, spending the first part of the day handling day-to-day enquiries, observing and taking action on the spot. As one production manager said, 'decisions made verbally can be relied on'.[38] Management tended to place a heavy reliance on the use of well-established recipes which, once uncovered, tended to be retained in the repertoire, often with only slight editing. Management believed that the appropriate knowledge required for running a car factory existed in the form of recipes rather than abstractions. Hence, the situated practices of management were regularized in a traditional format of social mores. Communication between management tended to be by personal contact, face to face, by telephone and by corridor meetings rather than by memos and forms. Only certain processes were recorded in formal memos, and these tended to be for irregular events linked to the design cycle for the cars. The best example of this was the Blue Book, recording the state of design for each new P range. There were other examples, including the record of alterations to existing cars. Generally, these pieces of formalization were confined to the car and did not cover the production process or forms of work organization at any level. The essential simplicity was also reflected in the means for handling future demand levels. The basic recipe was to ensure that there was always a waiting list for the saloons and the vehicles. Top management prided themselves on the unmet demand and seemed to have found an important degree of security in its existence.[39]

Overall simplicity in methods of co-ordination was complemented by the relatively complex forms of delegated control. There were three dimensions:

— the use of piecework and work group controls;
— the relative incorporation of trade-union representation;
— paternalism.

Each relied on informal, ideological and cultural forms of authority.[40] These strategies may be contrasted to the general use of hierarchies, technological pacing and formal rules in the American industry. Ford also used the technology as a means of control through, for example, the pacing and spatial deployment of work.

Piece-work was a well-established form of delegated control in Britain, and particularly in the engineering industry. British employers tended to

rely on the cash nexus.[41] Piece-work had replaced subcontracting from the
1890s onwards, when employers looked to eliminate the intermediate role
of the subcontractor and replace it by more direct internal supervision. In
practice the control over the pace of work, the choice of sequence of
operations, the ownership of the job knowledge and its learning were still
left largely to the operative. Because of the poor development of method
study and work measurement there were few accurate records of job
skills. Systematic corporate training of the kind developed in the United
States after 1910 was virtually unknown even in the 1950s. In practice
such training was developed more in the textile industry, often in the
suppliers to the major retailers. At Rover there was little training but
extensive use of piece-work. This had been established in the founding
period through estimating, and was only slightly modified by the Bedeaux
consultants (1929–30) whose main activities were at the Tyseley plant
which manufactured engines. In the 1950s the setting of piece rates for
individuals and for groups was done by estimation, not systematic time
study. Because of this approach and the relatively long work cycles—more
than six minutes for most car operations—there was considerable variability in the relationship between different types of work. However, the
looseness and incomparability of the prices were hidden by the social and
spatial divisions.

Productivity and wages are closely linked in piece-work. In the auto
industry wages formed a small, decreasing element in total costs, and
management were therefore often protected from the consequences of the
restriction of output.[42] Conversely, the operatives were anxious to avoid
any interruptions in the flow of work which reduced their earnings.
Operatives had a vested interest in developing collective, team-like forms
of shop floor co-operation, and these were also of obvious advantage to
management. Contrary to the image of fractionated car work, there were
many situations where shop floor co-operation by groups and gangs—as at
the Standard Works in Coventry—was highly efficient.[43] Management was
only required to give general orders because the operatives could be
expected to 'carry out the necessary detailed operations implied by these
orders'. On the other hand, piece-work often created problems for the
progress-chasers who were used to tracking the state and quantity of
components. Supervisors were expected to maintain control, yet the basis
for doing so was constantly undermined. At the shop floor level the
frontier of control was constantly challenged, though this was confined to
this particular level.[44] Union organization on the shop floor emerged out
of workers' attempts to bargain within the piece-work system. To a large
extent management sought to incorporate the shop stewards, especially in
the obtaining of overtime and in the regulation of bonus payments, and
via top management, dealing with the unions on an individual basis.

Paternalism was an integral part of a whole array of cultural and
ideological means of control aimed at preventing conflict through the
creation of a unitary, communal cohesion around managerial values.
Paternalism is a managerial strategy in which top management seeks to
obtain the employee's compliance with the belief that management

should be both judge and protector. Rover's management tended to adopt a belief in the simple recipe of high employee attachment to the firm, facilitating high productivity. At Rover the focus on a unitary vision of the workplace was pursued in a variety of ways. For example, these themes surfaced in the *Rover News*, in the many speeches made by management at occasions like the works' social and sports events, and in the rewarding of long service. They formulated images of the good employee as one with a strong sense of duty and service to the company. In return, the firm offered welfare provisions and social clubs.[45]

Paternalism at Rover made particular and extensive use of the family as an institution. In Solihull, as previously in Coventry, recruitment favoured members of families already known to be loyal employees: thus, husbands and wives were followed by sons and daughters. It may be argued that this procedure enabled management to simplify the selection process, as well as being able to benefit from the informal socialization of new members within the family. Although many employees were recruited from within the close neighbourhood of the factories, it cannot be said that Rover established a manorial labour market comparable to that of Cadbury's at Bournville, less than ten miles away. Management ignored the way in which the family can be a source and conduit of opposition to employer ideologies. Paternalism also placed extensive reliance on the image of the family as a cohesive unit. In doing so, Rover management were clearly unaware of anthropological claims that the family can be a centre of tension and tawdry secrets.[46] Rather, the family image was used to emphasize the need for close links between employees and the company. This theme was continuously emphasized at religious festivals (e.g. Christmas) and the secular events of sports, social meetings and dances.

Although paternalism was the dominant mode of authority, it was backed up by the occasional demonstration of sharp control. This was exhibited with respect to those executives who were considered to be responsible for failures and was shown occasionally to the shop floor. The combination of the two styles is not at all unusual. In the case of Rover the latent tendency to shift from paternalism to authoritarian stances was only rarely activated. Yet it was an integral part of the cultural repertoire.

This paternalistic posture of top management during the 1950s was reciprocated by the majority of the work-force. They believed in the good intentions of the management: 'Nothing was really written, but everyone knew, and justice was seen to be done'.[47] The relatively stable work-force possessed a high degree of manual skills and a strong craft consciousness. They believed that their work was varied, responsible and multi-skilled. This belief was tacitly reinforced by concessions in piece rates which were obtained through routine negotiation. Control is a frontier, and one which fluctuates. At Rover there was a form of complex social joint regulation which meshed with and supplemented the generally simple forms of management co-ordination.

Internal divisions of a hierarchical and sectional nature were typical features of Rover. Two examples will demonstrate the plurality of sub-cultures whose claims and domains were successfully sustained in the

1950s. First, the managerial division of labour was extensive. There was a hierarchy of specialist functions which directly shaped the ways in which problems came on to the agenda and were addressed. The hierarchy also determined that certain kinds of new knowledge would be under-represented. Because the core values of the firm highlighted 'engineering innovation' and 'car design' there was little attention to new areas of management and social sciences. Nor were specialisms like metallurgy and chemistry represented, even though both were increasingly relevant. Instead, the top management continued to rely on trusted external sources for expert advice and consultancy: the suppliers of equipment, the Pressed Steel Company which supplied bodies, the architects, and similar groups. Consequently, the analytic disciplines of management which were then burgeoning in the United States were virtually unknown. These gaps were not highlighted by contacts with the local universities, the most prestigious of which seemed to feel some reluctance to establish produc-tion engineering even when the giant Lucas Company provided the basic funding. Rover's focus on innovative engineering was lavished on the car rather than on the methods of its production. Yet their belief that the customer preferred advanced engineering was never put to the test of market research. The evidence that did exist via servicing and the Rover Clubs suggested that the buyers were rather conservative.[48]

The separations within management were paralleled by the divisions amongst the non-managerial employees, but they lacked the unitary ideologies to create collective forms of organization. The structure of the plant and the loosely coupled, highly buffered interactions between sections and departments facilitated a high degree of segregation in the labour-force. The various unions (eight main ones) each tended to occupy a particular craft-based constituency. There were few collective actions and no common mechanisms of joint committees. On the whole, the work-force was divided internally. The largest union was the craft conscious National Union of Vehicle Builders (NUVB), with 3,500 members at Solihull. This union grew rapidly during the expansion of the 1950s, when it organized the direct skilled workers in the body, trim and paint shops. The AUEW recruited the component workers at the plants in the Birmingham area. The other unions were smaller, more specialized and independent.

To most employees the 1950s must have seemed rather quiet and full of improving prospects for the future. Yet there were those in top manage-ment who sensed that there were problems ahead. Their diagnoses were not based so much on the analysis of the sector life cycle or similar templates, but were grounded in the revealing experiences of designing the P5. That iteration of the design process indicated that the costs of any new model would be at least four times greater than for the P4. The design of the P5 commenced in 1956. The basic layout was crystallized and the production tooling was ordered ready for manufacture in 1958. It was a large car, costly and unconventional, but its introduction created a gap for the future replacement of the P4 by a less expensive speciality car, the P6/Rover 2000, eventually introduced in 1963.

Whilst the production side of Rover seemed stable, the design teams were anxious to transform the exterior image of solid and rather stodgy shapes of Rover saloons, into something more exciting and stylish. The P6 became the mechanism by which S. B. Wilks introduced new designers and gave them their head. In 1956 he coupled the loosening up with a requirement for regular design meetings and some basic procedural features to shape and structure the free-flowing and organic relationships. The continuing sales success of the P4 provided the design team with time and opportunity.

Top management set a sales target for the P6 of 550 per week, which the sales force considered too high by a factor of at least two. By 1958 the solid clay mock-ups revealed a new model with a strongly sloping nose. From then on the design process became both a co-operative and a competitive process between the product engineers and the stylists.[49] The former preferred to add features and to introduce a brand-new engine whilst the stylists stressed simple clear lines and pressed for a layout with pillarless doors. The boot design was an issue of great debate. However, the design of the P6 demonstrated that Rover was aware of the need to adjust to the changing demand of the 1960s.

The 1950s closed with Rover looking comfortable to its major stake-holders, whilst its top management and the design teams were acutely aware of the need for important changes if Rover were to survive the next decade. Top management knew that they would have to raise some £15 million to finance the P6, and that it would be necessary to introduce dramatic expansions to the amount of work space and the number of employees.[50]

V P6: intended and unintended transformations

In the 1960s the two sides of the Rover business began to separate on to different trajectories. The saloon side became the focus of radical changes in the car and major changes in the work facilities and in the organization of work in the factories. The P6 series became the carrier wave for these intended changes—and also for some unintended changes. The saloon cars became highly successful in the growing British market niche for executive cars, where the Rover designers gained international recognition for their styling of the P6.[51] Meanwhile the other side of the business—the four wheel drive vehicles—also gained in reputation, particularly after the introduction of the up-market Range Rover series. Despite these changes in the saloon side and the increasing separation of the saloon from the four wheel side, the management attempted to utilize the existing structural repertoire. It was the saloon side which generated many of the unintended transformations which occurred, yet the consequences spilled through on to the whole company. This section focuses on the saloon side.

The P6 saloons were commissioned and launched in 1963 after Rover had spent more than £10 million on re-tooling and on the addition of 250,000 sq. ft. of new assembly area at the side of the already crowded

North Works.[52] The Board intended that the P6 would introduce certain alterations to the organization of work on the saloon side, but their intentions did not anticipate the raft of transformations which the P6 would introduce. The unintended transformations[53] included:

— the problems of logistics;
— the changing ownership pattern amongst the main suppliers of equipment and key components;
— the division of labour within management;
— the crises of managerial authority.

Each of these contributed to the uncertainties about an independent future for Rover.

The four problems arose, very largely, from the success of the P6. Its design by Spen King and David Bache was judged to be 'an imaginative and advanced design' which identified the designers as one of the key groups in Europe in the 'struggle between convention and innovation'.[54] From the perspective of the Rover company the new car was a radical design. For the first time the company had a car whose outer skin panels were detachable. Also the production engineering of the car introduced radical changes in the sub-assembly and in the final assembly. Few of the components were already in production, and so considerable pre-production care was required. The sequence of assembly was altered so that the outer skin was added *after* the engine, wheels and power train had been fitted to the base unit.[55]

There was a long period of commissioning the new facilities and the final assembly process, but this was very successful despite some initially unfavourable responses from the established work-force, who considered that their tasks had been de-skilled. Within three years the P6 range, known as the Rover 2000 series, dominated the market segment for executive cars. Rover began to gain a higher percentage of the total market (3.15 per cent in 1968 was a company record) and also to accumulate the profits necessary to pay off the investment and to build up reserves for the next design cycle. Demand for the car remained favourable, beyond expectations. The car ran from 1963–4 into 1976, by which time more than 325,000 had been sold. It was this level of success which heightened the four problem areas.

First, the growth in demand for the 2000 series increased the logistical problems of saloon car production. An ideal solution might have been to expand the Solihull site to contain additional facilities whilst also using factory sites in the nearby parts of Birmingham. However, the 1960s was the decade in which the Government used the auto industry as a regulator of the economy and as a means of reducing unemployment in the peripheral areas of the United Kingdom. Rover were more fortunate than Rootes (later Chrysler), who were persuaded to open a major plant in Scotland. Rover did have to accept a new plant in South Wales, and they were prevented from expanding the Solihull plant at the rate they desired. However, they were able to open branch plants in the local area. The result was that the internal transport system was totally reliant upon the use of road linkages to Solihull. This created immense strains.[56]

Logistical problems in the auto industry place a premium on the timing and the total reliability of delivery. In the 1960s the automobile industry became an important arena for the fractional bargaining between shop floor work groups and the management. These developments had a marked effect on the supply of components which reduced their reliability sufficiently to persuade the manufacturers that carrying stocks of components was the practical solution.[57] Because all manufacturers, British and American (e.g. Ford at Dagenham) adopted the same broad strategy, the overall competitive costs of inventories did not immediately become apparent. Yet even this strategy would prove insufficient to prevent some components from running out.[58]

Second, Rover depended for supplies of components, tools, equipment, dies and bodies on a number of independent suppliers who, during the 1960s, were progressively drawn into the ambit of the three major firms: Ford, Leyland and the British Motor Corporation. In certain cases, such as the Pressed Steel Company, the supplier was also the source of significant advice about the handling of new raw materials. Such knowledge was vital to a firm like Rover, which was not inclined to incorporate the full range of specialist expertise into its management structure. The independent suppliers were trusted to retain commercial secrets about future models, so when in 1965 the Pressed Steel Company was taken over by BMC, this created a very awkward situation for Rover. It meant that a major and larger rival was potentially able to acquire future knowledge of styling and other innovations.

Third, the development of the P6 had occurred within the established division of labour amongst management, but the growth in the size of the market share, coupled to the changing requirements of car manufacture, meant that changes were necessary. The division of managerial labour determines which specialisms are represented and how they are arranged. As indicated in the previous section, the Rover management lacked certain functions.[59] In the 1960s the Board were slow to create new functions and largely failed to incorporate new forms of specialist knowledge.[60] One example will illustrate the general point, and relates to industrial relations. At Rover there was a personnel function, but its remit was the selection and welfare aspects of employment. There was no specialist person responsible for industrial relations.[61] Consequently the Board lacked basic analyses of the events which confronted their strategies. It is evident that the forms of discourse used amongst management did not permit them to describe quite basic problems of inter-group power struggles.[62] The problems faced by Rover management were also those found in many other British companies. These problems became more serious in the auto industry because the prosperous 1960s could have been a time for learning how to incorporate the new skills. If that had occurred, the events of the 1970s might have been tackled differently.

Fourth, during the 1960s Rover faced a growing and novel crisis in managerial authority such that one manager described their approach to leadership as 'disenchanted paternalism'.[63] It is important to note that throughout its corporate history the paternalism which was highlighted as the style of authority was sometimes accompanied by short bursts of very direct and sometimes quite punitive actions which were directed both at executives who were considered unsuccessful (e.g. three previous managing directors) and at shop floor employees. Neither the Board nor senior management had felt the need to apply this back-up style of authority extensively until the 1960s.

The very success of the P6 meant that weekly output was almost doubled from 300 cars to 550. There was a need for a large additional work-force. This requirement had been anticipated. Top management intended to recruit a large amount of extra labour and locate them in the areas of least skill, mainly on the assembly lines, and to pay them at a lower rate than the existing work-force. These intentions were not immediately obvious when the new assembly lines were commissioned, because of the slow build-up of production and the redeployment of some existing employees to handle the uncertainties which always accompany the launching of a new model. Once this process was completed and the sales figures for the P6 were reaching the hoped-for targets, then the new labour force was introduced. In total almost 2,000 new employees were recruited at the Solihull plant. Their insertion into the established social organization of competing work groups sharply altered the existing rules of the game.[64] The existing craft conscious trade unions declined to recruit and to represent employees who were obviously doing less skilled work. The National Union of Vehicle Builders, the largest existing union, thus left the way open for the Transport & General Workers' Union.

Once on the assembly lines, the new workers found two sources of dissatisfaction arising from the methods of payment. First, the piece-work rates were based on a lower level than previously. Generally in the British context the relativities of wage differences between groups who regard themselves as equivalent has been a source of instability in piece-work systems. At Rover the multifarious small groups each regarded themselves as a bargaining unit within an implicit status hierarchy.[65] This hierarchy was challenged by the new workers who, when they found that the NUVB would not represent their interests against the established order of payment, then joined the TGWU. Second, piece-work earnings can be disrupted by uneven and varying amounts of work on the lines. In the 1960s workers used the tight labour market to bargain over allowances for disruptions—both those which arose from external sources amongst suppliers and those arising from within the company.[66] First-line supervisors were neither experienced enough nor had sufficient collective authority to comprehend and handle the new pressures.[67] In their place rose shop stewards, who gained influence through their representation of specific zones in the assembly process: they tended to operate opportunistically on behalf of the new work-force.[68]

Management resistance to this bargaining contributed to a rash of strikes which were so severe that they were investigated by an indepen-

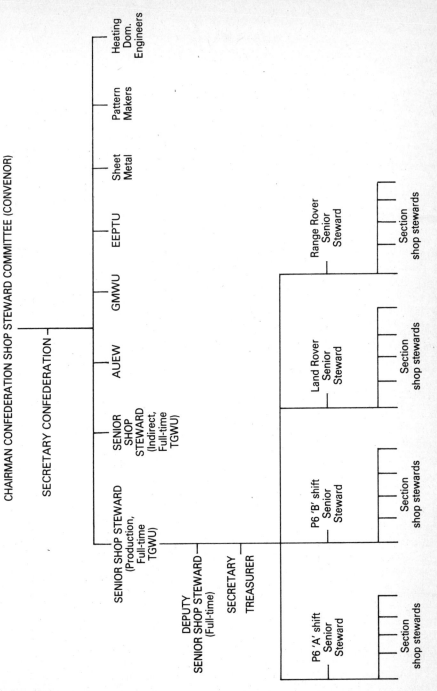

Figure 3.1 Shop Steward Committee Structure, Solihull Site, 1972.

dent committee under Scamp, whose report pointed to inadequacies in the industrial relations' procedures, channels and forums which were available.[69] Certainly the loose and informal relations amongst the existing craft-based unions could not absorb the new conflicts.[70] Thus management were unable to rely on the trade unions to contribute their authority to the regulation of conflicts. The available evidence suggests that management at Rover were implicitly aware of their usage of trade-union control as part of their own authority, but that they believed that this was relatively unimportant. Once again their forms of discourse did not permit them to analyse the new problems.[71]

The mid-1960s were a turbulent period for industrial relations. Most explanations attribute this to inter-union rivalry, but as indicated above, managements are involved because of their reliance—in the British situation—on devolved and delegated authority to shopfloor workers.[72] By the close of the 1960s the former paternalism had been fragmented and an industrial relations director had been appointed to implement the recommendations from independent consultants who did provide both the concepts for the analysis of inter-group struggles as well as some suggestions for their handling. By 1970 a new pattern of trade-union organization had emerged. Despite opposition from the NUVB there was an overall committee for the Solihull plant (see Figure 3.1) which both included the TGWU and reflected certain shifts in the composition of the work-force.[73] This new committee shared a determination to be included in the next P series design process, and they began to organize an intelligence network for reconstructing how future cars might affect work organization.[74]

The P6 is an example of the attempt by management to introduce new forms of de-skilled work organization which, once recognized, contributed to important transformations in corporate authority. Despite the turbulences of the mid-1960s, Rover was profitable and reached its highest profits in 1968. Even so, top management and the directors doubted that the company could survive as an independent car firm. The P6 clearly reveals the continuation of the Rover Company's structural repertoire, built up through the P series from the 1930s. It also shows the continued imbalance within the repertoire: between the growing strength of product design and the comparatively less developed components of production control or the organization of work. Rather, it is more accurate to say that the team management, paternalism and piece-work which had been appropriate for the markets of the 1932–60 period were unsuitable for the circumstances of the 1960s. Moreover, the difficulty in mounting an attempted radical change via the P6 productive unit, including the unintended outcomes, was indicative of the major upheaval which the SD1 project would represent in the 1970s.

Conclusion

The history of the Rover Company's design and innovation capacity has been examined by focusing on two sets of contexts—the external and the

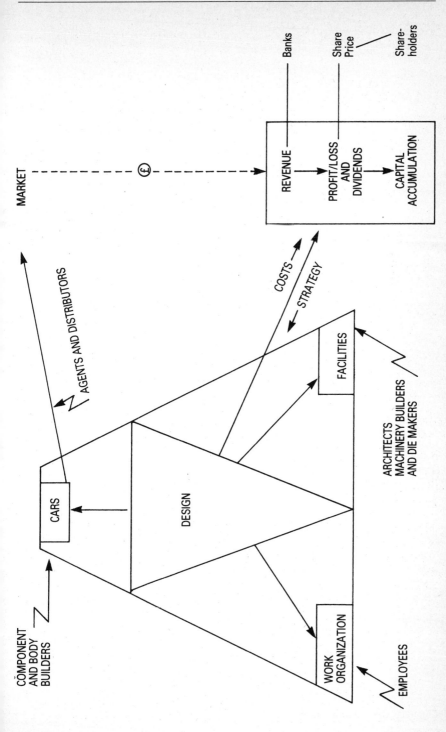

Figure 3.2 The design capacity of the Rover company: contexts and interdependencies.

internal—and their interactions. These can be expressed as in Figure 3.2. The link between the internal and external contexts can be expressed by reference to the company's design hierarchy. In the United Kingdom, unlike North America, the structure of consumer tastes for shapes and uses of the car were less homogenized. The generally smaller size of the car, its limited engine capacity and the more individual styling were all the results of varied consumer requirements. These tendencies have persisted over seven decades. Consequently, the founding period of the British industry was followed by a movement of the market structure towards multiple niches rather than to the routinized production of dominant designs for a uniform mass market.

The Rover Company, by remaining in the speciality niche of the British market, developed a distinctive design hierarchy. Instead of establishing an early dominant product design, as in the Abernathy model, leading to a diminishing rate of innovation, Rover continued to innovate both strategically and incrementally throughout the P series. In America the early dominant product designs lead to increasingly mechanized production and machine-based regulation of work. Whilst there was an overall tendency in the Rover case to greater automation, it was the late (post-1945), uneven and sporadic emergence of even flowline and then integrated production which stands out. The comfortable market position of Rover, which enabled its stable management to rely on piece work as the basis for its assembly work, resulted in an equally slow rate of change along the fluidity-specificity scale for work organization.[75] When the company's overall business strategy was severely altered by BLMC after 1968, the specialist groups within Rover, which were the bearers of its especial design capacity, varied widely in their ability to handle the radical changes required by the SD1 project.

In the internal context Rover seemed to stumble towards an awareness of the requirement for establishing a design capacity as a total process. This meant running an enterprise in two different time frames: a distant future and the immediate present. In the case of Rover, the Board and top management found the separation and linking of these time frames to be awkward. They were clearly lucky in the early 1930s when Lucas and Lloyds Bank chose to provide financial support. It was Wilks who installed a key process of car designing by showing how stretching a single design could produce a family of cars which achieved continued market acceptance over several decades rather than the conventional four- to five-year cycle. However, the acquisition of a capacity in design as total process requires continual editing. Organizational learning cannot remain static for long. In the 1960s the basic recipes came under severe pressure, given the imbalance within them.

Rover's experience is a sharp reminder of the wide variation in business operation with in the automobile sector. The company is an example of how a section of the industry can both embody the dominant logics, recipes and practices of car manufacture and yet also exhibit a distinctive variant when compared to Ford or Austin/Morris. Rover and Ford alike, as car manufacturers, conform to the general outline of car designing, manufacture and work organization; but it is the very different ways in which they chose to relate to the market and what strategies and structures they developed as a result which maintained the differentiation found within the sector even in the 1960s. Rover may therefore serve as both representative and distinctive within the British auto industry.

Above all, this historical reconstruction does not argue that Rover's history, in spite of the strong elements of continuity, was straightfoward or unilinear; quite the reverse. The firm's combination of policy and organization emerged through a pattern of events which have been identified with hindsight: yet each major event or crisis was a potential catalyst for change or modification, with the outcomes often entirely unforeseen to those involved, as the 1928–32 crisis and the P6 episode showed. Against this pattern, the SD1 project can now be seen as a 'transforming event', in Ladurie's words, which surpassed any in the history of the Rover Company.

Notes

1. E. Le Roy Ladurie, 'The "Event" and the "Long Term" in Social History: the Case of the Chouan Uprising', in his *The Territory of the Historian*, 1979, pp. 111–31.
2. R. Harré, *Social Being*, 1979.
3. P. Gardiner, 'Design Trajectories for Airplanes and Automobiles During the Past Fifty Years', mimeo., SPRU, Sussex University, 1983.
4. W. J. Abernathy and K. B. Clark, *Industrial Renaissance: Producing a Competitive Future for America*, Boston, 1983. For an extensive discussion of the long-term patterns of innovation in the British automobile industry see R. Whipp and P. A. Clark, *A Car Plant for the '80s: Work Organization and the British Car Industry*, Work Organization Research Centre, Aston University, October 1984, chap 2, 'The Auto Industry', pp. 45–84. See also Whipp and Clark, 'The British Auto Industry 1900–1982: A Sector Profile', ESRC Work Organization Research Centre, Working Paper No. 12 (1985).
5. Rover Company Directors' Minutes, Rover Archive (hereafter RCDMins), 18 April, 21 July, 19 August 1902; 19 December 1904; 20 March, 10 November and 8 December 1905. It was in November 1905 that plant and machinery were first separated from tools in the accounts.
6. R. A. Church, *Herbert Austin: The British Motor Car Industry to 1941*, 1979, p. 186 on the 'poor' production performance of the industry before 1914 and the refusal of large engineering firms to join the industry.
7. RCDMins, 1903, p. 829.
8. RCDMins, 1902, p. 662.
9. Shareholders' Minutes, The Rover Cycle Company Ltd, 1896–1936, Rover Archive.
10. RCDMins, 1907, pp. 278–9.
11. RCDMins, 1908, pp. 5904 and 1620.
12. R. A. Church, *Herbert Austin*, op. cit., p. 32.
13. See the collection of papers by J. Foreman-Peck: 'Tariff Protection and Economies of Scale: The British Motor Industry Before 1939', *Oxford Economic Papers*, **31**, 2, 1979, pp. 237–57; 'The Effect of Market Failure on the British Motor Industry Before 1939', *Explorations in Economic History*, **18**, 1981, pp. 257–89; 'Exit, Voice and Loyalty as Responses to Decline: The Rover

Company in the Inter-War years', *Business History*, **23**, 2, 1981, pp. 191–207; 'The American Challenge of the Twenties and the European Motor Industry', *Journal of Economic History*, **XLII**, 4, 1982, pp. 865–81; 'Diversification and the Growth of the Firm: The Rover Company to 1914', *Business History*, **25**, 2, 1983, pp. 179–92. We are indebted to their author for his thoughtful suggestions.

14. A. D. Chandler, *The Visible Hand: The Managerial Revolution in American Business*, 1977.
15. In 1910 the Rover Board sought to regulate the role of employees with respect to the ownership of patents: RCDMins, pp. 2787 and 2798, 1910.
16. Owen Clegg created an experimental section, RCDMins, pp. 2294, 1910, and a special agenda item on retooling for the Board, RCDMins, pp. 2366, 1911.
17. W. Lewchuk, 'The British Motor Vehicle Industry 1896–1982. The Roots of Decline', in B. Elbaum and W. Lazonick (eds), *The Decline of the British Economy* (forthcoming). We are grateful for the helpful comments of Wayne Lewchuk.
18. RCDMins, 1921, p. 191.
19. Op. cit., 1923, p. 4456.
20. Op. cit., 1923, p. 4536.
21. Op. cit., 1923, p. 4557.
22. Op. cit., 1925, p. 4635.
23. Op. cit., 1924, p. 4569.
24. Op. cit., 1924, p. 4780.
25. Op. cit., 1924, p. 4708.
26. Op. cit., 1925, pp. 4853 and 380.
27. Op. cit., 1926, pp. 4950.
28. Foreman-Peck, 'Exit, Voice and Loyalty', *passim*.
29. See Blue Book. Non-Current Details 1963 made up of the following sections: Engineering prototypes; Designing; Engineering Release; Specifications; Planning; Tooling; Tool Tryout; Production Prototype; Sales, Rover Archive. Interviews with ex-senior product engineer, Land Rover, 1 and product engineer employed on P series, p. 19.
30. G. Robson, *The Rover Story*, 1971, 1984 edn, Chapters 4 and 6.
31. See Rover Gas Turbine Project, ND, Rover Archive. *Stock Exchange Gazette*, 19 October 1904. *Birmingham Evening Mail*, 26 March 1970.
32. P. E. Shuttleworth, Rover: An Essay on Company History, 18 November 1977, Rover Archive. Rover employed 15,000 workers in the 1950s, yet only 2,000 were located at the main Solihull site.
33. 'Car Assembly. The Layout of the Meteor Works of the Rover Company Limited, Solihull', *Automobile Engineer*, September 1946, pp. 2–13.
34. P. A. Clark, *Organizational Design: Theory and Practice*, 1972, Chapter 9. H. A. Turner, G. Clack and G. Roberts, *Labour Relations in the Motor Industry*, 1967, pp. 105, 119 and 159.
35. S. Pollard, *The Genesis of Modern Management: A Study of the Industrial Revolution in Britain*, 1965.
36. Interviews with senior vehicle designer, 20 and senior Land Rover product engineer, p. 2.
37. H. Mintzberg, 'The Manager's Job: Folklore and Fact', *Harvard Business Review*, July/August, 1975, pp. 50–61.
38. Interview with ex-production director, p. 4.
39. Interview with senior executive in 'Rover at 70', *Motor*, June 1974, p. iii. RCDMins, 17 November 1960, p. 140; 13 April 1961; 2 August 1962, p. 251. *Rover News*, June and July 1971.

40. R. Whipp, '"The Art of Good Management": Managerial Control of Work in the British Pottery Industry, 1900–1925', *International Review of Social History*, **XXIX**, 1984, pp. 359–89; R. Bendix, *Work and Authority in Industry*, New York, 1956, pp. ix, 3, 13 and 115.

41. Lewchuk, op. cit.; R. Dore, *British Factory—Japanese Factory: The Origins of National Diversity in Industrial Relations*, 1973.

42. Lewchuk, op. cit.

43. S. Melman, *Decision Making and Productivity*, 1958, pp. 1–3.

44. C. L. Goodrich, *The Frontier of Control: A Study in British Workshop Politics*, 1920, 1975 edn; J. Zeitlin, 'The Emergence of Shop Steward Organization and Job Control in the British Car Industry: A Review Essay', *History Workshop Journal*, **10**, 1980, pp. 119–37; *A Workers' Enquiry into the Motor Industry*, Institute for Workers' Control, Motors Group, 1978, p. 45.

45. See Whipp, op. cit.; *Rover News*, 5 May and 12 April 1973; *Handbook for Supervisors*, 1965, p. 109, Rover Archive.

46. E. R. Leach, *A Runaway World*, 1967.

47. RCDMins, 21 January, p. 9856, 25 February 1960.

48. See Owners Club Correspondence, Drawer C, Filing Cabinet 21, Rover Archive. Interview with product engineer, p. 8.

49. See R. Whipp and P. A. Clark, '"A Car Plant for the '80s". Work Organization and the British Car Industry', Work Organization Research Centre, Aston University, October 1984, pp. 85–99.

50. RCDMins, 24 October 1960, p. 9951; *Financial Times*, 18 November 1964. *Investors Guide*, 18 July 1962. H. B. Light, 'The Rover Story', Chap. 26, p. 3, Rover Archive. In 1962 the declared profit for the year ending 4 August was £2,380,542 on a turnover of £50 million, and is representative of the company's performance in the 1950s and early 1960s. *The Financial Times* noted how 'the shares give a comfortable return of 6.1%' and were considered suitable for investment 'income rather than growth'.

51. J. Ensor, *The Motor Industry* (1971), 201.

52. RCDMins, 22 September 1960, p. 937 and 21 June 1961, p. 44. 'Rover 2000 Body Manufacture', pt. I–III, *Automobile Engineer* (January, March, April, **54**, 1964), pp. 1–13, 110–15, 152–7. See also November, **53**, 1953, pp. 466–515.

53. See note 1.

54. Ensor, pp. 30 and 201.

55. J. Sutherland, 'The Impact of Measured Day Work on Company Industrial Relations', mimeo., Warwick University, 1974, p. 8.

56. RCDMins, 30 April, 10 October (2465) and November (2496), 1969; 26 February and 24 March 1970.

57. RCDMins, 24 March, 4 September 1969. The loss of workers to Jaguar was particularly noticeable.

58. *Workers' Enquiry into the Motor Industry*, p. 45; Sutherland, op. cit., p. 19; interview with P6 rectification worker, p. 10.

59. RCDMins, 14 September 1971 (2465); 8 March 1968 and 30 January 1970; X Partners Ltd., Rover Co. Ltd Final Report, 28 October 1970, p. 1; RCDMins, 8 and 29 November 1968, 11 June 1971; Sutherland, op. cit., p. 19; interviews with senior P6 shop stewards, p. 21; P6 final trim worker, TI 16.

60. RCDMins, 23 October 1964 (627); interview with senior corporate IR officer, p. 9.

61. *Handbook for Supervisors*, p. 31; interview with ex-Ford product planner, p. 15.

62. Interviews with Rover IR officer, p. 14, and senior P6 shop steward, I, p. 2.

63. RCDMins, 24 June, 9 September 1968; 28 January 1969; 30 April, 1 May and 5 June 1970.
64. Sutherland, op. cit., pp. 8 and 15–16.
65. Sutherland, op. cit., pp. 18–19.
66. *Sunday Times* (16 August 1964); RCDMins, 5 January 1968, Appendix 2; interviews with senior P6 shop steward, p. 8.
67. *Birmingham Post and Mail*, News Archive, Rover Section, 28 Colmore Circus, Birmingham (hereafter BMNA), 14 December 1965; *Handbook for Supervisors* (1965), p. iii; Motor Industry Joint Study Group, 'Report of an Inquiry into the State of Industrial Relations at the Rover Co. Assembly Works, Solihull', 2 and 3 November 1965, Rover Archive; interview with P6 paint rectification shop steward, p. 13.
68. *Financial Times*, 25 September 1964; Turner *et al*., op. cit., pp. 241–4.
69. See note 67; Turner *et al*., *Labour Relations in the Motor Industry*, p. 119.
70. Interviews with P6 senior shop steward (TGWU), 1; P6 track worker, 23 and P6 shop steward, TI 162, 210 and 243.
71. See note 67; X Partners Ltd. Report, p. 4; interview with senior P6 shop steward, TI 179; cf. H. Wright Baker, *Modern Workshop Technology, Vol. II, Machine Tools and Manufacturing Processes* (1960), p. 54.
72. W. Lewchuk, 'Technology, Pay Systems and the Motor Companies', paper presented to SSRC Conference on Business and Labour History, London School of Economics, March 1981.
73. Foreman-Peck, 'Exit, Voice and Loyalty', pp. 196–7; interviews with ex-P6 NUVB shop steward, pp. 2, 3 and 12; senior P6 shop steward (TGWU), pp. 4–5 and 19 and senior AUEW shop steward, engine plant, pp. 8–9; Sutherland, op. cit., p. 25; cf. J. H. Clapham, *An Economic History of Modern Britain: Vol. II: Machines and National Rivalries 1887–1914* (1938), p. 335; BMNA, 1 January and 3 February 1970; interview with P6 shop steward, TI 730; cf. S. Tolliday, 'Trade Unions and Collective Bargaining in the British Motor Industry 1896–1970', mimeo., Cambridge University, 1984, pp. 29–30 and 41.
74. Interview with P6 shop steward, pp. 260–4.
75. See Figure 2.4.

4 The SD1 project—concept and translation, 1968–1974

Introduction

The first major project undertaken by the British Leyland Motor Corporation, code-named the SD1, is the centrepiece of Chapters 4 and 5. The starting-point for analysing the SD1 venture is the merger of the Leyland Company with Rover in March 1967 and the subsequent formation of BLMC in 1968. There were implications derived from the merger process which affected nearly every aspect of the Solihull project. The conceptual framework, discussed in Chapter 2, for understanding long-term change, suggests that the BL merger process represents a major 'transforming event'. For the Rover Company this led to direct challenges to its existing structural repertoire and design capacity. The extent to which the SD1 venture represented a strategic, radical or incremental innovation in Rover's story will be assessed and a comparison drawn with parallel changes in the auto industry of the 1960s and 1970s.

In Chapter 2, Section V an account was given of the model of the design process which informed our research into design and innovation in the car industry. The model was derived from the work of academic specialists such as Miller and Rice, combined with earlier observation of the design process in industry.[1] The design model is composed of four main stages: concept, translation, commissioning and operation. These stages, broadly speaking, are meant to run sequentially. Nadler[2] offers far more complex and highly prescriptive models of designing and planning, yet these are of little value for conducting new research. These models are meant to show how designing should occur. Instead, our comparatively straightforward version served two very useful initial purposes. First, the very basic four stages were generally consistent with both the general design sequence which appears in the secondary literature on the auto industry and with the overall intentions of the car companies. At the outset it enabled the researcher to come to terms with the massively intricate business of designing cars and their methods of production. Each person interviewed, from almost every background, was able to relate their particular set of activities before, during and after the SD1 project to our simple scheme. Every respondent, virtually, had their own conception of what the SD1 design process involved, and also what it should have included. Indeed, an important finding was the way in which those involved used words and labels in common to describe the design process, yet understood them in often differing and competing ways.

The second advantage of using this fairly crude model of the design process as a departure point lay in its simplicity. As each person we spoke to explained their experience and knowledge of the SD1 project, the model grew and was adjusted according to new evidence. Above all, by investigating how the design process embraces the three main areas of product, production process and work organization, the complexity of the design process from concept to operation becomes apparent. The multiple objectives and trajectories of the project, together with the many interrelationships involved, stand out as one traces how the SD1 car, the new Solihull plant and its form of work organization were conceived on paper, translated into prototypes, commissioned and finally put into operation. The combination of our model of the design process with the notion of the productive unit as the object of that process provides the basis for beginning to understand design as a totality rather than restricting attention to one area or strand of the more complex whole. Figure 4.1 is a graphic representation of that complexity as it appeared in the SD1 venture. Even so, the figure depicts only the main architecture of the project; its phases, events and the groups involved are only shown in summary form.

It must be made clear that the representation of the course of the SD1 project which follows in the next two chapters is a reconstruction mounted in the context of hindsight and reflection. As the figure tries to show, the design process was neither linear, nor straightforward, nor totally rational. The project, in common with others in the industry, was far too unpredictable for that to have ever been the case. Abortive subphases, repetitions of sequences after their initial failure and the collapse of key intentions concerning the car, plant and work organization rebut any assertion that this is a mechanistic model.

At the outset of this study the approach of historians such as E. P. Thompson, or geographers of Derek Gregory's kind[3] provided fruitful ways of viewing the process of change in terms of both structural determinants and human agency. Gregory's analysis of society maintains how,

> the creative interaction between the players, conscious or otherwise, reconstitute or re-fashion the structures within which (and through which) they take place. [Moreover,] this is a fundamental objection to the teleological ascription of such motivations to systems or structures; rather, people, in their conscious activity, for the most part unconsciously reproduce (and occasionally transform) the structures governing their substantive activities of production.[4]

Therefore, the account of the SD1 project which follows will try to convey both the corporate intentions and the imperatives which drove the design process as well as the 'creative interactions' between those involved. The way in which corporate strategy was reproduced and transformed during the design process is a major concern.

Chapters 4 and 5 represent an attempt to convey the logics and uncertainties, the intended and unintended outcomes, the strategic goals and the tactical responses, and the competition and interdependence within the SD1 design process. Chapter 4 begins with an assessment of the fateful significance for the SD1 project of the mergers which led to the creation of BLMC. The rest of the chapter examines how the three main elements of the SD1 productive unit were conceived and translated. Chapter 5 traces their path through to the commissioning and operation of the SD1 plant. There are a number of subsidiary questions which will be posed. What were the sources of the design concepts and how were the project's distinctive mixture of radical and incremental innovations generated? A comparison will be made between conventional and contemporary methods of project organization with the situated practices of the company and corporation. The patterns of involvement within the project and the multiple cultures, languages and their appropriate rhythms of reproduction will be revealed. A reconstruction of the contradictions between the design capacity of the Rover Company and the newly created corporate objectives is offered. The final operating system embodied both of these and yet at the same time was shaped by the interaction of management, community, suppliers, labour and the state. In particular, attention will be drawn to the high degree of uncertainty involved in such a large project which in so many ways came to register the problems and attempted remaking of the British car industry.

I Merger

The merger of the Rover Company with Leyland in 1967 can be explained primarily by reference to the financial pressures on Rover when set against the cost of technological change in the auto industry of the 1960s. Whilst considerable attention will be devoted to what turned out to be a major event for Rover, this particular path was by no means inevitable. The company could so easily have been acquired by Standard and/or Singer in the 1930s, and less spectacularly by Standard in the early 1960s. However, it was the lengthy independence of Rover down to the late 1960s which had implications for the merger with Leyland in two respects. First, the long period involved had enabled serious financial problems to develop at Rover. Second, the age of the company had perpetuated strategies and capacities which became so entrenched that their assimilation by a new corporation was always likely to prove difficult.[5]

In 1971 it was noted how the cost of competing in the world car market had become 'phenomenal'. Previously, manufacturers such as Citroën or Rover had been able to exist by making a specialized model for a mainly domestic market. By the 1970s the domestic market was too small a base, and international competition required a company to produce a model range. Costs increased so that £35 million was needed to develop and manufacture a new car in Europe. Ideally, new models should have appeared within a five-year rhythm. Renault's conventional requirements in this respect in the late 1960s were running at a cost of £100 million per annum.[6] Capital requirements of this order provided a major stimulus to the increased concentration of the auto industry. The larger corporations could contain product or plant failures which would be critical for the smaller producer and they were able to spread the growing burden of research and development costs over a wider range of models and returns. Few small producers could ever meet the capital requirements necessary to become mass producers. The volume manufacturers, meanwhile, were encroaching, by 1970, on the specialized market by producing adapted versions of their own standard models.[7] The independent specialist firms were therefore in an increasingly vulnerable position.

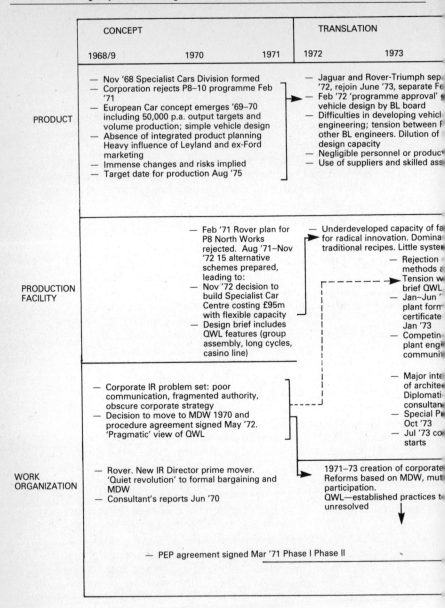

Figure 4.1 The SD1 design process, 1968–1982.

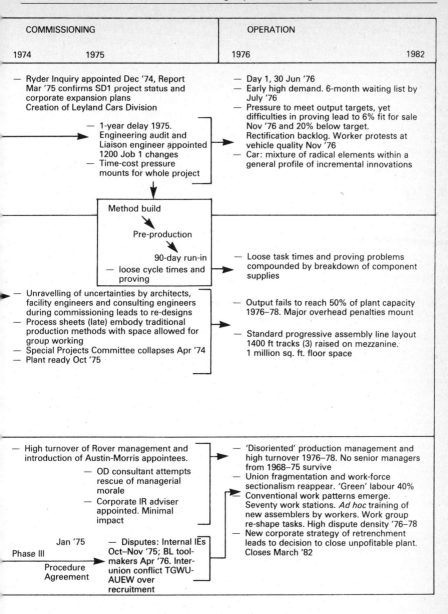

COMMISSIONING	OPERATION
1974 1975	1976 1982

— Ryder Inquiry appointed Dec '74, Report Mar '75 confirms SD1 project status and corporate expansion plans Creation of Leyland Cars Division

    — 1-year delay 1975. Engineering audit and Liaison engineer appointed 1200 Job 1 changes
    — Time-cost pressure mounts for whole project

— Day 1, 30 Jun '76
— Early high demand. 6-month waiting list by July '76
— Pressure to meet output targets, yet difficulties in proving lead to 6% fit for sale Nov '76 and 20% below target. Rectification backlog. Worker protests at vehicle quality Nov '76
— Car: mixture of radical elements within a general profile of incremental innovations

Method build

Pre-production

90-day run-in
— loose cycle times and proving

— Loose task times and proving problems compounded by breakdown of component supplies

— Unravelling of uncertainties by architects, facility engineers and consulting engineers during commissioning leads to re-designs
— Process sheets (late) embody traditional production methods with space allowed for group working
— Special Projects Committee collapses Apr '74
— Plant ready Oct '75

— Output fails to reach 50% of plant capacity 1976–78. Major overhead penalties mount

— Standard progressive assembly line layout 1400 ft tracks (3) raised on mezzanine. 1 million sq. ft. floor space

— High turnover of Rover management and introduction of Austin-Morris appointees.
    — OD consultant attempts rescue of managerial morale
    — Corporate IR adviser appointed. Minimal impact

Jan '75
Phase III
Procedure Agreement

— Disputes: Internal IEs Oct–Nov '75; BL tool-makers Apr '76. Inter-union conflict TGWU–AUEW over recruitment

— 'Disoriented' production management and high turnover 1976–78. No senior managers from 1968–75 survive
— Union fragmentation and work-force sectionalism reappear. 'Green' labour 40%
— Conventional work patterns emerge. Seventy work stations. *Ad hoc* training of new assemblers by workers. Work group re-shape tasks. High dispute density '76–78
— New corporate strategy of retrenchment leads to decision to close unpofitable plant. Closes March '82

Even by the late 1950s, Rover's capital was small in relation to the rising costs of research or re-tooling. The investment necessary for the Rover 2000 in 1960, for example, was almost equivalent to the issued capital of the company. The risk associated with each new project grew sharply, with less and less room for manoeuvre and the financial penalties of failure considerable. Rover realized the necessity of spreading its costs over a larger volume output in the 1960s, hence the simpler design of the P6 and the attempted increased production in 1963. There was also the need to purchase components made cheaply as well as to provide a wider range of models to dealers already under pressure by the larger car companies to sell their products alone. The circumstances of the 1960s auto industry, therefore, made Leyland and Rover likely, though not inevitable, merger subjects.[8]

Linkages with Rootes or Jaguar were unlikely, given their family control, while an abortive tie-up with Standard in the early 1960s regarding spare parts and engines ended the prospect of an alliance for Rover there. Rover was forced to evaluate its position in the sector as the 1960s progressed. In 1965 the Pressed Steel Company, which supplied Rover with car bodies, was taken over by the British Motor Corporation. By this time, financial commentators were openly speculating on Rover's ability to 'continue viable where increased competition makes economies of scale imperative'. Meanwhile, in response to such moves, Leyland M C wanted to prevent BMC becoming the largest British-owned car group. So when BMC and Jaguar merged in the summer of 1966, Leyland considered it vital to acquire Rover as a comparable, medium-priced luxury saloon unit. More particularly, Leyland was also anxious to add the Land Rover 4 × 4 models to its own commercial vehicle range. Rover's £7 million pre-tax profit in 1968, compared to its modest £3 million in 1967, made the company even more attractive in the short run. From Rover's point of view, by 1966 the company's existing overdraft requirements, combined with the need for capital to develop new models, made it especially receptive to merger proposals with Leyland. Negotiations were straightforward, were concluded successfully in January 1967 and the merger registered on 20 March. As in the major turning-point of the 1928–32 crisis for Rover, the company's bankers' advice proved critical. On this occasion they argued that a small independent car company was by current standards an anachronism,[9] an argument which Rover executives accepted.

In January 1968 the Rover Board welcomed the proposed merger between Leyland and BMH. The approval rested on the board's understanding that Rover and Standard-Triumph would be located separately in a 'quality car division independent of a volume car division, as it was recognized that it was undesirable to mix the two markets'. In February the Rover Board was apparently satisfied with the new British Leyland Motor Corporation chairman's 'definite intention that each company would preserve its autonomy, and particularly would be responsible for the design and engineering of its own products'.[10]

The collection of mergers and take-overs which culminated in BLMC[11] is represented schematically in Figure 4.2. How both major forces, BMH

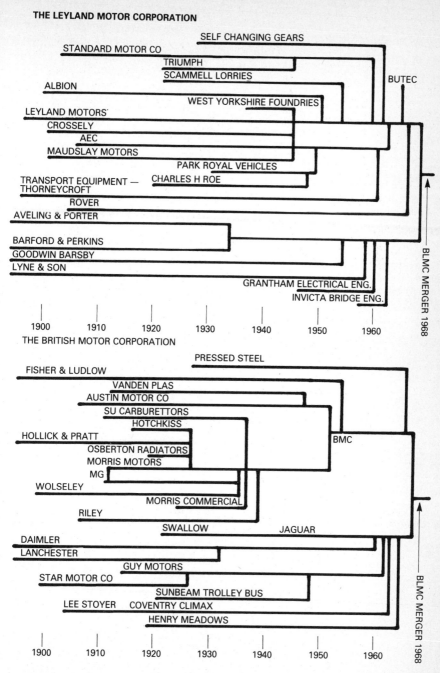

Figure 4.2 Mergers and the British auto industry: Leyland, BMC and BL.

and Leyland, were unable to unite and manage the companies they had acquired in the 1960s has been generally noted. The sales orientation of BL's senior management (exemplified by the appointment of Leyland's head as Chief Executive) did not make them well equippped to reorganize the firms involved. Neither was the problem given a high priority by the government sponsors or union supporters of the merger which, for Britain, produced a large corporation. The twenty-five manufacturing companies, employing 80,000 people, meant that the corporation could offer over 1,300 different vehicle types to the market.[12]

BMC's growth in the generally buoyant market conditions of the 1950s and 1960s had relegated the task of company integration to a lower order of importance, and long-term weaknesses in production, design management or industrial relations (Ford's strength) had been neglected. The Labour administration of 1964 admittedly reversed the trend in government policy by intervening directly in the restructuring of the auto industry, particularly via the Industrial Re-Organization Corporation. The IRC argued for the need to increase the scale of businesses and plant in order to match foreign producers as well as to prevent British companies being taken over. The Prime Minister and the Minister for Technology were in favour of the merger and were also instrumental in obtaining agreement between the managements of Leyland and BMC. The IRC provided £25 million for re-tooling. The Times commented that 'never before has a private enterprise merger been conceived with such close contact with government'. Yet the reliance by the Government on the existing management meant that any strategic weaknesses or deficiencies in product or design management were left untouched with, for example, model policy decisions postponed.[13] Whilst the role of the Government as financial and political broker within the merger has been widely commented on, few writers have drawn attention to the absence of practical advice or assistance in conducting the merger process. Most attention, both in 1968 and since, has been devoted to the initiation of the process rather than the way in which an appropriate means of executing that process might have been devised.

The problems facing the new corporation were immense. As is well known by now, the merger produced an 'ill co-ordinated empire of companies'. Jaguar, Rover, Triumph and BMC had hitherto designed their products in total isolation, in separate companies and plants. Jaguar, Rover and Triumph had three models in direct competition after the merger: the Jaguar 240, the Rover 2000 and the Triumph 2000. Besides the inevitable management rivalries between the constituent companies, there were separate distribution franchises for each BL company. The corporation owned sixty plants, some of which were very small, and which had never before been linked in any way. This compared unfavourably with Ford's four main assembly plants, integrated with their engine and body facilities. The divergent business strategies within the new corporation meant that BMH marketing, planning and design costing (similar to Rover) remained weak. At the outset the general paucity of communication or costing systems, compared to Ford's, meant that they

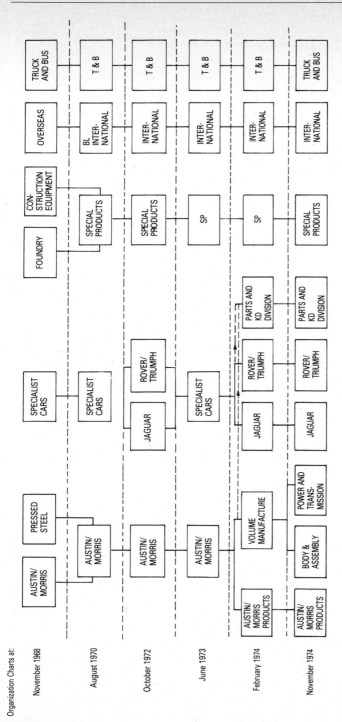

Figure 4.3 The British Leyland Motor Corporation. Development of operating divisions, 1968–1984. *Source: British Leyland: the Next Decade* (1975), 54.

had to be constructed from scratch. Ensor likens the internal problems of BLMC in 1968 to those of GM in 1923. Given the increase in foreign competition, the time available to resolve them was far shorter for BL.[14]

BLMC corporate management chose a modified version of the early General Motors strategy, based on centralized direction, combined with decentralized operations. The Truck, Volume Car, Specialist Car, Special Products and Overseas Sections were created as separate profit centres with their own management (see Figure 4.3), an arrangement adopted by Ford in 1946. Central management and staff were to provide financial and market information as well as retaining decisions over model programmes and major investment. Although BL's intentions went further than GM in the reorganization of plants, parts and processes, a coherent business strategy was very slow to emerge.[15]

Although Sloan's biography may have been required reading at the new corporation's London head office, the means of translating the divisional concept of organization into practice was poorly understood. As might be expected in a corporation where ex-Leyland management were in the ascendant position (Leyland had taken over BMH because of the former's stronger profitability), greater emphasis was placed on the market aspects (the Leyland Company's strength) than the managerial or production features of the GM strategy. The main emphasis was therefore placed on a divisional system containing a range of car products which would cover most of the expanding market and its segments. There does not appear to have been a profound understanding of the social transformation involved. One searches in vain for a theory of organization change or notion of corporate culture, for example, which informed the corporate executives in the 1968–70 period. The absence of an effective communications network or learning programme, whereby knowledge would be codified and preserved, were conspicuous. The GM administrative system helped to create a shared pattern of managerial thought which conditioned the routine activity of all levels of management. At BLMC the difficulties of weak mechanisms for communication and co-ordination were left relatively untreated in the urge to expand. Prior to the Ryder Inquiry's depiction of these problems, internal papers written in July 1973 already identified

— the loss of managerial authority brought about by the introduction of new divisional and corporate policies;
— the lack of information about Corporation plans, poor communication of the reasons for change and the remoteness of the top decision makers;
— the effects on morale of successive 'mergers' and the inevitable un-certainties with which these are associated.

Forty years after GM, the BLMC executives had adopted the elements of the American corporation's strategy but had failed to reproduce the central principle: the creation of a formal system for impounding the results of new market alignments and their integration with the daily management of the enterprise.

The use of largely ex-Ford marketing management led to a reorganization of retail operations: BL-owned importers now sold to dealers in place of the old independent distributor-to-dealer connection. Yet the lack of a clear model policy meant that these outlets still had to sell, directly competing, Jaguar, Triumph and Rover models. Poor profits in 1970 and disruption due to supply and industrial relations problems thwarted the planned progression of the business strategy. For example, the corporation could only find two-thirds of the £60 million required in annual investment, and it took until 1970 for a Group Standards Division to begin the job of establishing common coding and documentation. In the light of the slow realization of the original corporate policy, an early revision became necessary. Instead, each unit was assessed and then forced to concentrate on the products which appeared to be the most profitable. The original intention to leave the Specialist Car Division plants untouched was abandoned. Jaguar and Rover ranges were cut, Jaguar was to concentrate on the XJ6 and Rover, for the moment, on its existing P6 aqnd P6B (3500 model). Both of the model outputs were to be expanded, with Jaguar's production per annum doubling to 40,000 cars. Jaguar, Rover and Triumph hereafter would produce one saloon each, Jaguar in the luxury market, Rover in the quality, medium-size sector, and Triumph in small-size saloons and sports cars. The intention was that engines would be interchangeable across the whole range. As a result of the strategy revision, Rover's planned sports model and new 4 litre (the P8) were cancelled, since they would compete with Jaguar's E-Type and luxury saloon cars.[16]

The infant corporate business strategy was essentially overtaken by events and market changes, but above all by the enormity of the problems involved in reorganizing such an heterogenous collection of companies and plants. Figure 4.3 indicates the changes in divisional structure alone as central management grappled with the overwhelming problem of having too many plants, with too many workers producing product ranges with too many models. The instability of the Specialist Division is particularly marked. There are two important points to note here. First, in spite of the apparent advantages to both Rover and Leyland in their merging, the merger represents the intersection of two very different company trajectories. The divergence between Leyland's aggressive, expansionist, market-led approach and Rover's cautious pursuit of engineering excellence within a limited market niche was considerable even before the difference in managerial technique and practical operation are examined. The acquisition of BMC increased the range of approaches and methods which co-existed in the new corporation. Second, in the absence of a settled corporate strategy and without a mechanism for linking the market and managerial or administrative components of the corporation's divisional form, the 1968–71 period was conducive neither to the establishment of so large a project as the SD1, nor to the transitions which Rover management were attempting. Rover executives felt superceded by divisional management. The Rover Board's customary monthly rhythm of meetings, a rhythm which had structured the company's reporting and routine decision making in the past, were cancelled. The Board was now only required to convene once each quarter, together with divisional management. Without a clear set of standard operating procedures or a means of creating a 'shared pattern of managerial thought' in relation to corporate objectives, the Rover Board found themselves 'disoriented' and complained in writing in June 1971 of 'management by remote control'.[17] However, the SD1 project was begun at the same time as the corporation was wrestling with its new business strategy. The project at the outset therefore came to reflect many of the uncertainties and contradictions of strategy and practice which resulted from the collision of the Rover and Leyland trajectories. With no appropriate means of resolving such difficulties, the entire SD1 design process bears their hallmarks.

The BL founding experience also raises comparisons with amalgamations and mergers elsewhere. The difficulties of managing a large enterprise in the British car industry was discovered by Morris in 1939 as they tried to switch from central control by two executives over a decentralized organization to control by a specialist directorate over a four-group, divisional structure.[18] Ford in America experienced similar problems in the immediate post-war period. A major difference between the experience of restructuring in the British and American auto industries emerges. In America the merging independents had clear and successful models of the 'Big Three's' corporate mode of organization, and what Edwards termed 'the accumulative benefits of the corporate form of business'. In Britain no comparable models existed in the sector.[19]

There are two further findings related to BL's founding which are relevant to the prevailing views on the organization of large companies in Britain. The first observation is that BLMC's initial corporate organization in a holding company form (H-form) is consistent with long-term trends in British industry. In spite of their awareness of the existence of the multi-divisional form (M-form) elsewhere in the 1930s, British managers persisted with the H-form of organization down to the 1960s and 1970s. In 1960, forty of the ninety-two top companies listed by Channon were organized along H-form lines. The H-form in Britain, and the auto industry in particular, was not a transitional form, as Williamson argues more generally, but a stable and long-term feature of corporate organization. International competition, decline in profitability and the growth of shop floor union organization are seen as the triggers, in the late 1960s, to the increased adoption of the M-form of internal organization. This leads to our second observation. The generally agreed advantages of M-form are seen in terms of the reduction of control loss at the top of the firm by the separation of operating and strategic decision making, and by the creation by a central head office of control machinery to be used over the operating divisions. Marginson argues that M-form also had specific advantages for managerial control of workplace union organization.[20] However, the experience of BLMC indicates that these control benefits are highly dependent upon the ability of the organization to make the transition from H- to M-form in the first place: something which most accounts of the growth of M-form ignore. Given the persistence of H-form and the lack of an effective organizational learning programme outlined above, the slow emergence of the M-form apparatus in BL did not lead to the easy exploitation of its benefits. Indeed, the continual difficulty in establishing a central control machinery meant that not only was co-ordination of production operations poor, but many of the key areas of design activity also remained unrationalized and fragmented, as the SD1 project reveals.

However, recent research puts the merger problems of BL in a different perspective. Whilst Jones has concentrated on explaining the difficulties which BL faced, especially in the environment, and others have highlighted the comparative success of American corporations in reorganizing in the late 1960s and early 1970s, Prahalad and Doz's study provides a separate emphasis.[21] Their research on GM's 'large-scale strategic redirection' of its European operations from 1973 onwards suggests that it takes between three and seven years to complete such a manoeuvre. In this sense, given their inherited problems, the BL reorganization which arguably took up most of the 1970s is not nearly as exceptional as is generally believed. On the other hand, the authors identified the problem of changing corporate strategy and implementing it as central to the success of GM's European redirection. Here their conclusions support our findings that in both content and method BL's attempt to redirect corporate strategy was critically hampered by the lack of attention given to creating a dominant logic and communicating it to management. In BL the divisional system was expected to facilitate the growth of a multi auto product corporation. Yet in the case of GM, over twenty-four months in Stage I were devoted to 'developing an alternative world view and an emerging strategic consensus'. In Stage II of GM's strategic redirection, increasing global competition forced the European integration process to align with GM's world-wide integration. A separate three-year programme of changing managerial goals and winning their commitment (not compliance) was undertaken. As Prahalad and Doz observe, almost 80 per cent of the time taken for strategic redirection was 'devoted to changing the cognitive orientations of key managers'. The failure of BL to establish and sustain a dominant logic across the enterprise between 1968 and 1976 became critical not only for the viability of the corporation, but it will also appear as a vital means of understanding some of the contradictions, internal relations and peculiar dynamic of the SD1 project.

II Concept stage: the product, production facility, work organization

The SD1 project was intended to be a major event for both British Leyland and the Rover Company. The venture was meant to mark a clear discontinuity. In terms of a productive unit, each of the three main elements were to be innovatory. The project would produce a new product, with a new production process via a new form of work organization. The remainder of this chapter is devoted to an examination of the first two main stages of the SD1 design process: concept and translation. The way in which the SD1 car, plant and method of work organization were conceived will be reconstructed and in the way in which they were each translated into possible prototype forms will be traced. Besides assessing the sources of the SD1 design process and the contexts in which they emerged, the following sections will evaluate the degree of innovation planned in each of the three main areas against what emerged in reality, and the reasons involved. It will become clear that, although the project was structured at the outset by a series of corporate decisions, that framework was in turn restructured by subsequent actions of a range of key individuals and groups involved at all levels of the enterprise. Their interrelations not only shaped the SD1 design process but, together with their divergent motivations, were critical to explaining the dynamic of that process and its eventual outcome. As will become clear, the contradictions and tensions which appear in the concept stage were largely unrecognized and left unresolved. Even if the turbulent market environment of the 1970s is ignored, the subsequent phases of the design process were always going to pose major problems of coherence and co-ordination in the absence of a corporate capacity to understand or manage the design process as a totality.

The product
The SD1 car is best assessed as an innovation in relation to the Rover Company's design trajectory (see Chapter 3) on the one hand, and to the state of contemporary auto design on the other. It is notoriously difficult to determine precisely the novelty involved in a new car model, given the rhetoric which surrounds it. In the SD1 case, the detailed literature issued by the company plays down any innovative aspects: instead, it empha-sized the 'simple' engineering philosophy which 'inspired the design team who created the new generation of Rovers' (ultimately the model range of the 2300, 2600, 3500 V8 and V8-2).[22] The stress was on excellence and high standards (e.g. Rover will continue to set the standards of aero-dynamic design well into the 1980s') rather than new departures; an obvious attempt to connect with Rover's past image of product 'refine-ment' and to retain the company's high degree of customer loyalty. The V6 and V8 engine series and the safety features of the P6 car are shown as continuing in the SD1. Only in the later Rover 3500 V8 specification literature is the description 'the most significant new car development for many years' mentioned. The public statements by BL about the car were an attempt therefore to reflect marketing intentions, 'that the new Rover has to broaden the appeal of the marque ("simplicity") and at the same time retain the loyalty of existing Rover owners ("refinement")'.[23]

In 1977 the SD1 won the European Car of the Year Award. Although there are mixed views as to the value of this award in the industry, this would suggest that the model contained innovative features since a condi-tion of the award was that 'the design must be genuinely new, must offer substantial innovation in construction and technical specification'.[24] The degree of the SD1's innovativeness is a problem, however. The car is clearly new in the sense of being labelled differently from any other pre-vious Rover or BL model, yet its composition exhibits different degrees of change and certain key continuities. The details of the styling were

specific to the car, while the overall body shape was close to the contemporary norms in European car design. The chief styling engineer
admitted, 'Our solutions to the problems posed by all the many requirements (identity, low drag and general aerodynamics) is a sculptured form
in the increasingly important European hatch-back, five door idiom'.[25]
The monocoque body shell—body and chassis in one—was only partly
new for Rover, given the previous P6 base unit arrangement. Indeed, the
problems experienced with P6 body assembly led the SD1 design team to
ensure that body/unit fit was maintained in spite of 'the unavoidable
variations in production tolerances'. The five-speed, modular gearbox was
built not as a new departure but rather from common components across
the Rover-Triumph range and with a view to being used in other BL cars.[26]
The V6 and light alloy V8 engine was described as 'familiar to everyone',
having been used in the P6 range; the difference in the SD1 was its ability
to achieve higher bhp and revs (5,200–6,000 r.p.m.). Only the rear self-
levelling suspension appears as a patented feature of the car.[27]

The ensemble of the SD1's characteristics therefore appears very mixed
in innovative qualities. The major break made in the Rover P series design
family by the SD1 was made in body shape and in detailed engineering.
Rhetoric apart, the move away from traditional Rover engineering refinement was marked, although in practice, not straightfoward. In the corporate context, Rover engineers reported how they had 'to do great things
with simple means because we have been able to analyse more precisely
than before what the various parts of the car cost and what gives us value
for money'.[28]

Rover's traditional engineering specialisms could no longer hold, given
the corporation's injunction that they develop common components along
with the other companies in the Specialist Car Division. The production
volumes envisaged for the SD1 meant that engineering sophistication and
custom features had to be rejected, given the needs of semi-mass production. The SD1 was composed more straightforwardly than other Rover
cars in order that it could be assembled more easily. The back axle, for
example, was a single unit instead of a series of components. For this
reason, a Rover engineer, when asked, could not think of a single major
innovation on the SD1, and considered the back axle to be little different
from Ford's volume model except in suspension geometry. The SD1 was
'well engineered', but a more basic vehicle than previous Rovers; ease of
servicing for fleet buyers was a growing consideration at the time. By
comparison, the Rover P6 of the 1960s 'really was complicated'.[29]

An overall assessment of the SD1 car as an innovation cannot be
straightfoward, given the combined character of the technical changes it
embodied. An important distinction arises, however, if the car is viewed in
relation to the auto sector and then according to the experience of the
Rover Company and BL. First, for the international auto sector, the SD1 is
more properly described as an incremental innovation. It fitted the general
pattern of not dramatically altering the design of previous models;
instead, it followed the European direction, especially in body design.
Designs which are of high quality, market successes and initiate a new

direction as well as giving rise to 'design families' (that is, a collection of close variants which extend the original) are termed 'robust' designs.[30] While the Land Rover and P4 (60–110 versions) car qualify as robust, the SD1 does not. The SD1 was to use conventional unit-construction body shell, for example. However, in the eyes of the Rover Company, the SD1 ranks as a strategic innovation (see Chapter 2, Section V) at the concept stage. Set against the scale outlined in Chapter 2, the SD1 product was meant to represent a clear move away from Rover's original product market, with major implications for the character of the productive units within the enterprise. Above all, this single change at the conceptual stage, by implication, required a series of future changes in almost every specialist department of the company. The shift from limited production for a small, luxury market to semi-mass production of a more basic executive model could present a host of problems and situations hitherto unknown to almost every group within the Rover and Leyland operations.

The Rover SD1's product design process certainly emerges as distinctive by virtue of its length. While other car manufacturers regarded around four to five years as the norm in the 1970s to design and develop a car, the SD1 cycle lasted, strictly speaking, from 1968 to 1976.[31] The unusual duration of the SD1 project is best understood by first examining the objectives of those involved, their interrelations and the circumstances in which they operated at the concept stage.

Soon after BLMC's creation in 1968, the Rover Company's production planning was superseded by a central corporate planning function. Decisions already made by the company were overridden as the corporation drew up its own model policy. This act produced a cleavage between company and corporation at the outset, a schism which is referred to by everyone involved with the project. The impulse which led Rover to accept a merger with BLMC was in part derived from the company's desire to widen its car model range; to this end, Rover had already begun to work and spent £4 million on design work for a P8, P9 and P10 model series. From what we have already seen of Rover's late development of product planning, the company would always find it hard to match the specialist marketing expertise of the corporate staff. The two model series concepts were diametrically opposed. The company's characteristically cautious intention was to produce a 4 litre executive, luxury car (the P8) ready for 1972, with a P6 type base unit and panel construction, to be sold in parallel with a 'face-lifted' P6 which would reduce the risk involved in ceasing P6 production as the P8 began. The cost of the project would be £45 million. BL, however, saw the P8 as a competitor of the Jaguar XJ6. A totally different semi-luxury model was planned by the corporation: it would involve a completely new assembly and paint plant (Rover was going to extend the existing P6 plant) with 3,000 units per week production capacity; the project would cost around £90 million.[32]

Those who had already devoted time and resources to the P8/10 series were dismayed at the major change in policy and direction. In 1968 Rover had welcomed the LMC/BMH merger precisely because of the company's future independence. However, a succession of measures reduced Rover's autonomy. In February 1969 a three-tier capital expenditure control was imposed on Rover, with: (a) projects over £250,000 requiring the approval of the Rover and BLMC Board; (b) projects of £5,000 to £250,000 requiring the approval of the Group Chairman. The Rover Chairman could only authorize up to £5,000 of expenditure.[33] In May 1969 Rover's sales forecast pointed to little expansion in the home market for 1969–70 to 1973–4, and noted the increasing competition in its price range. Yet in September 1969 the purpose of the first appearance of BLMC's Director of Finance and Planning at a Rover board meeting was to announce a totally different set of projections. In February 1971 the implications of the figures from central planning became clear. The Managing Director announced that, 'the decision has been made by the Group Chairman, not to proceed with the production of the P8 car', or the P10. The Managing Director emphasized that the decision had been made with the full knowledge of the effects on utilization of resources, abortive expenditure and the effect on company profits.[34] By June of that year, Rover product engineers were drafting a new car's features according to the corporate planners' concept guidelines. The target date for production was August 1975.[35]

In contrast to General Motor's European restructuring and the experience of recent corporate reorganization, BL made little effort to resolve the deep-seated differences between Rover and central management. Incompatible imperatives were left to operate. Not only had a car model scheme for a P6 facelift and new P8 car continued down to 1971, but the company's plans for the conversion of the North Works, where the new models would be produced, had also progressed in parallel. There was no concerted attempt to begin an alteration of Rover management's world views via a systematic programme.[36] Instead, they were expected to accept a major shift in product philosophy almost immediately.

The testimony of an experienced organizational consultant who joined the corporation during the SD1 concept stage is instructive. First, he found that corporate executives did not conceive of BLMC as a single unit but as a federation. Second, to use his words, 'internal communication inside the corporation was a shambles' and led to his being directed to mount a study of the problem in 1973. His observations of the SD1 project are particularly revealing. The design process was what he termed 'step-wise' and relatively unsynchronized. Pre-Ryder, there were no common planning manuals. Instead, apart from the Board's validation of the original SD1 concept and programme in February 1972, the vertical linkages between Board, division and company, and the horizontal connections between functional specialisms (finance, product and production engineering) were left to operate alone. Each level and specialism developed its own part of the basic programme and then handed on its output to adjacent departments in the traditional manner of the 'sign off' procedure. As someone who was working in one of those departments, the organizational expert, highlighted the dislocation of the process as early as the concept stage:

The point about this system is that you never announce anything until you've got the money, which is when the programme starts as it were. Which means you don't tell anybody else until it's got to that stage, then it's too late . . . then traditionally you've got resistance of one sort or another. And this led to a number of things—the first thing, it (the project) was late . . . and it became a power struggle between functions.

The accuracy of these observations will be borne out during the translation stage of the SD1 project.

Unlike all previous Rover models, the SD1 was not only to be less refined and easier to build, it was to be built for a European market on a mass scale. The differences between the company's traditional operation and the corporation's conception of the SD1 were seized on by commentators on the industry. Their verdict was that, not since the new Ford and Vauxhall projects of the early 1960s, had 'so much been gambled by the British motor industry'. They questioned whether the transformation could even be made.[37] Why did British Leyland embark on such a major change and face the associated risks? The answer lies in the product planning capacity of the corporation in its first years of existence and the dominant influence of marketing during an important reordering of the European market.

The notion of BL's gamble with the SD1 at the conceptual stage should be put in perspective. It is generally accepted within the auto industry that all new model/plant projects—especially in Britain—involve a high degree of risk, given the range of interconnected variables involved. The risk is intensified by the high capital outlay and the inevitable continuing overhead costs. BL's position was more risky in a number of additional respects. The SD1 was the first totally new car and assembly plant project for the corporation. Although Ford and other mass producers attempted to upgrade their existing large car models, which were already being made in high volume, BL was isolated: the corporation was trying to produce a luxury model in mass quantities for the first time. Yet, in the crucial area of capacity planning, for example, BL did not have the experience of 'a continuous process of relating sales projections and the model mix to the available production capacity', either for the corporation as a whole or, more especially, in relation to the luxury car market. In addition, the degree of risk involved in the SD1 project was increased during the translation and commissioning stage as the first wave of oil price rises occurred in 1973–4 and severely disrupted the car market. The fuel-expensive executive car sector was reduced in size by one-third as a result.[38]

In order to assess the product policy of BL at the time of the SD1, a clear distinction should be drawn between practices in the early 1970s with product planning today. The overall design process in the auto industry during the intervening years has received sustained attention from practitioners and commentators alike. The risks involved in the design process—where 90 per cent of future costs are dedicated—have been intensified by the capital necessary to finance the process (especially research and development) or the plant and equipment for the production process. In the 1980s auto manufacturers now possess highly developed models of the design process: internal organization is elaborate and the recording of the process highly detailed. For example, Computer Aided Engineering (CAE) has facilitated fundamental changes in design; it has shortened the process, allowed greater flexibility in prototypes, thus enabling companies to respond to market requirements during the design process. CAE has been characterized by the current Managing Director of Operations at Austin Rover in the following terms:

> The creation of a fully integrated master data base holding all the engineering information on a product, and used by everyone involved in that product's design, development and manufacture, is the single most important development in our industry since the first continuously moving assembly track.

BL admits that the increased volatility and uncertainty of the market during the 1970s (i.e. the decade of the SD1's design and operation) made product design and planning more difficult. The process became more specialized and greater attention was devoted to an activity which in 1983 could cost around £100 million to mount. A current internal BL production planning paper explains the degree of risk involved:

> Motor companies the world over have been forced to improve their expertise to survive the increasing hostility of factors from oil crises to the massive increases in investment costs. It will not be possible in the future for companies to survive the launch of an unsuccessful product'.[39]

In particular, product planning has become not only a key input to the concept stage of the design process, but also a highly sophisticated activity with considerable responsibility within an enterprise. Product planners must ensure that it is feasible both to make a given product in engineering and manufacturing terms, as well as being financially desirable. Future market patterns are assessed by developing forecasts of macro-economic conditions, competitive activity and projections of vehicle sales performances. Car companies employ planners 'whose full time occupation is to build up a picture of competitors' business and product plans'.[40] Product design paths are projected for the forthcoming decade. Market trends, such as the movement of entire ranges up-market, are tracked and their implications assimilated. Moreover, the timing of the design process becomes critical. Product planners now seek to launch a product by a given date, but they also ensure the synchronization of each part of the process. The degree of integration between product and production designers has increased, as has their linkage with financial and commercial functions. The cost of new component development (a totally new engine and gearbox currently costs £200 million to develop) has led to increasing co-operation by production planners with other car companies.[41]

In the early 1970s, however, product planning did not exist as a separate specialism, nor did it contain the features found in today's auto sector.

Table 4.1 Models on offer in the British market by segment, 1975

Country	Manufacturer	Mini	Small	Medium	Large	Executive	Luxury	Sports
				Market Segment				
United Kingdom	Chrysler	Imp	Avenger	Hunter				
	BL	Mini	Allegro Toledo	Marina Dolomite	Maxi 18/22	Rover Triumph	Range Rover/ Jaguar	MGB, MG Triumph Stag E-Type
	Ford		Escort	Cortina	Capri Consul/ Granada			
	Vauxhall		Viva Chevette		Victor			
France	Simca		1000 1100	1301/1501	160/180			
	Citroën	2CV Dyane	Ami 6	GS	CX	ID		
	Peugeot	104		204/304	504			
	Renault	R4 R5 R6		R12	R15/17 R16			
Germany	Audi			80	100			
	Volks- wagen		Beetle Golf	Passat	Scirocco			
	BMW				1602	520	3.0	
	Mercedes				200		250/280	350 SL
Sweden	Saab			95	99			
	Volvo					244	264	
Italy	Alfa- Romeo		Alfasud		Alfetta			1300
	Fiat	500/850 126 127	128	124 131	132		130	Dino
	Lancia				Beta	2000		
Japan	Honda	Civic						
	Datsun	Cherry	Sunny	Violet Bluebird	Skyline Laurel	260C		260Z
	Toyota	1000	Corolla	Carina	Corona II Celica	Crown		
	Mazda		818	616	929			
Holland	Daf		44	66				

Sources: European Manufacturers' Car Lines by Market Segment (Ford of Britain): New Car Registrations in the United Kingdom (4 months, ended April 1975); SMMT (May 1975); CPRS, *The Future of the British Car Industry*, 1975, p. 66

Companies such as BL did not possess the capacity to assess a volatile market and continuously relate sales forecasts, model mix and production capacity. Design and operational costs were only beginning to rise on what later became a steep curve: the pressure to integrate the design process was therefore not so acute. The instruments available to product planners were comparatively simple. In 1970 (during the SD1 concept phase) the Economic Development Committee for the motor industry found it necessary to produce a model for forecasting car demand because of the absence of appropriate formulae within the industry.[42] Treasury assumptions relating to management of demand in the economy were not publicly available until the late 1960s. The motor industry EDC, established only in 1968, took some time to develop its advisory role. In fairness to BL, the CPRS Inquiry found that the forecasts used in the industry in the early 1970s relied on econometric models which used relationships based on past experience to forecast future levels. These models assumed that the explanatory variables would remain broadly constant over time.[43]

At British Leyland, after the formation, production planning was heavily influenced by the marketing emphasis of the senior corporate management. Perceived market opportunities drove the choice of a new model rather than the combined assessment of changes in model or production capacities together with their financial and operational implications. In comparison with Ford, BL lacked a clear model policy covering the entire range and gave less attention in relating model type and production implications at the conceptual stage. Interviews with contemporary production planners reveal that production logistics and costing aspects of a given model were not routine features of early BL product planners' work, nor were they concerned with the design process as a totality. In spite of the sales bias in the introduction of new models, as late as 1976, BL did not have sufficient sales and marketing expertise to feed market information into the whole design process. According to a product planning expert, the product planners 'did market research, there were things like clinics, but they were essentially reactive; in other words, they would use a clinic to suggest to them how they should market a specific car rather than helping in the design process.' As a result, 'they weren't the cars that the market wanted, they were cars which were full of engineering ingenuity and which pleased the people who produced them, but which didn't necessarily particularly please the market place.'[44]

The second main reason why BL took the risk of entering the international luxury car market with the SD1 relates to the perceptions of the market by central management. Table 4.1 indicates that in the early 1970s, as the SD1 was being conceived, Rover cars were generally seen to be in the 'executive' sector. Evidence to the House of Commons Trade and Industry Committee in 1981 by senior BL executives indicates that Rover's product market niches had shifted dramatically as a result of the SD1 project. The Rover product had by then moved down-market from a distinctive luxury car to a medium-sized semi-luxury model, during a decade of general redefinition of market segments. As the Chief Executive told the Committee, 'light–medium—the Austin-Morris through to

Rover—are more and more in world terms becoming one range of vehicles rather than two'.[45]

The decision by British Leyland's central management in 1970 was to aim for the European car market with the SD1, and thereby to alter radically the market position and hence product character of the new model. The intention was to move from a traditional specialist, luxury car to volume production of a semi-luxury saloon. Corporate model policy for Rover was signalled in 1967 by the then Chairman of the Leyland Motor Corporation (and later of BL). He declared,

> Rover must get much bigger—we intend that this company shall become the greatest manufacturer of prestige cars in the world. There is a tremendous and growing market for this type of car, and frankly I think that this country has not taken its fair share of it during the past few years.[46]

At the launch of the SD1 nine years later, BL asserted consistently: 'its main competitors are from abroad . . . Rover will take the sales battle into the home markets of its competitors in Europe [and] . . . broaden the appeal of the marque'.[47]

The break with Rover's previous market position was demonstrated by the Marketing Director of Leyland Cars in 1976. He argued how 'this car [the SD1] enables us to go for volumes and market shares we have never considered before for Rover'. He also identified the car's competitors as BMW, Peugeot, Citroën, Volvo and Ford, which represented a range of companies covering the luxury to medium car sectors. Output target levels were therefore set at the figure, unheard of for Rover, of 150,000 units per annum.[48]

Leyland corporate management found many changes in the motor industry in the 1968–72 period which supported their intentions. The logic behind BLMC's creation was after all one of exploiting growing markets via larger enterprises. The linkages of Citroën with Renault and Volkswagen with Audi seem to confirm that the alliance of quality models with mass production techniques was correct. The opening of the European car market via related EEC legislation invited an attempt to meet foreign demand for luxury cars. Indeed, Government reports on BL and the motor vehicle industry appeared to confirm this export strategy. In view of the Central Policy Review Staff in 1975,

> The British motor industry is already to a large extent, and will increasingly become over the next ten years, an integral part of the European motor industry. An updated range, spearheaded by the Rover Triumph and Mini replacements, could provide BL with the opportunity to recover some of the lost British share in Europe, provided product quality, delivery, performance and the distribution network can be improved.[49]

Growth rates in new registrations during the 1960s, when BL's market policy was conceived, were growing rapidly, at well over 10 per cent a year. The late 1960s decline in growth rates was recovering in the first years of the 1970s. BL's targets seemed to parallel the general increase in output volume necessary to achieve economies of scale in the world auto industry. This was especially important for BL, given its huge overheads. Mercedes and BMW production runs were increasing by 1970 to 240,000 and 140,000 units p.a. respectively. In addition, senior management were recruited from Ford to BL (for example, the marketing chief of Ford Europe) in order to reorganize BL's European operations to match the well-established continental arrangement of Ford, Fiat and Renault. BL is a good example, therefore, of those innovation theories which highlight the importance of competitive comparisons: one company, in comparing itself with others in the market, perceives a performance gap which touches off the search for innovation to meet the market need.[50] The SD1 innovation was therefore conceived in part as a result of the comparison which BL drew between itself and its competitors.

Whilst BL's intentions in model policy are wholly explicable, given the general market changes, the corporation's ability to translate intention into operation was always going to involve a very large element of risk. The complex strategic innovation which the SD1 project represented was risky for two main reasons. The problems which BL's restructuring left unsolved were added to an already weak corporate design capacity. Critical to the SD1 was the inability to inject market information into the design process—Rover car clinics were held *after* the product had been developed and its key features established.[51] The design process was not sufficiently integrated between product and production to handle the scale of the innovation involved, nor was it flexible enough to accommodate the market changes which were to assault it. Second, set in the context of Rover or BL's limited design capacities, the transformation which the SD1 concept implied in product and production engineering alone was immense, with similar upheavals required in distribution right through to organization in space in the new factory.[52]

The business strategy and model policy which provided the source of the SD1 design concept were clearly the creation of corporate management. Yet the influence of the product engineers and stylists on new model concepts should not be overlooked. The major responsibility for the broad characteristics of the SD1 rested with BL executive management throughout the approval schedule which the product engineers had to work to from February 1971 to February 1972. There were three main stages:

Stage 1: Original Concept Approval;
Stage 2: 'Soft' Concept Approval (first prototype with little attention to styling);
Stage 3: Programme Approval (capital committed to detailed programme of development).

Although the line of authority between corporate planners and product designers was sharply drawn, central management were highly dependent on the vehicle designers' expertise: there was an interaction between the two groups. With justification, the chief product designers and stylists argue that their ideas played a large part in the evolution of the concept even before the first physical prototypes were made. Apparently a succession of exchanges followed between the vehicle designers and the marketing and finance specialists.

The conventional view is of product engineers simply working to a remit handed down by corporate management. In the SD1 the remit could not be a clear directive since, according to an SD1 vehicle designer, 'the marketing people don't know what *can* be done in engineering terms'. Rather, the planners were largely dependent on the designers, who 'put foward possibilities to them of what can be done'. Therefore, the key features of the SD1—notably its five-door format and Italian influenced shape—are directly attributable to the arguments presented by the chief stylist. At the time these represented a 'jump in specification and credibility' for Rover's product line: the 'jump' was sanctioned by the Board largely on the strength of the Rover styling studio's 'impeccable' reputation.[53] Given the 'step-like' nature of the SD1 design project (see above), whereby each specialism was supposed to convey the results of its segment of the process to the next department, the opportunities for subsequent interaction and unintended outcomes in the SD1 project were considerable.

Production facility
The second major facet of the SD1 project at the concept stage relates to the design of the production facility. Until now, production and work organization have been separated as the three key components of a productive unit. While the production process is often isolated in examinations of the auto industry, in the case of the SD1 project such a label fails to capture the extent of the design activity involved. The SD1 project did not only envisage a new assembly line, but a totally new site and plant in which the tracks were to be housed. The inclusive term 'production facility', as used by the engineers at the time, is therefore more accurate.

The knowledge that the corporation's intention to create a totally new car product does not appear to have been fulfilled, suggests that the SD1 production facility requires equally careful scrutiny. The image of the new Solihull plant presented by BL was one of a major innovation in both the British and European context: it provides an excellent opportunity to compare the public face of industrial change in Britain with the reality. Initial research showed that the production facility which resulted differed widely from the original conception. The changes which occurred must be explained. This section provides the first step in that explanation, by tracing the source of the SD1 facility concept, the context in which it emerged and the range of intended features.

The 1960s and 1970s form an essentially flat and stagnant period in the development of either the production process or plant layout in the auto industry, and it is in this context that the SD1 project must be seen. The pursuit of certainty in mass production in America had, by the 1960s, resulted in the virtual ossification of the total fabrication cycle, and the assembly area in particular. Most changes elsewhere were associated with national auto industries attempting to initiate American methods. In Broomfield's opinion the period was distinctive for the absence of experiments. The dominant American design of integrated mass production had become established and was being copied and adapted more generally.[54] The Chrysler car assembly plant built in Adelaide, Australia in 1962 is an example of integration on a single site. It was only as a result of the events of the 1970s (namely, oil price upheavals, the rise of Japanese best practice techniques, and the need to distribute production phases world-wide, involving specialist plants with large production runs) that the dominant rationales for production facilities were radically altered.[55]

Senior executives of BL admitted at the end of the 1970s that the corporation could only hope to approach the best production standards in Europe; competition with Japan was out of the question.[56] British car manufacturers' post-war business strategies, in a period of excess demand, placed less emphasis on sophisticated production techniques and more reliance on delegated control and payment systems to create profit. Constraints such as investment diversion, fragmented markets and the persistence of almost archaic methods and machinery meant that British auto manufacturers were very slow to develop automatic machine tools and move towards the integration of the fabrication cycle.[57] Micro-electronic technology was only beginning to become widely available by the mid-1970s for auto production. Most of the changes in the 1960s and early 1970s (automated welding, automatic painting and computerized test equipment) did not require radical reorganization of production or novel plant designs. They were automating existing parts of the production process; they therefore reinforced conventional layouts.[58]

The claims by BL that the SD1 production facility would be one of the most significant projects in not only British but also European terms must therefore be set in context. The specific assertion that the plant would be the most important development in the British car industry for forty years would not require exceptional changes in production to meet the claim. In order to make a full assessment it is necessary to display here the intentions of the corporation for the plant, and then later to discover the way in which those were handled and reconstituted by the plant design engineers during the translation phase.

Corporate policy dictated that the SD1 plant should not only house production of the new model, but that it should also be a totally new centre for the 'Specialist Car Division'. The 'Specialist Car Centre' was to be flexible, not dedicated; that is, it would not produce just one model, but eventually a series of models under the same roof, with the ability to incorporate new models in the future. The Specialist Car Centre concept was taken directly from the corporation's market plans outlined above. BL wished to rationalize its dispersed production facilities by concentrating its operations. Longbridge, Solihull, Canley and Cowley were to form the 'Central Assembly Area'. Machine shops, for example, scattered over the Midlands, were to be brought together at Canley.[59] The poor profit performances of BL in 1970–1 impelled the corporation to accelerate the process of concentration.

It is quite clear that the conception of the new production facility followed the conception of the SD1 product. It was in February 1972 that the BL Board ratified the SD1 prototype, and yet it was November of that year before the Board took the decision to build a new paint and assembly hall. The corporation's assessment of the luxury car market set the tone for the production facility and its capacity. The Managing Director of Leyland Cars in 1970 was 'convinced that this product can sell world wide in exceptionally high volumes, so all of our planning capacity, product derivation, marketing and home and overseas selling was, and is, designed to ensure that this is a reality'.[60] However, there was no simple correspondence between the concepts of the SD1 car and the plant that would produce it. Instead, the concept stage of the SD1 production facility proved to be as contentious as the process from which the SD1 car had emerged. Rather than the production facility being directly derived, as a concept, from the SD1 prototype, there was a high degree of choice involved. There were two main areas of choice: first, between the Rover Company facility concept and the BL option, and second, over the scale of the new plant.

The differences between the intentions of the Rover Company and the corporation's were considerable. Rover production planners had intended to work to their existing strengths and with reference to their own repertoire and standard operating procedures. Their aim in 1969 was to add a second assembly line alongside the existing P6 track in their 'North Works'; this line would assemble the P8 model. Output was to be 900 units per week, using two shifts. The major concerns of the Rover planners was not novelty of production layout or capacity but the immense problems posed by the high water table and confined space of the North Works. In complete contrast, the senior BL executives (largely ex-Ford) were 'motivated by high volume output'. As in the case of the SD1 car, the corporate view prevailed and Rover's detailed planning work from 1969 to 1971 was rejected. The output capacity for the SD1 plant was to be raised to 3,000 units per week on two shifts. At this stage the corporate planners wanted one-minute cycle times, compared to Rover's six minutes. The gulf between the two concepts was vast. Not only was Rover's production planning capacity being rejected but, in the eyes of the Solihull planners, the preferred corporate concept was clearly derived from Ford-based models which were the antithesis of Rover's production methods (a senior Rover production planner referred to Ford as 'the four-letter word company'). Moreover, choosing a high-capacity plant model concept had immense implications for the following stages of the design process and relationships within the project. Whilst the Rover planners, according to their repertoire of the P series and the P6 and Range Rover in the 1960s especially, wished to 'convert' P6 into SD1 production via a 'slower processed way', the Ford-based approach was quite different. In the latter case the keynote was as short a period of production planning and change-over as possible, great emphasis placed on a simple-to-assemble model, and the use of detailed control of financial operation to remove any product-production problems. Above all, the responsibility for the development and translation of the plant concept was to be taken away from Rover; it was now to involve other groups from within the corporation.[61]

Why did the Rover Company accept the corporate concept when the difference was so marked? There are two main reasons: one relates to the politics of the design process, the other to the way that process moved forward. Rover's position was a weak one within BL. In a phase of rationalization following the poor corporate profit figures of 1970–1, Rover's products and facilities still overlapped with Triumph's and Jaguar's. The option of siting the new Specialist Car Centre at the Canley Triumph factory made Rover vulnerable. The prospect of the new Centre coming to Solihull, together with the SD1 project, was therefore immensely attractive to Rover's senior management. Rover executives were also convinced that, by accepting such a package, the relative independence of the Land Rover and Range Rover operations would continue.[62] Secondly, the increase in the scale of the plant, involving a doubling of the cost of Rover's original scheme to £95 million and a projected floorspace of 1 million sq. ft. did not occur in a single action. Rather, the final SD1 plant concept emerged from a key sub-phase of the design process. This phase lasted from August 1971 until November 1972. Rover and corporate planners between them produced fifteen major planning schemes during this period, each increasing in scale. Schemes 1 to 4 were based on low SD1 output levels of 1,000 units only and part use of the North Works, while Scheme 15 provided: 'A new Assembly Hall, single storey with stores, Major Rectification, Paint Rectification and Final Finishing Sections incorporated, capable of car production up to 3,000 vehicles per week'. The translation from Schemes 1 to 15 was accomplished, via a gradual incremental sequence, as the Rover Company became aware of their vulnerability in the light of the corporation's need to reorder production priorities across its sixty plants.[63]

Location theorists have commented on the long-term profile of the British-owned motor industry and the continuous trend to concentrate around production linkages and the framework of support services and suppliers in the West Midlands.[64] The location of the Specialist Car Centre at Solihull, however, was not solely a corporate decision: the role of the state was decisive. In the case of the P6 plant, the government policy of regional development had almost resulted in the location of Land Rover production not at Solihull but at Pengam Moor in South Wales. In the end a large components store was sited there by Rover in 1963.[65] In 1973 the Solihull site, with sixty-four empty acres adjacent and owned by BL, made it a strong choice against the corporation's Coventry sites, especially in view of its situation on the edge of the Birmingham road network. Yet the land in question was 'white land', designated for housing in government planning categories. To build an industrial unit required a 'change of use' authority which could only come from central government. The corporate plans for the new plant (it would require approximately 2,000 workers) seemed to fit the regional development plan for the Solihull, Bedworth, Leamington and Warwick area which projected a doubling of the one million population by the year 2000. The Industrial Development Certificate was granted in January 1973.[66]

The second main intention of the corporation was that the facility should make use of the available techniques of job improvement associated with the 'Quality of Work Life' literature. Public statements by the corporation, although unclear in this area, stressed the need for employee participation in the plant's design and the incorporation of 'human requirements' in its planning. In September 1974, as the plant was being built, an industrial relations manager in the then Rover Triumph division spoke of the intention of BL 'to find means of getting more reliable output ... at Solihull we will be concentrating heavily on the environmental side ... we want to make the environment in which men will be working far more pleasant'.[67] In a policy document of July 1973 the corporation had decided that it would be foolish to rush into a 'slavish imitation of the radical plans of its continental competitors, but unwise not to explore pragmatically the benefits which the re-structuring of work might bring'. The corporate policy was, *inter alia*, to include:

1. conducting independent small scale experiments in work re-structuring and job improvement;
2. a breaking down of the specialist departmental barriers between production engineering planners, industrial engineers and industrial relations staff at the *initial planning stages*; the invitation of employees and representatives to comment and advise on improving the physical detail of facilities plans, once broad investment decisions have been made;
3. ensuring that there is sufficient flexibility in physical layouts to allow for experimenting with the allocation of work.[68]

The Solihull plant (along with the O series engine plant and the Liverpool Speke plant, for instance) was to be one of the 'experiments'.[69] While Rover management in general gave such proposals a mixed reception initially, senior executives were concerned not to repeat the same mistakes encountered on the P6 line. There were a number of conflicting statements over the nature of the changes in job design, but two themes emerged: the SD1 plant should include participation in its planning, and new task arrangements should be devised. A form of 'modified group assembly' was chosen, whereby 'operatives attached to a workgroup were able to exchange operations with their colleagues on different work stations, provided that the station average was maintained'. Central industrial relations staff also wanted a 'buy off' system where rectification work was performed on the assembly track by the original work group responsible for the fault, not by separate specialist rectifiers at a later stage. The same staff also envisaged a 'casino' form of assembly line; in other words, three short lines with long (six-minute) cycles, similar to those used by Fiat as experiments at the time, rather than the conventional single long line with short (one- or two-minute) work cycles.[70]

If the two main aspects of the SD1 production facility concept are compared, important differences appear. Whilst there was a major conflict over the scale and character of the plant between the corporation and the Rover Company (involving detailed costing schemes), the 'human requirement' suggestions by the central industrial relations department were seen as less contentious at the concept stage. For the moment, these suggestions were passed on to the production planners with no precise indication of how these intentions would be incorporated into the development of the facility. In concept the SD1 plant appears as a strategic innovation, given the major change of product and production features that it embodied. However, translating that concept was always going to be difficult. The attempt to move from a traditional Rover production planning recipe to a Ford-based method was enormously ambitious. In addition, there was a sharp, yet unnoticed, contradiction between the proposed use of Ford methods and the intention of introducing participation and new task arrangements derived from the very different practices of other car manufacturers. The relatively loose concept of the SD1 production facility was always liable to be transformed in a number of ways which the original planners had not intended, as the fragmented, 'step-like' design process unfolded and as each department wrestled with the uncertainties and contradictions which the concept stage had left unresolved.

Work organization

The decision to examine the SD1 project in terms of a productive unit raises an important problem when tackling the third element of that unit. Unlike the product or the production facility, a projected form of work organization does not appear to have been conceived at an early stage. Instead, the major attention between 1968 and 1972 was devoted to the establishment of the new car and plant concepts and the initiation of their development programmes. No comparable activity related to a new form of work organization occurred at corporate or company level. The notion of designing a new method of working to match the SD1 car and plant seems to have been outside the frame of reference of the actors at both levels. Rather, the assumption was that the key changes which the new product and production facility involved would lead to adjustments in working methods which would be made in a traditional manner during the translation of the production facility's concept into pre-production form.

In the absence of a strongly developed sense of envisaging the form of work organization in abstract parallel to the SD1 product and plant, the eventual method of work which resulted in 1976 was not attributable to a single department or source. It is more accurate to identify two sets of forces which account for its final operating form. The objectives and pattern of relationships associated with the design of the SD1 car and the Solihull plant were a key context from which the eventual mode of work organization emerged: these supplied the broader secondary features of work organization (such as output capacity and market targets) and will be dealt with subsequently as the design process unfolds through the translation and commissioning phases. The second set of forces had a more immediate influence over the detailed or primary features (such as task profile, payment method and discipline). In this section the origin of the second set of forces is traced to the actions of two groups: one, the central industrial relations department, the other, a temporary alignment of Rover's IR management and work-force. The activity of these two groups was not systematically related to corporate objectives for the SD1 project and plant as outlined in the previous two sections; their actions pre-date the decision to begin the SD1 project. Yet although these groups (especially at Rover) were moving along a completely separate path, they must be considered legitimate actors within the SD1 design process. Indeed, it is the divergence and contradictions between their imperatives and those of the groups connected to the product and plant design which will help to explain the tensions and conflict of the later stages of the project.

The means of payment, the employment rules and the related methods of bargaining which emerged, quite separately, from the product or production design, stand as arguably the most innovative features of the project. If we conceive of these developments in terms of social innovations, then it is not difficult to understand how a Rover director saw them as 'the greatest change of the whole SD1 experience'.[71]

The corporate industrial relations department faced an array of difficulties in the early years of BL's existence and during the SD1 concept stage. It is necessary to understand the problems which BL faced as a corporation and the remedies it chose centrally before the actions of Rover management can be explained. The problems fell into two categories. The first related to that critical area identified by Prahalad and Doz: BL managers in the 1970–3 period could not 'see how their work relates to a total business plan', nor could they 'have confidence in the overall direction of the corporation and the sense of purpose that comes from having feasible objectives to which they feel personally committed and from having clearly delegated authority over the reasons required to achieve their objectives'.[72] This crisis, identified by a senior corporate IR expert, stemmed from the loss of managerial authority brought about by new corporate policies and systems of control, lack of information and poor communication of the reasons for change, the effect on morale of successive mergers, and increased pressure from senior management combined with growing desire for worker concessions.

The second kind of problems arose from the defects in the existing industrial relations situation in BL. In 1970 the corporation had only just decided to obtain 'its own procedure agreement for dealing with unresolved questions arising in its plants'.[73] There was no job evaluation guide available even by 1973, nor was there a common apparatus for measuring or monitoring plant performance. The decision to move from piece-work to measured day-work in 1970 notwithstanding, the payment systems in BL were chaotic, with grade structures varying considerably between plants. In 1973 only 71 per cent of BL workers were covered by reformed schemes. The same was true over differentials between hourly-paid workers, thereby setting enormous problems over parity.[74] Bargaining was decentralized, with large areas of plant discretion. Spheres of influence among staff employees were not arranged rationally, due to piecemeal recognition in the past. In spite of the May 1972 BL procedure agreement, which provided a framework within which plant procedure agreements could be negotiated, very few plant agreements had been concluded by 1974. Joint union negotiation bodies at plant level were not yet common, and 'the corporation was exposed to the power of small sections to disturb wage structures and provoke consequential claims'. There was no single bargaining unit covering the corporation, as in the case of Ford UK.[75]

The central IR department recognized that an attempt to change these characteristics was a 'huge task' when set against union strength and a managerial crisis.[76] An indication of the scale of the problems was set out in the Ryder Report. The department's response was to try to shift from their primary role of conflict (especially strike) resolution to a more preventative stance. They wished to reverse their position of being 'long on fire fighting, short on prevention'. This was to be achieved pragmatically by a programme of reform established in 1973. A BLMC memorandum on 'Corporate Industrial Relations Objectives for 1974/5' issued in July 1974 emphasizes three main objectives:

1. improving labour efficiency;
2. obtaining greater commitment to the corporation from its employees through the overhaul of our consultative arrangements;
3. the introduction in each plant of approved industrial relations programmes.

Mutuality was to continue as the basis of any reform: the 'key style' was to be characterized by 'negotiation'. The shift was to be gradual and cumulative, a long-term process, not an instant turn-round.[77]

The negotiation style was to be expressed thematically across management action. Improvements in 'non-negotiating' relations and 'participative' relations were seen as influencing traditional negotiating behaviour. It was decided to establish hourly-paid and staff committees and to construct divisional and corporate consultative bodies. Managers were to be assisted in leading and motivating their employees by: the establishment of briefing groups at each level of the organization, induction training, team development programmes, and the creation of manager-employee working parties on particular problems. The physical working environment was to be improved via a 'safety organization'.[78]

The adoption of a participative approach to management which recognized employees' needs and abilities outside of task execution, although influenced by contemporary academic thinking, was still based on pragmatism. The head of central industrial relations admitted that 'academic pressure' influenced their thinking as they tried to solve the problems of productivity and absenteeism.[79] However, in the formation of the new IR policy, the conclusions of 'socio-technical' or quality-of-worklife writers were reduced to what BL could accommodate without adding to the instability in plant industrial relations. The way in which the department perceived the social innovations on offer outside the organization is best summed up in the caution which surrounds Section 14 of the 1973 IR policy entitled 'The Work We Ask Employees To Do'. It reads as follows:

> Practical consideration of theoretical teachings can be limited to recognising that employees are likely to become less productive, that high pay will not cause employees to be productive, that much work does not use people's abilities, that unused ability may become counter-productive, that many people would respond to an improvement of their jobs which gave an opportunity for achievement, that the scope for change is limited by the availability of capital and by entrenched attitudes. It would be foolish to ape our continental competitors, but unwise not to explore possible benefits. The corporation should
> (a) play down job enrichment but explore job improvement;
> (b) conduct experiments;
> (c) improve liaison between the functions concerned with manpower and invite employee participation in the detailed planning of facilities;
> (d) ensure flexibility in layouts to allow for experiments.[80]

The corporate IR department, while aware of academic research and 'a feeling that the government will act sooner rather than later', were essentially reactive in their stance. In contrast to Volvo management, they were not convinced of the efficiency of the socio-technical analyses on offer. Management discussions around the 1973 policy indicate that the measures (a) to (d) 'on balance' were deemed to have potential advantages which outweighed the disadvantages. The conviction which drove the change programme of the entire Volvo business was absent.

The central IR department therefore set up a sub-group in 1973 to conduct experiments and supervise the four main proposals. The group of six externally recruited specialists in work design techniques faced major logistical problems. So small a staff, with only limited resources, was always going to have a restricted impact across a large corporation: at best they would perhaps be able to exert an influence on individual projects. Above all, the dislocation associated with the corporation's early years of merger had meant that by 1972–3, according to internal reports,

> there are indications that the corporation is in danger of losing the support of the middle rank of managers from superintendent to works managers and that there is a lack of common purpose between production managers and the newly imported finance, IE, systems and personnel specialists.[81]

The IR sub-group faced formidable difficulties, therefore, in influencing such divided management interests in a time of suspicion, if not open conflict, and in the absence of a clear corporate policy, rationale and means of communication which the department's own reviews of 1970 and 1973 had highlighted.

The qualified acceptance of a 'job improvement' approach by the central IR department apart, the sub-group's proposals seem ill-suited to the problems at which they were aimed. At a general level, the papers produced by the group are notable for their imprecision and an almost apologetic stance. A 1976 paper, 'Job Improvement—Analysis of Costs and Benefits' (a title suggesting measurement), includes this paragraph, which is indicative of their tone and stance: 'Deciding whether improvements in performance are due to enhanced opportunity or a new attitude is difficult but it is important because opportunities are limited in scope and number, but attitudes can be altered and/or amended over time'.[82] 'Participation' or 'consultation' are offered repeatedly as the answer to any conflict which the proposed schemes of job redesign or organizational restructuring suggested. The ways in which these problems would be resolved practically and in detail are not addressed.

Chern's 'Principles of Socio-Technical Design'[83] is a useful measure, from an acknowledged expert in the field, to apply to the BL job improvement projects. His checklist of nine principles emphasizes the importance of restructuring the relevant parts of an enterprise around the project in question. There should be 'compatibility' between the design of a new system and its broad objectives, with no boundaries erected which interfere with the sharing of knowledge or experience. Systems of social support should reinforce the behaviour which the new organization structure is designed to elicit. Yet, as we have seen, BL was poorly placed to provide these features, given its own continuing attempt to develop a corporate identity and set of commercial and organizational rationales. On the evidence available and from the testimony of those involved,[84] there was no clear compatibility between the job improvement projects and corporate or company objectives. The corporate IR review and policy stresses how information should not be available on certain project issues; it also displays the urgent problem of poor communication in the enterprise. Each of these problems should have been solved prior to attempting the job improvement projects, according to the socio-technical orthodoxy.

In individual projects the contradictions between the job improvement scheme and corporate directives appear stark but unrealized by the sub-group. In a report on 'Methods of Vehicle Assembly at East Works, Solihull' (the SD1 plant) in August 1976, a 'job improvement officer' notes on page 3 that 'one of Leyland Cars' essential basic industrial relations policies [is] that of reforming wage structures away from individual or small group piece-work'. On page 10 however, he advocates 'fully autonomous group working, in which operators are responsible for the day-to-day operation of part of the production process.' He was seemingly unconscious of the contradiction between his advocacy and BL's policy of moving from piece-work to measured day-work in order to achieve stricter control and more tightly defined tasks.[85] The critical sensitivities around the wage issue for workers are side-stepped. The role of the job improvement group will be looked at more closely when we deal with the SD1 project's commissioning phase in the next chapter. At the moment it is sufficient to note that when a final review of the group's projects took place in 1978 (prior to the group's demise), their minimal impact was only too clear.[86]

The contrasting method adopted by Rover management, in introducing major changes in work organization, could not have been more different. Prior to the establishment of the corporate IR job improvement sub-group in 1973, Rover management had already begun a process of restructuring its work organization in relation to a new payment system and a newly created industrial relations apparatus. The contexts and objectives of the sub-group and the Rover management, although in some respects they appear similar, contrasted sharply in their methods.

The first executive Industrial Relations Director appointed by Rover in 1969 immediately realized the scale of the company's problems, as outlined in Chapter 3. The solution he proposed was two-fold. There was a need for a formal collective bargaining framework and code of practice. Through this new system the company's method of payment would be changed from piece-work to measured day-work. Commentators on payment systems from Rowe through to Brown agree that changes in payment systems involve questions of work organization, but also have implications for the power relations which underlay any method of regulating the wage contract.[87] It is understandable therefore how, for those involved, both management and work-force, the change could be seen as 'the greatest change of the whole SD1 experience'.[88] Perhaps the reason why these changes received less public attention than the experiments associated with job improvement or participation was the method of their conception and introduction. The change process took nearly seven years, and was as skilfully handled by the managers responsible as it was thoroughly thought out. One commentator described it as a 'quiet revolution' compared to the intense conflict which arose at the Longbridge and Cowley plants of BL over the introduction of measured day-work.

Three basic questions present themselves: why was the change attempted, what was its source and why was the proposal accepted and implementation begun smoothly? The change in payment system at Rover centred on one 'prime mover'. The new IR Director at Rover, following his experience elsewhere in the engineering industry, was convinced of the need for formal bargaining practices and an official set of employment rules. His experience in the electrical components supply industry, where manpower costs as a percentage of sales were almost double those in the car industry, had led him to admire the more developed personnel and IR departments. In Lucas, Wilmot-Breeden and Smiths, data on labour turnover and absenteeism were routinely available and training schemes and procedure agreements were, compared to the car industry, more sophisticated. In Rover, lack of basic records was obscuring the precise measurement of the generally evident problems of wage drift and high dispute intensity. The changes proposed by the Director were sanctioned by the Rover Board because the 'industrial relations situation was having such an impact in terms of loss of output'; they were accepted as a solution to a crisis.[89]

The choice of measured day-work was common to both the corporate and company heads of industrial relations, set against the background of a general expert and car sector consensus, as an internal BL paper on payment systems made clear. These influences were summed up by Rover's IR Director thus:

> A window opened and we went through it. We went through that window not only because it seemed the right thing to do in Rover, but at that time, after [a corporation IR director] had come, the general feeling among personnel people in British Leyland was that piece work was no way of running a motor car operation. And the evidence for this was Vauxhall and Ford . . . who were doing much better than the BL companies and whose production seemed more reliable . . . it was seen as a cure for the incidence of industrial relations disputes.[90]

The reasoning of the corporate IR chief was very similar. He felt that the 'payment system was symptomatic of a much deeper, deep-seated malaise. Things like management inconsistency and managerial disciplines'. As his 1970 and 1973 IR reviews indicate, there was a double need—for a reformation of the payment system, but allied with the creation of comprehensive procedure agreements and bargaining frameworks. The twin objectives were seen as means of 're-introducing some elements of discipline'.[91] Measured day-work and a more formal bargaining structure would necessitate the development of work measurement to underpin the establishment and maintenance of payment grades rather than the 250 bargaining units at Rover. These objectives are clearly implied in the internal papers on payment systems which defined measured daywork as,

> payment on a time basis with a fixed bonus for maintaining standard performance based on work measurement. Hourly rates are set for each job classification and a bonus curve established to reward performance based upon standard times arrived at through work study. In other words, the system is basically a time rate with bonus for specified performance. . . . The role of management in maintaining work flow and monitoring the work measurement function is crucial, as is the establishment of a sound labour relations climate.[92]

The paper also stressed how measured day-work systems 'seemed preferable for the added impetus it gave to increased centralization of bargaining and to reduced numbers of bargaining units, as well as facilitating the introduction of annual contracts'.

A further impetus was given to the changes at Rover by a firm of management consultants. Like the architects and consulting engineers in relation to the production facility in later stages of the design process, the consultants turned out to be key change agents. The use of a firm of management consultants by Rover was explained practically by the lack of resources within the IR department and their inability to mount a comprehensive study of forms of payment in the company. The study was endorsed by the trade unions during the 1970 piece-work negotiations after they had complained once more about the instability of earnings.

The consultants were offered and accepted as an independent body to conduct the investigation. The unions were already considering modifications in payments systems following the NUVB's national policy on seeking wage security.[93]

The report delivered by the consultants to management and union representatives on 28 October 1970 on the P6 wage structure made an immense impact. The recipients were presented with a total picture of Rover's problems for the first time, ranging from detailed measurement of hours lost through disputes, to broad strategy options for conflict resolution and wage stability. The consultants' 'Survey of the Rover Company' (dated 12 June 1970) gave a clear analysis of conflict at Solihull. It identified the causes of conflict across a range of levels from individual, work group, and plant to the company and expressed it concisely in everyday language. The union representatives, who at the time were in the middle of constructing their own company-wide organization, were impressed by the way the report faithfully echoed their problems over the lack of information, the need for shop steward training, erratic production and unstable and unequal earnings. Their shock on discovering the extent of Rover's problems were comparable to the reaction of those union representatives on BL's Joint National Committee and its survey of European production methods in 1973–4. The recommendations of the report were therefore treated seriously.[94]

The broad idea which emerged from the negotiations which followed was the establishment of a payment system based on five performance bands using 100 BSI standard performance in the middle band. The eventual agreement, known as 'The Protected Earnings Plan' (an astute label offered by the consultants), was signed on 12 March 1971. The agreements embodied far more than just a new wage payment system; it represented a long-term programme of change with manifold implications for future work organization.

The IR Director of Rover observed that, for the first time in the company's history, negotiations had taken place which covered the terms and conditions of all hourly-paid employees. Mutuality was accepted as the legitimate basis for future negotiations, and union representation enshrined as a right in Clause XXV. It was admitted how, 'attitudes and powers of employees are now such that significant changes can no longer be imposed and can only be implemented effectively if they are accepted by employees and their representatives'.[95]

The subsidiary features of the agreement were as momentous for those involved as the broad change in payment system. In return for a commitment to measured day-work, workers were granted the right to full shift work as long as they attended and non-availability of work was not due to industrial action. Waiting time was to be credited as 66.66 per cent of standard performance pay—an earlier major grievance of the Rover shop floor related to erratic production in the 1960s. Moreover, it was agreed that not only would work standards be studied and officially set (in order that variations in effort levels or conditions could be taken into account), but six union representatives would be trained in work study so that they could monitor the operation and mount their own 'check studies'. Audits of work standards would be annual. The first formal industrial relations procedure was also part of the plan. Specific provision was also made regarding statutory sick pay, medical provision and job training. In the eyes of those who had been struggling merely to establish the basic framework of union representation in the 1960s, these features represented enormous gains. Taken together, the 'Plan' cannot be understood simply as an attempt to 'buy off' piece-work. Indeed, as will become increasingly clear, the SD1 project does not fit with Noble's conclusion that labour's choices are not registered in the design process. An examination of the multiple phases and sub-processes of the design process, as in the SD1 project, reveals both the direct and indirect impact of labour.[96] More especially, the strength of the Rover work-force's commitment to the Protected Earnings Plan accounts for the bitterness of their reaction to the way the competing interests within the SD1 project led to those agreements being broken later in both letter and spirit.

These parallel yet separate paths of the central IR department and the Rover management–union alignment are indicative of the character of the concept phase of the SD1 project. This first key phase is notable for the ambitiousness of the innovations which were intended in all three aspects of the SD1 productive unit. In terms of the BL or Rover enterprise, the project's intention included a series of strategic innovations. Put another way, the concept of the SD1 project implied a major shift in Rover's location within the auto sector's design hierarchy, from sophisticated to simplified product, from small-scale to semi mass-production plant, and from devolved, piece-work based work organization to a system resting on measured day-work. Yet, in spite of the scope of these intended changes, there appears to have been no comparable alteration of the design process which would develop and implement them. On the contrary, the inherited conventional and fragmented, linear sequence seems to have been adopted with little trace of any holistic conception of the design process. Inconsistencies between the product, production facility and work organization concepts remained unresolved at the end of the first phase, and their competing logics were left to operate with serious consequences for ensuing stages. Without an effective formal organization learning programme, centrally directed, a variety of more informal learning paths are discernible within the process, as those involved attempted to cope with the incompatible intentions of the project within increasingly unstable corporate and market contexts.

III Translation stage: the product, production facility, work organization

The translation stage of the SD1 design process began in February 1972, when the BL Board granted programme approval to the SD1 car concept, and ended with the appointment of the government (Ryder) inquiry into the corporation in December 1974. It was a major phase of the SD1 project. The actions of the range of groups involved, both from within and outside the corporation, transformed and even in some cases defeated the intentions laid down at the concept stage. In the translation stage the multiple cultures that co-existed within BL became apparent and the detailed forms of each specialist department's dominant logics and situated practices were thrown into sharp relief. The scale of the project and the high density of interrelations was notable in the British context, features which became clearly visible between 1972 and the end of 1974. The translation phase was also distinctive for the degree of organizational turmoil. The already fragile, infant corporate structure was beset by a sequence of upheavals. The Specialist Cars Division, established in 1968, was first broken down into the separate Jaguar and the new 'Rover-Triumph' units in October 1972. The difficulties of integrating the Rover and Triumph operations notwithstanding, the Specialist Cars Division was re-formed in June 1973 and then broken down once more into Jaguar and Rover-Triumph in February 1974.[97] The problems facing the development of a new design capacity, the management of a formal organizational learning process, or simply the direction of a complex design sequence were therefore formidable.

The product
Once product programme approval is given, the vehicle designers and engineers can play an enormously important role and their actions carry immense significance for the subsequent design process. How they develop the model concept affects not only the performance characteristics of the car, but also the way in which it will be produced, the costs involved in facility building, and even the eventual details of job design. The growing importance of this function is shown by the labour involved. In the 1960s, Rover designers had spent the equivalent of around sixty man-years developing the Range Rover, whereas Ford devoted over 1,300 man-years to the Fiesta design in the 1970s. Ford has eschewed fundamental design research. Instead, the company concentrated their resources on ensuring that any new model was both easy to build and assemble and was being costed precisely during the vehicle design so that profit targets were met. Ford planners in the early 1970s were advising the adoption of new panel shapes and solder types in order to minimize current production difficulties. The specialisms within product engineering of body engineering, power engineering, body electrics, engine electricals and electronics, together with the current or future model specialists are indicative of the range of operations involved in vehicle design.[98]

    In the case of the SD1, the characteristics of the product design staff, combined with the difficulties associated with organizing a new set of designers within the corporation, led to a series of unforeseen difficulties, with grave effects on the subsequent design phases. First, BL tried to make a virtue of how the SD1 was 'to a large degree due to the bringing together of separate design groups within Leyland Cars'. Rover's records show that the best design talent then available was employed on the SD1. Yet the problems which the dispersal of the product design among separate BL companies created were immense. The organization and management of the SD1's design were the antithesis of those which created the Land Rover, Range Rover or P6. Critical differences in philosophy, procedure and emphasis developed into mutual hostility between staff of companies which had previously been close competitors (especially between Rover and Triumph). A Rover product engineer complained how 'BL took away large parts of our design'. As in many other respects, the SD1 project overlapped with the lengthy attempt by the new corporation to draw its engineers together within a single department of the Specialist Cars Division in a new central engineering centre.[99]

Second, deficiencies in the available product design staff became apparent. These became acute when one realizes that although BL had more design engineers than Ford or Volkswagen, the latter companies worked to five distinct models whereas BL were handling fifteen. Basic equipment was lacking, down to 1976. There was insufficient transmission testing, and whole-vehicle and hydraulics test rigs. An engineer explained how, during product design 'we could only carry out one test at a time, we were not able to carry out any multiple testing'. Instead, reliance was placed on government research departments. Many of these gaps were realized in a systematic way when the new engineering centre was being planned, between 1973 and 1976. The building consultants needed to understand the design and development of a motor car, the skills and technology involved. Their questions pushed BL engineers to compare themselves with other producers internationally and to discover their own limitations.[100] Yet it was still not until 1978, two years after the SD1 plant opened, that BL even had a central corporate technology centre which could begin to supply the necessary test facilities.

The constraints imposed by deficiencies in design technology were compounded by the shortage of sufficient high quality staff. Rover reviewed the problem almost annually in the late 1960s and early 1970s. A good example came during product development in 1970. Due to changes in brake specifications made by a supplier, a problem arose of accessibility and servicing of the rear brakes, but, as the department's report concluded, 'we have nothing in hand in terms of staff, facilities or time, so that each of these problems inevitably affects the programme'.

One of the reasons why BL collaborated recently with the Honda company over developments of new medium-sized models was the 'haemorrhage of design talent' in the early 1970s. Bhaskar found, therefore, in 1980, that BL was both short on design and technical staff and its resources were 'fully stretched' to produce the mini replacement.[101]

Comparing Ford's deliberate build-up of university-trained engineers and management since 1945, or the qualifications of engineering staff in the American car corporations, an American engineer brought in by BL was appalled at the low qualifications of BL staff. The British motor industry has not figured prominently in graduate recruitment. National tables drawn up in 1981 show BL recruiting one hundred graduates out of a work-force of 50,000, whereas IBM had the same number of graduates but only 14,700 employees. In 1975 a senior engineering manager at BL discovered how 'in the studies that we did to review the training of engineers at high levels, with my HNC in Production Engineering I was one of the better qualified individuals, which I think is absolutely ridiculous.'[102]

Engineers brought in from other car companies to BL felt that the relatively low level of engineering qualifications prejudiced the introduction of new design technology. Computer Aided Drawing or Design (CAD) is now used to give complete three-dimensional access to vehicle design via mathematical modelling of the body structure using 1,300 simultaneous differential equations. This enables engineers to model 'the whole dynamic behaviour of the car'. Lack of investment apart, the outside experts found that BL engineers were extremely wary of CAD and questioned whether there were sufficient engineers qualified to assess the new technology. The Pressed Steel Company had been one of the earliest users of CAD in the late 1960s; yet two years after their acquisition by BMC in 1965, the corporation's CAD capacity had been outstripped by a factor of eleven when compared with Nissan.

However, BL engineers felt that they lacked recognition within the corporation in terms of rewards, power and resources, which eventually led to the exit of engineers to other functions or enterprises. The view of a senior SD1 product engineer is instructive:

> I think there is a set of double values actually, because I think that a lot of people realise that these [engineers] are really crucial and respect them for it, but in the end . . . they always end up by being desperately undervalued. We have done a lot of analysis lately of people's rewards relative to areas inside engineering as a whole, and relative to outside engineering; you're a mug to be inside engineering. You're very considerably underpaid.[103]

The view taken of engineering as an 'overhead' by finance departments was especially wounding. In addition, BL product engineers felt that not only did the national education system not provide relevantly trained engineers, but that the corporation lacked the ability to develop design engineers. A representative of the Finniston Commission admitted that it was a real problem of how to educate someone in the 'creative skills of synthesis' which design involves.[104] A number of those interviewed referred to the social networks engineers developed in each company as a defence against the disadvantages of their status. These networks were also the effective means of insulating the apprentice-trained engineer from outside developments, a feature of the engineering culture of BL which was left untreated during the early 1970s.[105]

The third main obstruction to the translation and development of the SD1 product was derived from the accumulated difficulties of insufficient design staff, operating in separate companies, with differing philosophies and practices. The market conditions and the environment in which design took place were also contributory factors. Product engineers at Rover were used to operating with a high degree of discretion during the 1950s and 1960s when overall demand was high and waiting lists existed. A Rover product engineer, comparing the earlier period with the 1970s and 1980s, thought the difference in the context of design was 'shattering'. In the first era, the Rover product designers developed their own 'rhythm':

> You could get away with doing something on the quick [i.e. an experiment] because the managing director thought it would be a good idea, because it was an easy world. Now it's much tougher . . . everything's getting more and more competitive. You're competing in a world market with things that are better value for money or else you just don't compete. The effort has got to be put into every individual little bit [of the car] to squeeze the last ounce out of it and get the best value for money.[106]

The SD1 project stands at the transition point between the 'easy world' and the new, intensely competitive market conditions. In the absence of CAD (with its central computer storage of information and the necessity for procedural conformity), the perpetuation of traditional areas of discretion by designers in the separate companies meant the SD1's design and development was ill-coordinated. CAD could have saved time in many areas, especially given the novelty of both designing a volume-produced, semi-luxury car and apportioning the design to a number of separate companies. The way in which, for example, the 'general practice' was to store design data in filing cabinets and the method of recording was 'enormously variable' meant that access and retrieval was slow and unpredictable. Mistakes were not recorded accurately, and therefore the designers found that they often repeated 'the same errors over and over again'.[107]

The complexity of product design and the tensions and conflicts which arose around the SD1 car proved critical for the successive stages of design, and most especially for the production operation. Design experts in the auto industry now recognize how 'quite frankly you only get one real chance to do anything about production, and that is at the outset; you certainly can't afford major cost changes later on.'[108]

Yet within BL the integration of product design costing and production engineering was weak. In the SD1 project the involvement of design engineers from the range of subsidiary companies meant the problem was exacerbated. The links between the companies and between the separate phases of design were poorly framed. Rover's design capacity—based on small design teams, with a priority on high-quality engineering—was broken open by the allocation of parts of the product's design to other BL companies.

The degree of uncertainty in the process was intensified by two additional pressures. Rover engineers, according to corporate policy, now had to design a much less refined product and with great stress on its suitability for manufacture in large numbers. Second, there was immense friction as a result of the differing design philosophies experienced by each company. The contrasting traditions derived from volume production or specialist manufacture threw up detailed contrasts in emphasis. A senior engineer appointed to resolve these difficulties found that Austin-Morris engineers concentrated on 'pure design' while Rover's were seen, by comparison, as 'development oriented'. In other words, Longbridge product engineers put most effort into the elaboration of the concept and tried to resolve major product characteristics at the blueprint stage. Rover's technique was more experimental. Rover engineers would be 'very much involved in doing a quick scheme for a car, then get something on wheels as fast as possible and run it around for a while to try and get the bugs out, which with the available technology . . . [was] a very expensive and slow method'.[109] Those Rover engineers involved in the SD1 project found the fragmentation and resulting tensions to be serious obstacles to their work. The spatial and conceptual separation was acute. It was, according to one designer,

> a very difficult organisational situation with people on different sites and so on. People who have spent many years working in a particular place and being associated with a vehicle aren't easily dragged out . . . If you've got to try and do that *and* actually bring new vehicles through, it makes it extraordinarily difficult. I mean there is a limit on human nervous energy to be able to cope with it all.[110]

A very powerful styling studio, together with a notable tension between engine and transmission design specialists added to the difficulties of integrating product design. Inside the Rover Company at this time, product and production engineers were engaged in a political battle with each other over seniority and resources, with the result that data and equipment were not easily shared.[111]

The most notable feature of the SD1 product design in terms of project management related to the degree of co-ordination and control. BL's attempt to imitate Ford's 'Red Book' system, whereby all aspects of a given project were conducted according to a detailed central manual and code, met with little success. Rover product engineers had worked experimentally but were directly answerable to a managing director with an engineering background. Most problems were resolved via a relatively loose and organic style of working which was a core feature of Rover's long-established design capacity. In the SD1 project, although the BL Board laid down the policy requirements for the new car, the novel requirement of so complex a project following the creation of the hybrid corporation received less attention. Product engineers therefore felt that the issues relating to product resolved at board level were resolved in a rarified way, leaving a host of practical difficulties unresolved. The Government inquiry into BL in 1975 identified this lack of integration as a major weakness. Moreover, the Chief Engineer who was appointed to oversee the design of the SD1 car admitted that as a project it was 'incredibly difficult, because I was put in charge of something which I had severe doubts about—which was running a totally integrated engineers department.'[112] Instead, he favoured a 'strong central product policy' with company autonomy on product development and project conduct.

The SD1 car not only highlights the difficulties facing a newly formed corporation in monitoring a major design project in the 1970s auto industry: it also reveals the relevance of certain parties not commonly recognized by the literature on the industry or on innovation in general. In

the case of the SD1, both component suppliers and labour played significant yet hitherto unnoticed roles in the design of the new car.

Component supply companies did not only furnish almost 70 per cent
of the car's parts and equipment on a simple commercial basis, they also
injected information and expertise into the design process. The degree of
reliance on the suppliers was marked. The growing costs of design and the
scarcity of qualified staff meant that the Rover Company could not afford
to devote the resources necessary for such work. Component firms were
given the task of both developing and supplying components. While the
company engineers realized the effect on product cost, in the circumstances they had little choice.[113] Reliance on Lucas or Pressed Steel was of
long standing. The influences of the latter can be clearly traced on Rover
body design throughout the P8, P10 and SD1 models from 1968 to 1971. In
1968, for example, it was 'agreed that they be asked to co-operate in the
engineering of the prototype, so that advantage could be taken of their
expertise'. Rover also purchased competitors' models in order to gain
information on components: a further corroborative reason for the
convergence of car designs and the parallel development of product
design trajectories.[114]

At first sight the secrecy which surrounds new car models and projects
would appear to preclude the direct involvement of the work-force who
would assemble the car. The SD1 project, however, provides a useful
insight into the relationship between labour and design which has barely
been noticed in social science accounts of the industry. Labour's involvement in the design of the SD1 came in two main related forms. Official
exclusion notwithstanding, certain skilled workers were not only
intimately bound up in the development phases of the product, they were
also key sources of information for the Rover unions. They also kept the
existing P6 work-force acquainted with the car's progress by many ad hoc
means, such as the numerous social networks of the Solihull site. The
senior stewards relied heavily on jig-shop workers and the highly experienced, multi-skilled car builders who were used to producing the prototypes of the SD1 in 1973.

As will become clear in Chapter 5, during the pre-production stages the
product and production engineers 'continuously consulted' these workers
over detail modifications to the car. An experienced engine worker
stressed the informality of the consultation and its contrast to bargaining
or negotiation. In the engine design department 'it would be a case of [a
senior engineer] going down to the job or somebody being sent down . . .
but no question of collectively sitting down and having a talk.'[115] Other
workers felt it slightly ridiculous that the company tried to keep the
product design a secret in the light of such contacts.

An analysis which only concentrated on the skilled workers directly involved with the product's development would not uncover wider aspects of
the Rover car workers' consciousness and motivations during the SD1 project. Independent studies of skilled workers have remarked on the intimate
knowledge which craftsmen develop of a product. In spite of the objective
physical privations associated with toil, workers have none the less been

observed as identifying, though not invariably, with the final product; this identification does not necessarily signify allegiance to the firm or its management. These studies[116] sit uneasily with the dominant orthodoxy on work experience in the car industry and its emphasis on alienation.[117]

At Rover, production workers as well as craftsmen appear to have been genuinely inquisitive about the vehicles they made, and proud of their technical knowledge of the car's operation and commercial position. They took the trouble to monitor their model's performance, given the effect such movement had on jobs. In the course of the SD1 project, therefore, workers tracked the fall in demand for the P6 in the early 1970s (learnt from delivery drivers) as an indicator of the project's development. Workers recalled how they used their own knowledge of Rover's product policy, model specifications and market to interpret official contacts with management during the SD1 project. The close association which a track worker builds up with a given model (especially the snaggers) makes him acutely aware of its design and construction and ways in which it can be improved. Almost every track worker interviewed had clear views on product design and how it could be improved.[118] Indeed, it was the groundswell of anxiety on the shop floor among P6 workers (i.e. those who had endured the difficulties of the 2000 model's new body construction) regarding the new SD1 product and its apparently radical implications for work organization which led the P6 shop stewards to press for formal meetings with the company over future plans in 1972. Routine shop floor practice was seen to impel union action.[119]

The design and development of the SD1 car, if taken in a comparative sense within the auto sector, can be illuminating of a major issue: the interrelationship of product and production. More features of this relationship will be teased out in the next section, but for the moment the role of labour can be used as a lens through which the product/production relationships can be viewed. Abernathy's model of the American car industry demonstrates how product and process were matched to facilitate high-volume, low-cost products. Innovation was at a low level as the complexities of both were reduced in pursuit of a single goal. He also shows how production process requirements (high predictability) came to dictate the character of the product (low innovation).

Information supplied by product and production engineers from Ford and Chrysler's British operations in the 1960s and 1970s confirms the relevance of relating not only product and production but also work organization. These companies set out systematically to link these areas together early in their respective design projects. Ford, in the early 1970s, set up a major review of its product planning with direct input from its industrial relations department. One of their planners involved described their thinking in the form of the following question:

> How can we design models to get rid of some of the IR problems we face in plants? Let's construct cars in ways that are easier to put together. For example, we don't have to use lead solder on joints because lead solder always causes endless arguments and bother.

The same planner was later employed by Rover. He observed how in the SD1 car there was little industrial relations influence 'in either the design or the concept', and 'as far as the product design was concerned, generally you didn't feel there was much personnel input'.[120] Similarly to Ford, Vauxhall product designers were acutely aware of the implications of body design for smooth assembly operation as, for example, in the case of the location of body 'pick-up points'. Unsuitable sitings make for unsteady, even dangerous conveyor transfers.

In the SD1 project the connections between product, production and details of work organization were never of this order. The fragmentation of product design personnel alone militated against it. Product designers at Rover, given their background, only concerned themselves with the character of the product and the intention to produce it in large numbers. There was no systematic connection of product design or IR functions, or their concerns. The public statements of the SD1 product designers make 'simplicity' the keynote of their design policy. Yet this general intention was not applied to work organization implications in detail; besides, the injunction to aim for simplicity in the broad sense is an established axiom in engineering design anyway.[121] In the language of the SD1 product design, 'simplicity' was a sufficiently broad notion which came to obscure some of the connections between product and production.

The example cited earlier of the SD1's back axle being a single unit rather than a set of components refers to an attempt to simplify the engineering work associated with the model. It was not a move to relate the detailed aspects of product design and task content. None the less, it will become clear how, in later phases of the design process, features of the car such as exhaust pipe or body dimensions had immediate impact on track design, paint plant and assembly layout, and cycle times.[122] The comparison between the practices around the SD1 with those of Ford or Vauxhall return us to the special nature of Rover's overall design capacity. A senior industrial relations manager who had to deal with the problems which arose on the shopfloor from the incongruities between the SD1 product and the production process, summed up the persistence of Rover's traditional attitudes. To Rover designers: 'these cars weren't volume cars, they were cars which were special and therefore some of the ordinary disciplines that you associate with motor manufacturers were disciplines which [to the designers] were still not needed.'[123]

Production facility
The 'design brief' given to the plant engineers was drastically transformed in its complex translation by a combination of forces. These forces may be grouped logically around, first, the design capacity of BL and, second, the politics of design and its effect on project operations. One of the chief characteristics of the £90 million plant's creation will become increasingly apparent: its high degree of uncertainty as a process.

The broad policy intentions of the BL Board resulted in a design brief for the plant project design group which appeared quite clear. The object was to design and build a single-site, non-dedicated, final assembly car

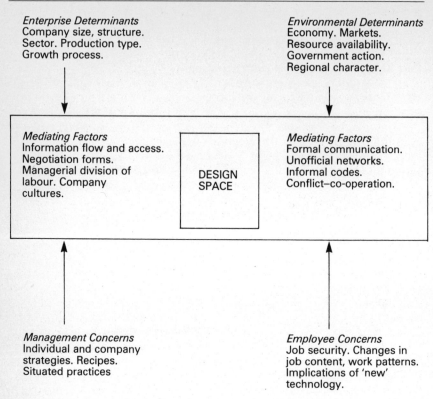

Enterprise Determinants
Company size, structure.
Sector. Production type.
Growth process.

Environmental Determinants
Economy. Markets.
Resource availability.
Government action.
Regional character.

Mediating Factors
Information flow and access.
Negotiation forms.
Managerial division of
labour. Company
cultures.

DESIGN
SPACE

Mediating Factors
Formal communication.
Unofficial networks.
Informal codes.
Conflict–co-operation.

Management Concerns
Individual and company
strategies. Recipes.
Situated practices

Employee Concerns
Job security. Changes in
job content, work patterns.
Implications of 'new'
technology.

Figure 4.4 A design space model. *Source*: After Bessant and Dickson,
Determinism or Design, 10.

plant capable of producing 3,000 units per week, flexible enough to
accommodate a range of low- and high-volume models, and via a participative planning operation with related experiments in work restructuring. The final outcome, as will be shown, in Chapter 5, was a traditional
car assembly plant with forms of working not very different from the P6
line and with output levels never going above 1,000 per week. The difference in intention and final form requires careful reconstruction of the
translation of the plant concept. An explanation can be offered by employing the concept of the design space.

Bessant and Dickson have shown that there is a general acceptance by
social scientists of a single 'implicit logic' in management action in
general and in production planning in particular, centred on the increase
in profit and managerial control over production. There are in fact
multiple logics in play which affect the choice of designers, their implementation of design briefs and the commissioning of new technology. The
space in which the design of new plant (or product or work organization)
occurs is not unilaterally controlled, but rather influenced by five main
potential classes of variables, as Figure 4.4 indicates. The model points to
the range of possible influences on designing; it also suggests that the

design arena is highly malleable. In conjunction with our findings in Chapter 2 and in the light of this model, the transformation of the SD1's project objectives during the design process is not surprising.[124] As Bessant and Dickson observe, 'the view of technology as an imperative solution bringing with it inevitable and pre-determined types of change must be revised: it becomes a case of "it's not what it is but how you use it".'[125]

Figure 4.4 represents a range of possible influences on the design process. The case of the SD1 plant reveals its own set of variables. This account will emphasize specific elements from each of the four main areas and offer a synthesis of the mediating factors. In addition, the SD1 experience stresses the way in which these forces not only constrain the design space but also how, in interaction, they impel and even transform the actions of designers. Some of the mediating factors (such as the state of production innovation in the auto industry) have already been suggested; others will be dealt with in Chapter 5's account of the commissioning phase of the SD1 project.

The factors which influenced the translation of the SD1 plant are best grouped under two main headings: those which affected the production engineers' design capacities, and those which converged around the political issue which the SD1 project became for British Leyland.

The capacity of production planners for major innovation in BL was not strongly developed. Government reports found experiments in the United Kingdom were rare, with little inclination shown to emulate Fiat's, Renault's or Volvo's new departures in production layouts or techniques.[126] Few of the planners generated in-house appeared to enjoy high prestige in the corporation or had international experience, with the exception of the chief production planner. Most of the production planners were used to designing dedicated, single assembly lines and using the highly mechanistic methods of determining their dimensions and operating characteristics. 'Line balancing' calculations, despite their contemporary sophistication, are notable for the tightness of their limits and the lack of flexibility they allow.[127]

Interviews with production managers in both American and British-owned car firms showed that most motor companies were similar in this respect. A consultant production planner was horrified, therefore, at even the intention that the SD1 line should ultimately handle a series of models on the same assembly line (such as the 2000, 2600, 3500 models and Triumph cars) owing to the difficulties this raised for line balancing.[128] A BL production planner expressed the generally overwhelming concern with line co-ordination and the extreme reluctance to tamper with it thus:

> the mix is the most important thing, getting that work balance down there. I mean the whole object of the exercise is to build cars in the most effective manner. So the purpose of starting right from the body in white, through the paint shop, right through the whole factory, is to be able to get the right labour done at the right time for continuous building of the model.[129]

Table 4.2 Reconstruction of conventional production line planning in the Rover Company, taken from the Range Rover project, 1969–1971

— Vehicle concept introduced to planning engineers by product engineering.	
— Concept line layouts offered by planning engineers to board. Prototype vehicles developed off-line; engineering tests leading to modifications.	
— METHODS BUILD	Prototypes built experimentally to indicate likely tool needs and line sequence. Planning engineers write 'preliminary planning sheets'. Assembly line laid out provisionally with component sequence. Line stations allocated. Inspection stations derived.
— PRE-PRODUCTION	Experienced workers assemble vehicle (and its variants) on the provisional line. Proving of tools, component flows. Time study engineers derive appropriate work cycles.
— INITIAL PRODUCTION RUN	at low-level line speeds (25 per week). Time study engineers carry out 'proper time study'. Leads to re-allocation of tasks along line. Line balanced so that full interdependence of sequence established and adjusted to four-minute time cycle. Time studies negotiated with operators under piece-work.
— FIRST PRODUCTION YEAR	Initial vehicles sold. Customer feedback leads to vehicle engineering changes with need for new task arrangements. 'Season' changes after ten months, including new trim, fixings and specifications. Need to adjust tasks and re-balance line.
	Operating production rate of 250 units per week. Maximum of three weeks between need to change production details.

Rover production planners, in their reconstruction of the planning techniques they used, proved to be more empirical. Trial and error played a large part, and it was regarded as inevitable that adjustments and changes would continue throughout the final operating system. Table 4.2 shows the highly contingent method used by Rover experts to plan the line layout and balance. They also confirmed that they did not have any great input into product design, instead they received the product and adjusted the line layout accordingly. The relationship between the specialist functions was so distant that a formal procedure had to be gone through in order to obtain changes which production planners required to make production feasible (a so-called PAR, or Production Action Request).[130]

British Leyland in the early 1970s did not possess the technology which could have obviated the need for such elaborate and repetitive procedures and increased the accuracy of the whole process. Although the corporation had individual systems analysts, there was no central system department until 1978. Simulation based on computers was not used until the Metro project. SD1 production planners were using wooden models linked to traditional planning sheets. The great advantages (as Volvo had found in the early 1970s) of simulation are, according to a consultant production engineer,

— an interactive model of line layout which rejects at an early stage decisions which violate layout rules;
— control rules operating on both normality and crisis can be tested at the outset of planning;
— facility designers and production management can be brought together immediately—under the traditional system 'problem owners' from production remained isolated.[131]

These limitations on the BL and Rover planners' design capacity meant that they were unlikely to be exceptionally innovative in what they planned. Yet, what of the much publicized experiments in production planning in Volvo, especially at this time, and their potential 'demonstration effect'? A close examination of the BL planners who were given the task of evaluating these new forms of layout shows that they did not fully comprehend and assimilate these ventures, and especially Volvo's. The production engineers seemed to follow the general approach to Volvo, centring on the 'bending' of the traditional assembly line and the use of autonomous work groups.[132] No one among the BL planners we talked to showed an appreciation of the major corporate restructuring of Volvo in the early 1970s; this had involved the creation of independent divisions for each major product group and all main market units becoming separate profit centres within the division. The restructuring involved over one hundred countries. Substantial investments were made in truck, bus and equipment activities in order to balance income from the hitherto dominant car area. The official account of the process by Gyllenhammar shows it not to have been a trial of new production lines and working methods only, but a total recasting of business policy and corporate structure comparable to the reorganization of GM's European operation at almost the same time.[133]

As far as the SD1 production line was concerned, its planners concentrated mostly on Volvo's experiments on the shop floor. Despite the attempt by social scientists in this country, among others, to widen the debate around Volvo's experience, the need to tackle the concept as a totality was ignored by BL planners. In the Rogers sense, they opted out of the chance to 're-invent' the Volvo concept inside their own organization, that essential remodelling of a potential innovation which must take place before adoption and operation.[134] The partial view and ultimate rejection of Volvo's ideas and methods is echoed by both BL's official response and the attitudes of individual production engineers. In May 1973, just after the Board had sanctioned a new SD1 plant, a group of production planners from BL (including a representative of the SD1 project) attended an international conference on 'the working environment' held by Volvo. They reported back[135] that the problems facing BL and Volvo were similar: high profile in respective countries, core problem of alienation, large numbers dependent on the enterprises. The report concentrates on the differences between the two regarding their industrial relations climate and the quality of management. Whilst there was praise for Volvo's efforts and an acceptance in principle that certain of the changes might be suitable for BL, there was no indication of how these changes would be assimilated, nor of how they related to BL's corporate strategy. The piecemeal approach is revealed in the final line of the report, which reads, 'The chief lesson which the experience at Volvo has for BL is in adopting this pragmatic, problem-solving approach'.[136] The formulation of a clear strategy to implement any or all of Volvo's programme of change was not forthcoming. This was due not only to the formidable restructuring problems of BL; there was also deep-seated resistance from key individuals. As in the case of BL's business strategy, there was no concerted action to change managerial world views. In the words of a production planner,

> I don't honestly think that all the implications of the Swedish experiments were fully appreciated and understood ... there was no more than lip service paid to the conditions of work life. There was a lack of intellectual appreciation of the Swedish experiments and an almost instant readiness to dismiss it on the grounds that it was different.

Others complained that there was insufficient training for those who were sent to Europe and Japan to assess foreign production methods.[137] Personal antagonisms between those who championed such experiments, as well as departmental barriers, were additional obstructions.[138] The notions of autonomous work groups (AWGs) current in the early 1970s were, ironically, remarkably close to aspects of the group piece-work arrangements of Rover's P6; as was said at the time, AWGs and job design techniques were 'only suitable for small volume, high quality vehicles'.[139]

One crucial feature of the translation experience associated with the SD1 plant was its novelty, both in the relative and the absolute sense. As Gregory shows, few industrial engineers have experience of very large, multi-million pound projects, if at all. An assessment of production planning at BL at the start of the ADO88 (Metro) project in the mid-1970s showed that there had been very few major projects which had involved radically different objectives. It is understandable, therefore, how BL's production engineers came to reject the Volvo programme either in detail or more generally.[140] The notion of breaking up the assembly line into smaller sections, a form which had remained unchanged since the early part of the century, and the order of uncertainty it posed for a group of Rover planners already being asked to make the jump from quality to volume production was immense. Volvo had predictive techniques, such as MTM in its production planning in the late 1960s; BL had still to develop them by the mid-1970s. In the broader sense, the way in which Volvo's programme relied on the equally novel integration of functions, the dilution of hierarchies and made change a virtue, presented a huge risk to BL engineers. Plant life-cycles of around twenty years and the large capital outlays involved reinforced the danger of adding to the novelty; as Gyllenhammer admitted, 'there is no way back from major changes in working patterns. The Kalmar plant, for example, is designed for a specific purpose: car assembly in working groups of about twenty. If it didn't work, it would be a costly and visible failure'.[141]

Scarborough[142] had suggested that technological change is 'inextricably intertwined' with the political relations of an organization. He found that the political conflict which results takes place upon several different planes, from the corporate to the shop floor level. Our research points to the parallel importance of the politics of the design process and the associated contests for control of design space. In the SD1 project, the resources allocation or the uncertainty over the final operating system, for instance, ensured that questions of power arose between competing groups within the enterprise. The politics of the Solihull plant's design involved a dense fabric of issues and relations. The main lines of cleavage were between company and corporation, company and work-force, and the corporation/company versus the community. The next chapter will show how shop floor politics in the new plant extended the contests which had been started in the early design stages.

The basis of the struggle between Rover management and the corporation has already been explored in the assessment of their differing product and production concept intentions. Whilst the corporate formula was accepted, this did not mark the end of the political struggle, rather, it was the beginning. Competition between central corporate departments and Rover management or SD1 project members continued at all levels. The casualty list of those involved in the project became notorious.[143] At the executive level, for instance, the conflict between Rover and headquarters planners over production totals and cycle times meant that the ex-Ford advocate of one-minute cycles left when the idea was rejected. Although they admired their general standards, Rover management's antipathy to the one-time Ford executive's concepts and practices was acute, and they were resisted throughout the project.

An example of the corporate versus company contest and the way in which the political relationships were engaged on multiple levels was in the relations between central BL production engineers and Solihull production and industrial engineers. A senior Rover engineer, when asked who he thought was ultimately responsible for the design of the SD1 line, could only complain of the dominance of central planners. He replied how 'everything was brought in over our heads and we just had to try our best with it'. The competition in the relationship stands out. There was

Engineer: 'a lack of liaison between the various departments, particularly from people outside the Solihull plant. When I say outside ... we used to call them divisional, and divisional people to us were a load of dum-dims, who didn't know what car manufacture was about at all'.

Interviewer: 'Why didn't they?'

Engineer: 'Because they thought they were superior to the plant
people and when it came to the actual building of the car,
we didn't see them again, they were gone, to make
another botch up at some other place'.[144]

The head of the corporate plant engineers was seen as a 'rank outsider'. It
is interesting that Rover production engineers expressed views similar to
the company product engineers over the project: they felt 'sidelined', to
use their word. Their anxiety to define their status and assert their competence at a time of major change such as the SD1 project led the Rover
production experts to interpret and modify the intentions for the plant layout in the light of their own standards and objectives.[145]

The political relationship between the Rover Company and their work-
force over the details of the new plant centred on knowledge and control.
At the very basic level, Rover production planners were highly reluctant to
divulge information on the details of the new plant to workers or their
representatives. The planners were highly aware of the ability of workers
to reorganize elements of tasks and whole phases of production (as on the
P6 line), resulting in the diversion of planning intentions. So fearful were
the planners of this aspect of labour power that they became even more
resolved not to attempt the creation of large autonomous work groups,
given the increased opportunity such schemes afford to shop floor
control. Instead, as one of the consulting engineers found, the Rover planners reverted to standard line layout with conventional work stations.[146]
Labour therefore clearly had an indirect role in the design of the plant,
given the planners' perceived view of workers' ability to re-occupy the
design space at the operational stage.

The corporation's stated aim, and the public image of the project, was
clearly one of a more participative design process which included labour.
The corporate IR policy documents referred to above cite the need to
'invite employees' participation in the detailed planning of facilities'.[147] In
reality, the union representatives found that they were barely being
informed, let alone consulted, over the new plant. The unions took the
Special Projects Committee (established by central and Rover IR departments in October 1973, following the complaints of P6 shop stewards over
the rumours surrounding the new project) very seriously; they held
lengthy internal debates and mounted shop floor elections for representatives to sit on the committee. It soon became clear that they could do little
to change what had already been decided by management. As the union
convenor put it, 'we were merely given the courtesy of being told'. A shop
steward representative described the meaninglessness of the situation in a
simple image: as he looked out of the window of the room where the committee met, he could see the footings of the new plant already being constructed.[148] The union representatives never met the plant designers, or
the architects.[149]

It is vital to appreciate the subjective views of those trade unionists
involved. It was in October 1973, two years after the Protected Earnings
Plan had been agreed, that the unions at Rover (especially the TGWU)

committed themselves to both the Special Projects Committee and joint action with management to sell the idea of the new plant to the community.[150] It is all too easy for academics to dismiss such activity as evidence of the incorporation[151] or emasculation of labour power. The newly formed union framework from 1969, recently legitimized by the PEP, represented a major breakthrough for the P6 workers; the Committee offered the potential for another. The promise by management of discussing such subjects as working methods, training, track-side amenities and colour schemes for working areas seemed an opportunity hitherto unheard of. One of the senior TGWU stewards was in principle opposed to the idea of co-operating with the Committee, but was persuaded by the chance to effect basic changes.[152] The investment of the plant convenor in the Committee was enormous. After years of sitting on old boxes or 'stillage' at the track side and eating meals there, the concept of the plant presented to the union representatives embodied huge improvements.

In April 1974, as the increasing costs of the total project mounted and as profits, confidence and the corporation's liquidity fell, the SD1 plant's budget was cut unilaterally by the corporate finance department.[153] It was both the act of cutting and its manner which angered the unions. The convenor's reputation had virtually been staked on the usefulness of the Committee during the shop floor debates and ballots in 1973. The Rover unions had also been under great pressure from their counterparts in other Leyland plants not to co-operate in the Special Project Committee. The departure, coincidentally, of the company Director of Industrial Relations to the divisional level before the opening of the new plant added to the dismay felt by the Rover unions at the action of higher management over the Special Project Committee.[154] Their feelings of bitterness were later intensified by the crises of the commissioning and operation phases. The union leaders denounced the exercise as a 'deflating failure'. The inability of the unions to gain knowledge of the planning of the plant did not lead them to direct conflict. Instead, they decided to defer engagement until the plant was operating.[155]

Why did the unions choose to postpone action? First, it was entirely outside the work-force's experience to be consulted over such matters. It is often alleged that a contemporary demand for participation by labour existed. At Rover (as elsewhere), members and activists were divided over the issue. Some were deeply critical of any involvement with management outside of face-to-face bargaining over the employment contract. One senior Transport and General Workers' Union steward argued that not only should they not attempt to run the business for management, but realistically 'by the nature of the subject to be discussed (i.e. the new plant), our involvement had to be limited because we didn't have the expertise'.[156] In addition, the recently formed union structure which covered the company had more urgent preoccupations. The union officers were primarily concerned in the 1971–3 period with containing the level of disputes and monitoring a totally new bargaining and payment system. It was only via the efforts of an especially energetic, autodidact convenor that the unions at Solihull began to discover the current interest by academics and industrial commentators in job design. The TGWU research department and a Cambridge-based advisory group supplied information.[157] Furthermore, the unions were prepared to jettison the Special Projects Committee since they could fall back on the traditional, informal information networks of the Solihull site. Union officials were especially reliant on the jig-makers who built the wooden scale models of the plant used until computer simulation replaced them. Knowledge of these models (in tandem with similar information on the new car) enabled the unions to develop their own plans for line zones and steward organization in the new plant.[158]

The third major contest over the design of the SD1 plant was between BL/Rover and the community,[159] the outcome of which had one of the most direct impacts on the plant's final form. In January 1973, when the corporation applied for local planning permission for the plant, Solihull opinion was divided over the prospect of such a large industrial development. A fierce debate ensued through the summer of that year. A local 'Residents' Action Group' was not only opposed to the loss of the sixty-four acres of land designated for residential use, but also to the projected changes in local roads. Above all, they objected to the invasion of light and space around the Elmdon Park and Damson Wood estates. 'The area would become an industrial suburb' was how the Group's leader saw the result of the project. Dorridge Residents' Association argued that 'the whole scheme as it stands is too massive, too rapid in its growth concept to be even remotely within our [the borough's] structure plan'.[160] However, the Rover workers who lived on the estates argued publicly that 'quite a lot of Rover workers live on the Damson Wood estate and their views should be taken into account. They bought houses here because of the job security offered to them at Rover'.[161] On balance, the local council was persuaded by the prospect of a £400,000 rate income from the plant and 2,000 new jobs, and it declared the project 'vital to the town, future employment and to the nation's economy'.[162] Planning authority was granted in June 1973.

The local controversy over the plant may have generated division within the community, but it also produced a reformation of relationships inside the company. Representatives from BL and Rover management joined with Rover workers to argue the case for the new plant—an exercise which looked especially ironic when the plant was mothballed nine years later. The price which BL had to pay for local acceptance was of more immediate significance. The original concept of the plant, given the centrality of the component supply, envisaged a two-storey arrangement: production area on the ground floor and component storage on a separate floor above. Parts would be lowered through the ceiling to the track side below. Local protests forced the company to dispense with the top storey. The plant had to be reorganized on a single level involving a 28 ft. reduction in height and a doubling in width to 500 ft. (the length of the plant remained 2,000 ft.). Component storage and floors had to be totally redesigned. The council also made conditions regarding landscaping, noise and emissions which became key articles in the construction contracts.[163]

The set of major political forces associated with the design of the production facility was completed by an external grouping. These were the
architects, consulting engineers and equipment suppliers who had far
more impact on the plant's final form than is generally supposed. The
group's activities point up the high degree of uncertainty and even chance
which such large projects as the SD1 involved. The firm of architects used
by the plant planners had a long and continuous association with the
company, and had worked on major projects such as the P6 plant and
many smaller ones, since the 1930s. However, the consulting engineering
firm which the corporate planners chose to handle the engineering installation, manage the contractors and design the paint plant after the failure
of BL engineers, wanted total control of the SD1 plant's construction,
including architectural work. The consultants wanted a turn-key operation. A dispute ensued between the architects and the engineering firm.[164]
The architects did not want to be subcontractors to the consultants, and
convinced the corporation that they needed an independent role, given
the complexities of designing and developing a physical structure to
encompass such a complex plant.

The tension between the architect and the consulting engineers for the
project was far less momentous than their respective roles in designing
the plant. In their translation of concept into reality, both worked with
large areas of uncertainty. The architects found that, even though tenders
for contracts are by definition 'full of guesswork and probabilities', the
specifications in the tender documents were extremely loose compared to
previous joint work. A member of the architects' team described how this
made for a larger number of 'unknowns' throught the project, and set in
motion a series of 'learning by doing' exercises. At the outset 'the only way
to get the job moving was to design the building work as it was being built,
and as they [the company] gave us information'.[165] In the paint plant, an
architect explained how

> we were asking [the engineers] for information for us to design the
> building around the plant [machinery] without the specifications being
> firmed up . . . we wanted to know what discharges there were, and they
> couldn't tell us because they hadn't done it before in this way. And they
> in turn, to be fair to them, were going back to Rover and asking them
> about what sort of vehicles and what sort of paint they were going to
> use; it went on from there. It's a series of decisions which almost go in a
> circle.[166]

Time was a major constraint. The pressure on the project cost/time
relationship was so strong that the architects and engineers felt they were
forced to design, develop and redesign the plant almost continuously, a
complete contrast to the 'slow processed way' the Rover engineers
worked. In addition, there were different time frames for engineers and
builders. Architects spoke of the clash between 'engineering' and 'building' time and their respective imperatives. The result was that 'the
engineers know the engineering problems . . . they don't know a lot about
the building process'. Engineers were late in giving architects informa-

tion, which meant that the building sequences were disrupted. The chief architect explained how, during the commissioning phase, therefore, 'in the paint shop, as an example, a 900-foot long building, the paint equipment was going in [installed] one end when the builder was still working at the other'.[167] As a result of these high levels of uncertainty, the architects and engineers did far more than fulfil the strict letter of their contracts: they had to provide organizing and liaison roles, which were not formally defined, in order to complete their tasks. In the engineering consultants' case they were most concerned with the relationship of the project to government bodies and statutory regulations.[168] The architects were more concerned with the day-to-day co-ordination of concepts, information and detailed operations. In the same way that the architects for the new corporate engineering centre at Canley needed to know the practical details of product engineering work, so the SD1 architects had to extract relevant information from the plant planners, compare it with material from the engineers and building firm, and assess the implications against the original concept and contract. This process would go through numerous iterations. The engineer/architect relationship was a close, often informal one in the early stages, with a need to 'look over the engineer's shoulder' irrespective of official procedures. One architect described how

> I used to go into X's office, walk round the drawing office and I'd see work being done; you can catch an awful lot. You can go to the managers' meeting and ask, are there any drains wanted? They reply, no, and you can then go to the drawing office and see someone putting in the drains . . . an awful lot is picked up like that . . . we saved a lot of time and bother that way.[169]

The rejection of the company planners' ideas (in the SD1 case, for example, on flooring) by the outside group owing to cost or practical implications had an immense impact on the details of the plant. None the less, the general image of the architect, for instance, in the industry, is of a 'wall builder'. The cost of the shell is always much less than the equipment, hence the relatively low recognition given. In the SD1 project, their liaising role apart, the architects' continuing presence became a real source of knowledge and stability, given the tremendous upheaval in management which afflicted the corporation and the SD1 project:[170] only five managers involved in the project lasted its entire course to 1976.

The combined result of the corporation's slowly emerging, fragile design capacity and the operation of the relationships both inside and outside the enterprise are embodied in the final form chosen for the SD1 production facility. Figure 4.5 gives a representation of paint plant and adjacent assembly hall. As with the SD1 car, the innovative qualities of either are at first unclear. The corporation's public statements celebrated the £6.2 million paint shop as 'the largest and most technically advanced ever to be commissioned in the UK'.[171] Yet paint experts and the consulting engineers were quite clear, the paint system using electro-coat or dip and thermoplastic paint, derived from a General Motors concept, was not

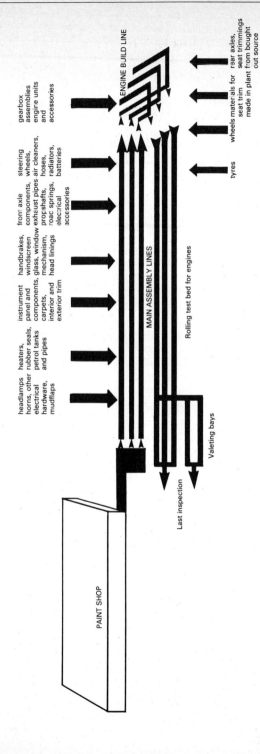

Figure 4.5 A diagrammatic representation of the SD1 assembly hall layout.

new, although it was widely regarded as one of the best systems available.[172] A similar system was already in operation at a plant in Ellesmere Port.

The real innovation for both Rover and the engineering contractor was very specific: it was the spatial arrangement of the paint process in being, one, adjacent to the assembly plant and, two, compact in a single unit. Each of the sub-processes involving automatic control of flow and electronic monitoring had 'been used elsewhere', according to the consulting engineers, but 'to put them all under one roof was something special', in a three-tier arrangement of pre-treatment, paint spray and oven floor.[173] The tiers allowed the oven and pre-treatment stages to be isolated and unmanned, with obvious implications for the traditionally hostile working environment of the paint plant. The plant planners were undoubtedly reliant on the consulting engineer, given the shrinking number of specialist paint plant engineering companies. The corporation admitted how 'having satisfied Leyland of the feasibility of the advanced plant design [the consulting engineers] adopted the combined role of diplomat and technical consultant'.[174] In a similar way, the assembly hall, to use BL's own words of 1976, was 'comparatively conventional and straightfoward in design and layout'. The building structure and the assembly track can be taken separately. If we accept the opinion of the architects who designed the shell structure, there was little that was new. The roof system was a variant of the conventional 'Monitor' designs, taken almost directly from the Leyland Speke plant, and was very similar to the Rover Company's plant roofing of the 1950s. The system's main advantage was its ability to allow uniform levels of daylight, although it is now seen as energy-expensive, given the heat loss involved.

Once more, it was in the details of the new building structure, compared to past Rover practices, that innovation occurred. The architects were told in their design brief to assume that one- to two-thirds of the assembly area would be for component storage or movement. Component flows, following the recent problems of the P6, were to be a priority. Loading bays of 150 ft. by 150 ft. and improved road access were planned and special reinforcement of the lower walls added. One of the few detailed influences of the Volvo project to seep through the resistance of the BL and Rover engineers was the provision of amenity areas at the outer edge of the building. Most of these changes were ones of detail, not fundamentals; they were rearrangements or refinements of existing forms, not radical innovations. One element of flexibility which the company asked for in the fundamental sense remains curious and so far to be explained: the floor of the plant was designed to provide dual purpose use—by taking one-ton panel point loading, the floor could be used as either an assembly plant or a machine shop.[175]

The main equipment housed by the factory shell was the assembly track and related conveyors. The same mixture applies of generally conventional equipment assuming innovatory qualities, in the eyes of the Rover Company, when they first used the machinery. As a piece of equipment, the assembly line (supplied by a separate specialist firm) was not new, as the suppliers' records of their lines for the 1959 Mini, the 1963 Rover P6, the 1971 Marina and 1973 Allegro show. In their words it was 'a traditional chain link' system, motor driven, with standard car sledges. It was of standard 'pitch' or speed capacity.[176] When the roof was lowered, after local protest, the lines were lengthened to 1,400 ft. The line had a degree of flexibility consistent with the corporate anticipation of future model series, in that the sledges could accommodate different body sizes.

The major novelty of the track turned out to be its mezzanine character; in other words, the assembly line was raised on supports and operated 8 ft. above the ground on a separate level.[177] The explanation for raising the track rests on three elements. First, it had been used very successfully by Mercedes Benz in their conquest of the European luxury car market. The raised track was a well-established idea in the 1960s.[178] Second, and more importantly, the mezzanine enabled a greater flexibility in track-side storage and component flows,[179] of vital concern after the problems of the P6. Parts on the conveyors, trucks or gravity feeds could, if necessary, move freely underneath the line and from one side of the track to another. The third reason was related to waste. Put simply, in civil engineering terms the time and cost of excavating a large pit and reinforcing it in order to accommodate a ground track was seen as too expensive: putting the track above the ground eliminates the excavation cost.[180]

In short, the SD1 facility, seen as a building structure or an assembly operation, cannot rank internationally as being highly innovative, the corporation's intentions and declarations notwithstanding. Instead, it represented a major departure for British Leyland in general and the Rover Company in particular. On reflection, given the corporate or company inexperience of such projects, their considerable reliance on architects, consultant engineers and specialist suppliers to provide them with both ideas and hardware, design and development competence, is understandable. The conflicting imperatives and priorities within the host organization, its differing capacities to assess contemporary changes in plant design, and the high degree of uncertainty generated by the design process itself made radical innovation less rather than more likely.

Work organization
The problem in dealing with the work organization features of the translation phase of the SD1 project are similar to those raised during the account of the equivalent concept stage. In the formal sense, the continued development of the Protected Earnings Plan was not an integral part of translation work in the SD1 venture. Yet, one can see with hindsight how the experience of the PEP's evolution clearly accounted for important actions by both management and work-force in the new plant relating to the detailed organization and regulation of work. The actions of the production engineers, however, can be considered as part of the official translation phase. Although their title suggests that they should have been dealt with in the preceding Production Facility Section, their assessment and interpretation of the corporate concept of the SD1 plant had direct consequences for the profile of work organization in the new plant.

Nowhere were such assessments more relevant than among the production engineers. A process engineer explained how: 'The product engineers supply us with the documents, the drawings for manufacturing to build the vehicle, and it's production engineering's job to be able to interpret the drawings'.[181] The act of interpretation takes place within the context of the relationship between product, production engineers and plant management. Engineers in general argue that the communication between these groups should be regular and the relationship a close one. One vital aspect of the relationship is the conversion from product prototype to pre-production model to work planning sheet. Product and plant engineers should, according to conventional practice, hand on their plan drawings to specialist product process planners who develop 'process sheets'. The process sheets are derived from the general production concept of the project, allied with the detailed parameters of the car, line machinery and component flows. The sheets are essentially graphic representations of the layout and dimensions of the assembly line and its associated functions (conveyors, line feeds, work stations, etc.).[182]

In the SD1 project this abstract model was transformed by a combination of events and relationships. One manifestation of the traditional aloofness of the product engineers at Rover and their attempt to control the broad engineering function was their use of the design process to exert pressure. Not only did they make a large number of changes in the product but in the absence of stable divisional production management the product engineers were slow to release the so-called 'issue points' (officially finished product drawings) to production engineers. The second disruption resulted from the resentment by process/installation specialists over the way plant specifications were 'handed down' to them. In conditions of uncertainty which the corporate concept requirements produced for these specialists (one thought it 'a colossal change in philosophy and practice' to move from specialist to volume production), they looked to protect their own interest.[183] It was these problems of separation and competition in these departments which so shocked the 'liaison engineer' later appointed, although experts on design have come to regard such problems as almost commonplace on such large projects.[184]

In the climate of increasing divisional upheaval and internal competition the engineering groups fell back on their safe traditional strengths. The way that their vision became dominated by practical considerations meant that their interpretation of the corporate concept emerged as a standard, assembly line formation. There were seventy successive work stations arranged for progressive assembly (see Figure 4.5). The main vestige of novelty which remained from the original corporate concepts of work organization was the layout of the work stations with sufficient space for both group working and the necessary component buffer zones. Indeed, although the production engineers had been very cautious in the assembly layout, the process sheets had been drawn up with sufficient gaps between work stations so that 'on-line' inspection and rectification could take place. In their view it was now up to production management whether they chose to make use of that capacity of the line. The head of the facility planners pointed out after the plant had opened in 1976 that the raised track, component floor and three tracks allowed for long cycle times (up to four minutes), autonomous working and a programme of job redesign, if desired.[185] The response of the production management will be dealt with in the next chapter.

The parallel and quite separate phased development of the programme of changes contained within the Protected Earnings Plan was to be of great significance for both the context and operation of work organization in the SD1 plant. In recognition of the degree of change involved and the pressures with which the negotiations were associated (note the pressure applied by other BL plant unions on the Rover officials not to accept measured day-work), the Rover IR Department made a critical choice.[186] The decision was taken to set up a programme of changes, phased over three main stages. Separate details were related to each main occupation category (hourly paid staff, etc.), as 150 grades were reduced to eight main types. This phased programme from 1970 to 1975 not only enabled current legislation (such as the Equal Pay and Employment Acts) to be incorporated, but because of its starting date the company was not included in the Government's pay freeze. The process enabled joint union and management working parties (with sixteen senior stewards), meeting monthly, to monitor the adherence to the letter of the agreement. It was these practices which explain why management felt that 'a durable basis for relations between employees and the company' had been laid.

The outcomes of this episode may have been novel for the company, yet they had been arrived at by a technique rooted in customary bargaining, based on a realistic assessment of worker power and an acceptance of work place contest as natural. The attempt to construct participation artificially (via the Special Projects Committee, for example) which ignored such fundamental power relations of the work place were doomed to failure. In short, the Rover workers took up and sustained the PEP precisely because it was located in the arena which they saw as legitimate and purposive. The PEP can be regarded as a 'transforming event' (in Ladurie's sense) for industrial relations in the Rover Company; the Special Projects Committee was merely transitory. Poole distinguishes between mere co-operation and, more strictly, co-determination. The PEP was the outcome of a process which could be justly termed co-determination; the Special Project Committee barely deserved the label of co-operation.

The analysis of industrial disputes between 1966 and 1974 by the Incomes Policy Research Unit of the Department of Employment suggests a caveat to our conclusions on the relative success of introducing a new form of bargaining and payment system at Rover. They discovered that: 'the introduction of such schemes ... is probably relatively conflict free. The far higher proportion of disputes over the operation of payment systems suggests that it is operating a system, not changing it, that involves conflict'.[187] This finding will be tested when we examine the running of the new system and plant. But there were a number of very important consequences of Rover's successful introduction of the Protected Earnings Plan. The first relates to the impact of industrial relations on the phases of the design sequence. The apparent stability in industrial relations which accompanied the new agreement came at a critical time in the SD1 design process. It was at the stage that the corporation had decided on a new model (the SD1) in February 1971, and was considering a location of the new specialist production facility. Management believed that it was more than coincidental that the IR department should receive a letter from the BL Chairman on 4 November that year, congratulating them on the reduction in man-hours lost through disputes from 1969–70 to 1970–1.

There were also implications for future management/worker relations and work organization embedded in the new agreement. In the case of management, total responsibility for the maintenance of supplies and labour was ascribed to them in order that they fulfilled their obligation to provide a basis for workers' achieving standard performances. The legitimation given to the shop floor union structure, and especially the stewards, was a major event for labour which raised expectations regarding the style of management in the future and therefore when the SD1 plant opened. As the operation of the facility will show, it was the process of change which the PEP began which stands out. Management and workers alike attempted to shape and direct the operation of measured day-work as they responded to the intense pressures which the SD1 project's later phases developed. Moreover, there were two contradictions inherent in the creation of the new agreement for other aspects of the new plant's work organization. The logic of measured day-work, with the onus on workers to deliver standard performance, sits uneasily with the spirit of autonomous work groups where workers decide on component ordering and effort rating. Second, compared with other car companies, and especially Ford, the absence of production engineers and plant management inputs into the negotiating process points to the very optimistic expectation that the payment system *itself* was somehow going to solve the major problems of productivity, problems which were in part caused by separate factors such as supply breakdown, quality control, or inter- and intra-site production flows.

Finally, the experience of Rover and BL lends qualification to some of the models of industrial change which have gained currency in recent years. Bardou and others argue that, across Europe in the 1960s, management was rationalized and became more centralized as they followed methods pioneered by American corporations early in the century. The example of Renault's Billancourt works is cited quite aptly, with the creation of a central personnel office in 1950, the growth of systems of job descriptions, co-ordinated production plans and the installation of a central computer in 1960. This account differs markedly from the experience of Rover and BL. While American ideals were acknowledged in BL's restructuring and in Rover as early as the 1930s, the pace of change was much slower and the degree of realization compared to Ford or GM blueprints only partial.

The national annual contract model of bargaining developed by the United Auto Workers and GM in the 1945–6 disputes in the United States and used by Fiat, Renault and Peugeot in Europe in 1955, finds only a faint echo in the attempts by Rover and BL to win once-a-year agreements for each plant only. The use of national union confederations in Europe after the Second World War, and the subsequent evolution of decentralized plant-based bargaining lent a very different character to European industrial relations. Some maintain that in Europe this led to

> the institutionalisation of the union as a guarantor of labour peace as the other side of its involvement with managing the work force, even if it did not recognise it and even if it retained the option of using its power as it chose, placed the union nonetheless in a contradictory situation: between demands from the workers and managing the same workers . . . This change also set the stage for the appearance of autonomous forms of labour organization.[188]

In Rover, and across BL, the opposite was true: it was the lateness of union development which stands out, together with the long-term absence of national bargaining. Unofficial shop floor unionism grew spontaneously in Britain (as on the P6 line) and was the precursor of broader union strength, not the result of it. In passing, those models which allege that formalized national collective bargaining essentially created a major turning-point in the early twentieth century are seriously questioned by the experience of the British-owned car industry.[189]

The translation phase of the SD1 project stands as a key episode. The actions of each specialist function involved both confirmed and compounded the inconsistencies within the original concepts of the SD1 production unit. In the absence of a formal design process appropriate to the scope of the intended innovations, the departments responsible for translating concept into prototype form fell back to conventional practices and their own dominant logics. Whilst the Rover Company's recipe for design and innovation was rejected, no new total process was created in its place (the creation of a corporate total design capacity was in fact to occupy BL for the rest of the decade). Instead, in assuming that an essentially linear sequence would suffice, the corporation allowed both a high degree of fragmentation and political contest to develop, given the many uncertainties generated by the concept phase. The translation phase is indicative of the interdependence and contest which characterized the whole SD1 project. Adjacent groups (such as the Rover product and production engineers) depended on each other for information in order to fulfil their roles within the process, yet at the same time could use such critical translations to demonstrate or augment their own interests and power.

The extent of political activity involved in the attempts to occupy the 'design space' of the SD1 apart, the most distinctive feature of the translation phase was the density of 'unknowns' and unforeseen outcomes. The impact of external community pressure resulting in the reduction of the plant's height, or the experience of the plant's architects, are just two examples. Indeed, the concept and translation phases of the SD1 project confirm the conclusions of those writers who stress the 'streams of problems, solutions, participants, and choice opportunities interacting almost randomly to carry the organisation toward the future.[190] This was particularly so in a corporation which, with little experience of strategic innovation, attempted such a large-scale project within the context of increasing organizational and market turbulence. On the other hand, even thus far the SD1 project's first two phases confront the dominant picture of car design and innovation derived from the American producers. Whilst commentators on the American auto corporations in the early 1970s bemoaned their predictability and lack of even attempted radical innovations, in Britain the reverse was true. It was the collection of intended strategic innovations and their unforeseen transformations which marked BL's experience during the concept and translation phases from 1968 to 1974, and which continued throughout the rest of the SD1 project.

Notes

1. E. J. Miller and A. R. Rice, *Systems of Organization: The Control of Task and Sentient Boundaries*, 1967, pp. 146–57. See Chap. 2, Note 118.
2. G. Nadler, *The Planning and Design Approach*, New York, 1981.
3. E. P. Thompson, 'On History, Sociology and Historical Relevance', *British Journal of Sociology*, **27**, 1976, pp. 387–402. D. Gregory, *Regional Transformation and Industrial Revolution: A Geography of the Yorkshire Woollen Industry*, 1982.
4. Gregory, op. cit., p. 14.
5. J. Foreman-Peck, 'Exit, Voice and Loyalty as Response to Decline: The Rover Company in the Inter-War Years', *Business History*, **XXIII**, 2, July 1981, pp. 199 and 204.
6. J. Ensor, *The Motor Industry*, 1971, p. 34.
7. D. G. Rhys, *The Motor Industry: An Economic Survey*, 1972, pp. 59–60. Austin Rover Group Product Planning Dept., 'The Right Product for the Right Market', mimeo., 1984, p. 8.
8. G. Turner, *The Leyland Papers*, 1971, pp. 30 and 70–1. Rover Company Directors' Minutes (hereafter RCDMins), 5 January 1968.
9. Turner, op. cit., p. 72. RCDMins, 23 March 1967, item 1091.
10. RCDMins, 9 February, 2 April 1968 and 6 February 1969.
11. *The British Leyland Motor Corporation* (ND BLMC), 1968?
12. D. Jones, *Maturity and Crisis in the European Car Industry: Structural Change and Public Policy*, 1968, p. 25. The British Leyland Motor Corporation, pp. 14, 15, 22 and 40.
13. Jones, op. cit., pp. 45–7 and 108. L. T. Wells, 'Automobiles', in R. Vernon (ed.), *Big Business and the State: Changing Relations in Western Europe*, 1974, p. 244.
14. Ensor, op. cit., pp. 114–19. K. N. Bhaskar, *The Future of the World Motor Industry*, 1980, p. 148.
15. Ensor, op. cit., p. 119. G. Bloomfield, *The World Automotive Industry*, 1978, p. 99. Rhys, op. cit., p. 77.
16. M. Jelinek, *Institutionalizing Innovation. A Study of Organizational Learning Systems*, New York, 1979, p. 139. British Leyland's Industrial Relations Policy 1973, 31 July 1973, Section 6, p. 6. Ensor, op. cit., pp. 122–6. On internal model competition see M. Edwardes, *Back from the Brink: An Apocalyptic Experience*, 1983, p. 33.

17. RCDMins, 17 June 1971, MD's report.
18. R. J. Overy, *William Morris: Viscount Nuffield*, 1976, pp. 96–9.
19. C. Edwards, *The Dynamics of the United States Automobile Industry*, Columbia, 1965, p. 266.
20. P. Marginson, 'The Historical Development of the Firm's Internal Organization in the UK—Managing the Work Process', mimeo., Warwick University, July 1983, pp. 3, 6 and *passim*; D. F. Channon, *The Strategy and Structure of British Enterprise*, Harvard, 1973.
21. C. K. Prahalad and Y. L. Doz, 'Managing Managers: The Work of Top Management', mimeo., University of Michigan and INSEAD, 1982, pp. 8, 13 and 15.
22. Jaguar Rover Triumph, *Rover* (ND 1978? Publication No. 3458), p. 1 and sections entitled: the design difference; aerodynamics; designed-in safety; the Rover standard; the Rover 6 cylinder engine; and the Rover V8 engine.
23. *BL Mirror, Special Edition*, 30 June 1976, p. 1.
24. *The Car of the Year Today* (ND BL Cars Public Relations News Services), pp. 1–4.
25. Op. cit., p. 8.
26. Op. cit., p. 5.
27. Op. cit., p. 4. Jaguar Rover Triumph, *Rover*, the design difference. P. Turner, 'The V8 Engine', *Motor*, Special Supplement (June 1974). Cf. Jones, *Maturity and Crisis*, p. 30.
28. *Car of the Year Today*, **4**.
29. Interview with Rover facility engineer, TI 24. RCDMins, 31 January 1969.
30. P. Gardiner, 'Design Trajectories for Airplanes and Automobiles During the Past Fifty Years', mimeo., SPRU, University of Sussex, 1983, pp. 1–7.
31. Interview with ex-Ford product planner, pp. 12–13.
32. Interview with ex-Rover senior executive, p. 2. RCDMins, 9 February, 8 March and 13 September 1968, 10 October 1969 and 11 September 1970.
33. RCDMins, 6 February and 10 October 1969, 'information [was] required to be kept to the minimum consistent with that required to exercise proper control by the Central [corporate] staff'.
34. RCDMins, 9 May, item 1483, 12 September 1969, item 1534 and 26 March 1971, items 1724 and 1729.
35. RCDMins, 15 June 1971, technical director's report.
36. Prahalad and Doz, Managing Managers, pp. 4, 8–13 and 16. Interviews with ex-Rover senior executive, p. 2 and senior Rover production engineer, p. 12. G. Robson, *The Rover Story*, p. 154.
37. Quotation is from an interview with a corporate job improvement adviser, pp. 1, 5, 15 and 25–6. Bloomfield, *The World Automotive Industry*, p. 110; *The Future of the British Car Industry*, Central Policy Review Staff, HMSO 1975, p. 23.
38. S. Sinclair, *The World Car*, 1983, pp. 10 ff. Evidence of M. Edwardes to *The House of Commons Industry and Trade Committee: Finance for BL*, HMSO 1975, p. 43. Bloomfield, op. cit., p. 110.
39. Austin-Rover Product Planning, 'The Right Product for the Right Market'; I. G. Volpato, 'Product Market Changes and Firm Strategies', mimeo., University of Venice, June 1984.
40. A. R. product planning, in loc. cit. and p. 4. Interview with senior ARG product planner, p. 4.
41. AR product planning, pp. 6 ff.
42. A. G. Armstrong, *The Demand for New Cars: An Econometric Model for Short-Term Forecasting*, 1974, *passim*.

43. Rhys, *The Motor Industry*, p. 257; CPRS, *Future of the British Car Industry*, p. 34.
44. Interviews with ARG product planner, pp. 6–7 and senior SD1 vehicle engineer, p. 1. Jones, *Maturity and Crisis*, p. 25.
45. See Note 38.
46. H. B. Light, 'The Rover Story', November 1967, p. 30, Rover Archive; speech dated 22 August 1967.
47. *BL Mirror, Special Edition*, 30 June 1976, p. 1.
48. *BL Mirror*, in loc. cit., p. 13; BMNA, 27 and 30 June 1976.
49. Turner, *The Leyland Papers*, p. 95; CPRS, *Future of the British Car Industry*, pp. 8, 28, 31 and 107.
50. Ensor, *The Motor Industry*, pp. 123–6 and 149. Rhys, *The Motor Industry*, p. 282. Interview with consultant engineer, p. 5. E. M. Rogers and R. Agarwala-Rogers, *Communication in Organization*, 1976, p. 159.
51. *BL Mirror, Special Edition*, 30 June 1976, p. 13.
52. Ensor, op. cit., p. 87; Bhaskar, *Future of the World Motor Industry*, pp. 20 and 81.
53. Interviews with senior vehicle design engineer, pp. 1–2 and senior Rover production engineer; Robson, *The Rover Story*, p. 155–6.
54. Bloomfield, *The World Automotive Industry*, p. 39.
55. Ibid.; Jones, *Maturity and Crisis*, p. 6; interview with European manager, assembly line engineering contractor, p. 2.
56. Evidence of BL executives to *The House of Commons Committee: Finance for BL*, pp. 54–5.
57. *British Leyland: the Next Decade. An Abridged Version of a Report Presented to the Secretary of State for Industry by a Team of Inquiry Led by Sir Don Ryder* (HMSO 1975), p. 6; CPRS, *Future of the British Car Industry*, p. 21.
58. Bhaskar, *Future of the World Motor Industry*, pp. 78–9.
59. *A Workers' Enquiry into the Motor Industry*, 1978, Institute for Workers' Control Motor Group, p. 38.
60. BMNA, 29 April 1970.
61. Interviews with senior Rover production engineer, pp. 12 and 17 and senior Rover production director, p. 7.
62. *BL Mirror*, in loc. cit., p. 4; interviews with senior Rover production engineer, pp. 13 and 28 and senior Rover production director, pp. 1 and 3.
63. SD1 Cost Estimate Schemes Nos. 1–15. Rover Archive. See No. 15 for summary.
64. For a useful overview, see Bloomfield, *The World Automotive Industry*, pp. 110–41 and 201–3; D. Massey, *Spatial Divisions of Labour: Social Structures and the Geography of Production*, 1984, pp. 89–93.
65. RCDMins, 21 January and 22 September 1960.
66. Interview with construction engineering manager, p. 19.
67. BMNA, 6 September 1974 and 29 July 1976.
68. British Leyland's Industrial Relations Policy 1973 Onwards, pp. 38–9 and Sections 14.2 and 14.3.
69. 'Job Design and Work Organization in BL Cars, Period 1973–78', mimeo., Personnel, Manpower, Projects and Resources, BL Cars, 8 August 1978, *passim*.
70. Interviews with: corporate job improvement adviser, p. 20; BMNA, 27 June 1976. A comparison was also made with the work of Lucas at Renault.
71. Interview with Rover director, p. 17.
72. British Leyland's Industrial Relations Policy Review, 1973, Section 6.1.

73. In loc. cit., Section 2. For the text of the agreement of 1972 see 'Memorandum of Agreement between British Leyland Motor Corporation Limited and 18 unions listed from Amalgamated Society of Boilermakers to the Union of Construction, Allied Trades and Technicians'.
74. British Leyland's Industrial Relations Policy Review, 1973, Section 10.
75. In loc. cit., Section 10, pp. 27 and 31.
76. Ibid. See also B. Malcolm, 'A Note on the UK Motor Industry', mimeo., BLMC, 1971, pp. 10–11.
77. 'BLMC Memorandum, Corporate Industrial Relations Objective for 1974/75', 30 July 1974. CLNO 74/146 passim.
78. In loc. cit., Sections 13–14.
79. British Leyland's Industrial Relations Policy Review, 1973, p. 37.
80. In loc. cit., Section 14, p. 7.
81. In loc. cit., pp. 40, 41.
82. 'Job Improvement—Analysis of Costs and Benefits', corporate job improvement officer, 16 December 1976.
83. As discussed in F. H. M. Blackler and C. A. Brown, Job Design and Management Control: Studies in British Leyland and Volvo, 1978, p. 84, from A. Cherns, 'Principles of Socio-Technical Design', Human Relations, 29, 1976.
84. Interview with corporate and Rover job improvement advisers, passim.
85. 'Methods of Vehicle Assembly at East Works, Solihull', mimeo., BLMC, August 1976, pp. 3 and 10.
86. See Note 69.
87. J. Rowe, Wages in Practice and Theory, 1928, pp. 22 ff. W. Brown, Piecework Bargaining, 1973, p. 174.
88. Interview with senior Rover IR manager, p. 17.
89. In loc. cit., pp. 1 and 2; BMNA, 27 November 1970 and 29 March 1972; A Workers' Enquiry into the Motor Industry, pp. 13, 15–16.
90. Interview with senior Rover IR manager, pp. 7–8.
91. In loc. cit., p. 8. 'British Leyland and Measured Daywork', mimeo., BLMC, ND, pp. 14 ff.; CPRS, The Future of the British Car Industry, p. 102.
92. British Leyland Measured Daywork, p. 1.
93. Interview with senior Rover IR manager, p. 10. X and Partners Ltd to Rover Company Ltd. Final Report P6 Wage Structure, 28 October 1970. Rover Archive. J. Sutherland, 'The Impact of Measured Day Work on Company Industrial Relations', mimeo., Warwick University, 1974, pp. 30–1.
94. X and Partners Ltd to Rover Company Ltd., 'Survey of the Rover Company', 12 June 1970, pp. 1–16; Rover Archive; Interview with senior engine plant shop steward, P6 and SD1, p. 5.
95. Industrial Relations Director Rover, 'The Protected Earnings Plan. A Review', 21 December 1973, and 'Review of Rover Agreements, Main Works' 1971, ND, p. 3, Rover Archive.
96. Interview with senior P6 and SD1 shop steward, p. II, passim. All references to shop stewards are for the Transport and General Workers' Union unless otherwise stated. The best detailed account of the PEP's features is found in 'Memorandum of Agreement, British Leyland Cars, A Collective Agreement for a Protected Earnings Plan, Hourly Rated Employees, Rover plants, January 1975'. See especially Section B, pp. 1–5 and Section D, pp. 7–10. D. Noble, 'Social Choice in Machine Design: the Case of Automatically Controlled Machine Tools', in A. Zimablist (ed.), Case Studies in the Labour Process, New York, 1979, p. 45.
97. British Leyland: the Next Decade, BMNA, 14 May 1973, p. 54.

98. Interviews with senior vehicle design engineer, pp. 7 and 29, and ex-GM corporate liaison engineer, p. 2.

99. RCDMins, 26 March 1971; interviews with BL liaison engineer, pp. 1–10; ex-senior Rover product engineer, pp. 1–2; *Car of the Year Today* (BLMC ND), p. 4; Robson, *The Rover Story*, p. 155.

100. Interview with BL liaison engineer, pp. 4–6; cf. Edwardes, *Back from the Brink*, p. 64.

101. RCDMins, 11 September 1970; Bhaskar, *Future of the World Motor Industry*, p. 148.

102. Ensor, *The Motor Industry*, p. 87; interview with BL liaison engineer, p. 4; Cambridge Careers Research and Advisory Centre, *First Destination of University Graduates*, 1982.

103. Interviews with BL liaison engineer, p. 4 and senior vehicle design engineer, p. 6.

104. In loc. cit., p. 3.

105. Interview with BL liaison engineer, p. 10. We are grateful to P. Gardiner, SPRU, University of Sussex for his confirmation of the phenomenon from his own BL fieldwork, reported at the Royal College of Art, 12 May 1983.

106. Interviews with senior vehicle design engineer, pp. 29–30 and ARG product planner, pp. 1–10.

107. Ibid., especially p. 26–7.

108. Interview with BL liaison engineer, p. 6.

109. *Car of the Year Today, passim*; BL liaison engineer, p. 3.

110. Interview with ex-Rover product engineer, p. 17.

111. Interview with Rover facility engineer, TI 669.

112. See chapter 3, Sections III and IV; *British Leyland: the Next Decade*, p. 5; interview with senior Rover Triumph engineer, p. 16.

113. Interviews with ex-Rover production director, pp. 2–3 and ex-GM liaison engineer, II, p. 13.

114. RCDMins, 9 February, 28 April 1968, 28 and 31 January 1969, and 8 May 1970.

115. Interviews with: ex-snagger worker on P6, SD1, I, 1 and II, p. 1; engine plant shop steward, pp. 23 and 28, and senior shop steward for Land Rover and P6, p. 10.

116. See R. Whipp, 'Potbank and Union: A Study of Work and Trade Unionism in the British Pottery Industry 1900–1925', unpublished Ph.D. thesis, Warwick University, 1983, chap. 2 *passim*; T. Matsumura, *The Victorian Flint Glass Makers 1850–1880: The Labour Aristocracy Revisited*, 1983.

117. See H. F. Moorhouse, 'American automobiles and workers' dreams', *Sociological Review*, **13**, 3, August 1983, pp. 403–26.

118. Interviews with SD1 assembly track worker, p. 15 and 'internal transport driver, p. 2. Sutherland, op. cit., p. 2.

119. Interview with senior P6 and SD1 assembly shop steward, TI 351.

120. Interview with ex-Ford product planner, pp. 15 and 25. CPRS, *Future of the British Car Industry*, p. 17 takes the relationship for granted.

121. *Car of the Year Today, passim*; Cf. N. L. Svensson, *Introduction to Engineering Design*, New South Wales, 1976, chap. 1 *passim*; S. Dickerson and J. Robertshaw, *Planning and Design*, Lexington, 1975.

122. Interviews with Rover facility engineer, TI 44 and contracts manager assembly line supply, TI 410–413.

123. Interview with senior corporate IR manager, p. 3.

124. J. Bessant and K. Dickson, 'Determinism or Design: Some Notes on Job Content and Micro-electronics', mimeo., Technology Policy Unit, Aston

University, 1982, p. 8; A. Sanders, 'Construction of a Car Plant for the 1980s', Viscount Nuffield Memorial to the Royal Society, 28 July 1976.

125. Bessant and Dickson, op. cit., p. 11.
126. CPRS, *Future of the British Car Industry*, p. 22; cf. H. Wright Baker (ed.), *Modern Workshop Technology, Part II, Machine Tools and Manufacturing Processes*, 1960, p. 589.
127. See R. N. Basu, 'The Practical Problems of Assembly Line Balancing', *The Product Engineer*, October 1973, pp. 369–70; II. G. Van Beek, 'Assembly Line Organization', mimeo., N. V. Phillips, Gloellampenfabrieken, Eindhoven, ND; G. Buxey, 'A Guide to the Selection of Methods for High-Volume Assembly', *Production Engineer*, December 1974, pp. 503–11. We are indebted to Peter Burcher, Aston University, for his guidance in this area.
128. Interviews with ex-Vauxhall production engineer, pp. 1–2 and consulting production engineer, pp. 1–10.
129. Interview with corporate production planner, p. 2.
130. Interview with senior Rover production planner, pp. 1 6. 'Vehicle Sub Assembly—Job Improvement Concept. A Report on the Methods of Vehicle Sub Assembly at East Works, Solihull', Report No. S0001, August 1976, Appendix 4, p. 5.
131. B. Fiddy, J. G. Bright, R. Hurrion, 'See—Why: Interactive Simulation on the Screen', *Automotive Manufacturing Update '81*, No. 13, 1981, pp. 168–71. P. Hill, 'A Job Worth Doing?', *Work Study and Management Services*, January 1976, pp. 5–9.
132. Hill, in loc. cit. Report by Participants from British Leyland. Information Conference on the Working Environment Held at Volvo, Sweden, 10 May 1973.
133. P. Gyllenhammar, *People at Work*, Reading, Mass., 1977.
134. Rogers and Agarwala-Rogers, op. cit., p. 160; F. Heller, 'Some Observations with Special Reference to Saab Scania', paper presented to SSRC Anglo-Swedish Conference, Changes in Work Organization and Work Design, 25–6 March 1974.
135. See Note 132.
136. In loc. cit., p. 19.
137. Interview with Rover production planner, p. 11.
138. Interviews with: corporate job improvement adviser, p. 16; senior Rover production engineer, p. 2 and senior Rover IR officer, p. 15.
139. Blackler and Brown, *Job Redesign and Managment Control*, pp. 25 and 47–9.
140. S. Gregory, 'Large Technological Projects', mimeo., Aston University, 1983; interview with Austin Rover product planner, p. 9.
141. Gyllenhammar, op. cit., p. 12.
142. H. Scarborough, 'The Politics of Technological Change at British Leyland', mimeo., Aston University, 1982. See also his 'The Control of Technological Change in the Motor Industry. A Case Study', unpublished Ph.D. thesis, Aston University.
143. Interview with assembly line contractor, TI 403.
144. Interview with senior Rover production engineer, pp. 18 and 28.
145. BMNA, 29 July 1976.
146. Interviews with Rover job improvement adviser, TI 770 and consulting engineer, p. 40.
147. British Leyland's Industrial Relations Policy, 1973 Onwards, p. 7. BMNA, 27 April 1974.
148. Interviews with senior P6 and SD1 assembly shop steward, TI 343 and P6 shop steward representative on the Special Projects Commitee, pp. 13–14.

149. Interviews with senior P6 and SD1 shop steward, II, p. 2 and architect, TI 404; Rover Trade Union Works Committee, Solihull: 27 June, 4 July, 14 and 21 November and 5 December 1974.
150. Interview with senior P6 and SD1 shop steward in loc. cit.
151. Ibid., and interviews with senior shop steward for Land Rover and P6, p. 11.
152. Interviews with senior P6 and SD1 shop steward, II, pp. 2 ff and Rover job improvement adviser, TI 600.
153. Ibid.
154. Interview with internal transport driver shop steward, p. 2.
155. BMNA, 27 April 1975, interview with senior shop steward for Land Rover and P6, pp. 1–2 and 11.
156. Ibid.
157. Interview with senior P6 and SD1 shop steward, TI 1000. See, for example, 'Versatility at Work', Industrial Training Research Unit, Cambridge, ITRU Research Paper TR6.
158. Interview with senior P6 and SD1 shop steward, II, p. 2.
159. See R. Whipp, 'Labour Markets and Communities: An Historical View', Work Organization Research Centre, *Working Paper Series No. 3*, Aston University, June 1984.
160. BMNA, 13 June and 4 July 1973.
161. In loc. cit., 2 May 1973.
162. In loc. cit., 25 May and 4 July 1973.
163. Interviews with consulting architect, TI 13, 60 and 250; and ex-Rover production director, pp. 1, 5 and 9; BMNA, 5 and 12 June 1973.
164. Interview with architect, TI 26–34.
165. Interviews with architect, TI 118 and consultant engineer, p. 4.
166. Interview with architect, TI 148.
167. In loc. cit. and 640.
168. *BL Mirror, Special Edition*, p. 19.
169. Interview with architect, TI 940–969.
170. In loc. cit., p. 980.
171. *Project Solihull* (BL News Series, ND), 'Building the Car'.
172. Interview with paint plant consultant, TI 80–111.
173. Interview with architect, TI 108 and consultant engineer, p. 149.BMNA, 26 August 1976.
174. *BL Mirror, Special Edition*, pp. 19 and 24.
175. Interview with architect, TI 490, 542 and 795.
176. Interview with assembly line contractor, pp. 5 and 165. Cf. Weldall Engineering Ltd., *Mechanical Handling Techniques*, Stourbridge, ND, *passim*.
177. BMNA 30 June 1976; *The Car for Tomorrow, Today: From Leyland Cars*, BLMC April 1976, 'The Factory'.
178. BMNA, 29 July 1976; interview with ex-Vauxhall production engineer, p. 2.
179. RCDMins, 10 October 1969. Interview with Rover facility engineer, TI 268.
180. Interview with consulting engineer, TI 690.
181. Interview with Rover facility engineer, TI 174–80.
182. Interview with liaison engineer, II, pp. 5 and 7. See, for example, 'Frame One Proposed Distribution of Shop Floor', Rover, British Leyland, Sheet 41/0062.
183. Interview with installation engineer, TI 180–190 and 291.
184. Gregory, op. cit., p. 546.
185. BMNA, 26 August 1976. Cf. Blackler and Brown, op. cit., pp. 90 and 107.
186. Interview with senior Rover IR officer, pp. 17–19; *PEP, Review of Human and Industrial Relations Aspects*, 21 December 1971.
187. As quoted in British Leyland, Measured Daywork, para. 26. R. Whipp,

'Management Design and Industrial Relations in the British Auto Industry', *Industrial Relations Journal*, 1986.

188. J-P. Bardou *et al*., *The Automobile Revolution: The Impact of an Industry*, Chapel Hill, 1982, pp. 240–44 and 246.

189. R. Price, *Masters, Unions and Men: Work Control in Building and the Rise of Labour 1830–1914*, 1980, pp. 55–7 and 184 ff.; K. Burgess, *The Origins of British Industrial Relations*, 1975.

190. T. J. Peters and R. H. Waterman, *In Search of Excellence: Lessons from America's Best Run Companies*, 1982, p. 7.

5 The SD1 project—commissioning and operation, 1974–1982

The following chapter completes the reconstruction of the SD1 design process by examining the commissioning and operation phases. The commissioning phase ran from January 1974 until June 1976, while the plant operated until March 1982. It is in the commissioning stage that the various elements of designing derived from conception and translation are supposed to converge as the productive unit is 'set up', tested and 'run in'.[1] In the case of the SD1, that convergence did not occur smoothly. Whilst continuities of theme and practice are noticeable during the SD1's commissioning, there were major disjunctions which arose from the range of social and technical interactions involved. It is possible, therefore, to trace the corporate intentions for the project together with the way they were refashioned by those who bore the design process forward. The technological contradictions and the political conflicts of the concept and translation phases were intensified as the corporation's environment and internal position worsened. The pressures within the SD1 project became acute. A processual analysis of both the Rover Company's progress and the SD1 design process offers a more satisfying explanation of what happened in the Solihull facility when compared with the existing accounts.

I Commissioning

There are a number of features of the SD1 project which both underline and help to explain the loose connections within its design process which are in sharp contrast to the dominant images of design presented in the auto industry literature. These include: the lack of information in the project and appropriate methods of recording, the breakdown of Rover's traditional practices and implicit rules around design and lack of communication both between those involved and between the different phases. These aspects of the early stages of the project set up a number of pressures which meant that the SD1 design process continued to develop its own dynamic during commissioning, other than the one intended by corporate headquarters. Crises arising at corporate level, within management and most especially during pre-production will be examined as key events in further transforming the original intentions of the project.

The product
The lack of a comprehensive record of the activities of almost every part of the project, and in so novel a venture for all concerned, meant that the degree of certainty and co-ordination was always likely to be low. In the design of the car, an engineer admitted that it took almost all of 1975 to unravel what different engineering groups had been working on (such as electronics, power-train, etc.). A complete inventory had to be taken and

the inconsistencies and contradictions resolved. One design expert involved in the design of the product did not consider this unusual in essence, but rather in degree. His experience elsewhere led him to view such delays and enforced learning paths as almost inevitable.[2] Moreover, it is interesting how future corporate projects have planned or incorporated 'engineering audits', using either internal specialists or contract arrangements with outside firms. Production engineers also related how, in the early 1970s, there was little recording of procedures or detailed project manuals, as used by Ford, which offered models of company or corporate practice to replace the traditional Rover methods. Nor was the general engineering literature helpful in their precise role when faced with uncertainty, according to the engineers we spoke to.[3]

The difficulties experienced during the SD1 translation and development stage in combining the various parts of the car which had been designed by different companies led the corporation to appoint a 'liaison engineer' in 1975. His job was to co-ordinate all the engineering activities associated with the SD1 (although at a very late stage), and to supervise the creation of a body which would bring together all engineering specialisms within the corporation for the first time. He therefore found the SD1 to be 'an excellent motor car', yet it was 'laboured' [i.e. took a long time to develop] and it was not really developed for production. In fact there were over 1,200 'job one' changes made to the vehicle before it even approached being ready to go into production (a job one change is a basic yet detailed revision of the model without which a car cannot be offered for sale). Current product engineers maintain that the divergent tendencies and tensions we have identified persisted until the late 1970s, over a decade past the original merger; an indication of the embeddedness of such relationships and the amount of time necessary to change those practices in the British context. The SD1 project could not effect that transformation, rather it became a graphic means of illustrating the strength of traditional methods and mentalities.[4]

There were two important problems which arose from the commissioning of the SD1 car. First, the virtual year's delay in synthesizing the product engineering work, though masked somewhat by the attention commanded by the government inquiry, set up enormous time, and therefore cost, pressures related to the £95 million devoted to the SD1 car and the assembly plant. It was from this point that the stresses within the project mounted, resulting in a continuous struggle to meet even rearranged deadlines. The effect was cumulative, and especially discernible during the plant's early operation. The one year delay in 1975 would have been ever more disastrous financially, had not the Government accepted the Ryder recommendations to fund this existing BL project.

The second problem emerged during the transition from the so-called 'engineering and development' of the SD1 car within the translation phase to the car's 'method build' during commissioning. This sequence is one of many sub-phases of the SD1 design process. The intention of 'method build' was to construct the vehicle prototype experimentally, yet starting from the skills and approaches already being used on the existing models. The method of building the car was to be refined during the subsequent 'pre-production' phase. Method build and pre-production take place 'off-line', away from current assembly using skilled, experienced workers. The assemblers who rehearsed the tasks involved reported on their feasibility within the time allocated and suggested modifications to task, tools and, if necessary, body dimensions. This procedure was well-known to one car assembler who had worked eighteen years for the Rover Company. This phase was usually difficult, and in his experience 'manufacturers [of cars] always get it wrong going from the design to the production process. There always seems a lack of clarity between design and production'.[5] Indeed, this experience was not uncommon among specialist car markers. The SD1's contemporary, the Triumph TR7, needed 1,300 modifications during pre-production. However, for many of the skilled assemblers at Rover, the method build revealed a major change in the product and hence their future work. The poor quality of materials used and the low standard specifications compared to past Rover cars threatened dilution of their skills and a lowering of their status and pride, with the result that many left the company.[6] This 'exodus of discontent', as one P6 worker put it, was to gather pace during pre-production; it was also only one of the series of social upheavals which the later stages of the project contained.

One additional feature of the transition from 'engineering and development' to 'method build' deserves highlighting. The inability of product engineers, or others, to change the product concept in any major way stands out. Their overwhelming objective in the SD1 was to develop prototypes and pre-production vehicles according to the original product programme: this was a task which consumed all their resources, given the growing pressures on the project. As one SD1 product engineer put it,

> if you do the job right you need to build a lot of vehicles and do your method build work on them to make really sure that your build process goes right and also to prove your engineering ... but when you'd committed all the money for the production machinery, everybody was screaming their heads off, because of cash flow, to get production going. So you've got a conflict of interests, the financial interests short term and making a job of the thing [i.e. in engineering terms] ... you really do your proving tests to make sure that when it's [the car] off tools, it really works as well as you said it was going to when it was at the prototype stage.[7]

It was hardly surprising therefore that when commentators questioned the product engineers in 1976 on the appropriateness of such a large, fuel-expensive car as the SD1 (following the oil price rises of 1973–4), the Rover men had to reject the criticism. Even if they had wanted to alter the car so dramatically, their version of the design process would not have permitted it.[8]

The commissioning stage of the SD1 project also shows how, instead of witnessing the bringing together of the concept and the translation work, it came to reveal the fragmentation of effort and direction. It has already been shown how 'clan loyalties' became reference points for action among engineers from the different BL companies during the product translation. Yet it was at the beginning of the commissioning phase that the problem was raised and shown to be of wider relevance. The major difficulty of integrating Rover and Triumph management and operations, from October 1972 to December 1974, was readily apparent. The best indication of this element of uncertainty within the project and the powerful competitive dynamic of the design process occurs in the internal Rover-Triumph Report submitted to the Ryder Committee investigation of BL on 31 December 1974.[9] It is highly indicative of the problems facing both BL and the SD1 venture. The notes on 'Divisional Personnel and Staff Planning' include the following observations:

— at least one year before Divisional MD appointed;
— 1974 was only the target date for 'organizational integration';
— 'unwanted integrated organizational plans given to reluctant managers who are unwilling to accept change to modes of operation practised over many years';
— integration of departments from a system and physical point of view is only about one-third complete;
— finance, systems and personnel have recruited and grown in the last two years: 'manufacturing and hard-core technical areas, Production Engineering, Quality Control, Engineering have by comparison done little or no recruiting'.

In January 1975, by which time the pre-production of the SD1 should have begun, another internal study discovered that of the twenty-two Rover-Triumph 'top management', most had only a half to three-and-a-half years' experience in their present job.[10] The final report of the Ryder Inquiry in April 1975 noted how:

there were conflicting schools of thought within the Corporation—some working towards full integration and others hoping to preserve the independence of the old company structure. [And yet] there are, however, no agreed plans within BL about the eventual form of organisation which should be adopted or the timetable for achieving it.[11]

The outcome of the continuing uncertainty over corporate organization was disastrous for both Rover's product engineers and the company's management. One of the SD1 vehicle engineers characterized the attempted changes as 'a sort of dance' where 'there was a lot of tension' which made his job 'incredibly difficult'.[12]

However, for the Rover management the pre- and post-Ryder reorganizations resulted in the removal from office of senior Rover executives and their replacement by ex-Austin Morris personnel.[13] The conflict over the concept of the SD1 car had already led to a reorganization of the Rover Board; after Ryder, Rover management at all levels felt extremely uneasy about their position in a corporation whose managerial instability was becoming notorious. The imminent crises of management which the corporate industrial relations chief identified in his review in 1973 became reality in the Rover Company in 1975.[14] Perhaps the best way to convey the impact of the major blow which had been dealt to Rover's design capacity is to use the testimony of the managerial victims. One observed how, at corporate level,

> the theory I think was that it [the SD1] would require management with experience of volume production. And that really was criminal because what they proceeded to do, you see, post Ryder, was to take out the management [of Rover]—and it wasn't just at the top, they went right the way through down to even foreman level—they tore out the guts of the management really and they put in people from Austin Morris.[15]

Another Rover manager felt, post-Ryder, that

> they had been sold down the river. A and B [senior managers in Rover] had been made scapegoats. It was generally felt that it was a time for the Cowley [Morris] ascendancy. There was a basic tribalism in British Leyland and the Ryder Report represented the Cowley tribe coming out on top.[16]

This second major upheaval in management, following the earlier clashes over product concept in 1970–1, was disastrous for the commissioning stage of the SD1. What a senior product engineer required was,

> not that the decisions and detail have to come from the top, but making sure that the organisation is right, so that you've got a proper exchange of information and a proper manufacturing feed in at an early stage; to ensure that that happens, it's got to come from the top. You've got to make sure that you've got a set-up where people really will work together and do the job properly.[17]

The results of the Ryder reorganization produced the opposite conditions.

The problems of the traditional Rover management are best summed up by two advisers who were brought in to rectify them. The 'Liaison Engineer', brought in to the project in 1975 to co-ordinate the by now intensely fragmented product and production planning, described the Rover management as 'disoriented' by the whole experience. The removal of the person who was to be the plant director with just over a year to go before the plant opened, owing to his disagreement with the semi-volume production imperatives,[18] added to the alienation of Rover personnel from corporate aims and objectives. The result was that the SD1 project was one of the first occasions when BL called in an 'OD' consultant to try to rescue the by now seriously demoralized set of actors. The political pressures in operation, combined with the divergent goals and practices of the various engineering or other functional specialisms seen in Chapter 4, led the consultant to characterize the SD1 design process and the commissioning stage especially as 'haphazard . . . with no formal structure'. The series of team building workshops which he held at weekends with their focus on clarifying personal and group objectives came, as he admitted, too late.[19] As the Liaison Engineer had found, the only chance to change such fundamental aspects of the design process comes at the outset, not during the commissioning stage.

Production facility

At first sight the Ryder Report, which provided the basis for BL's rescue from bankruptcy by nationalization, would seemingly have been to the SD1 project's benefit in that it endorsed the finance for the venture. As later BL management have confirmed, the final report of the inquiry team underwrote the volume concept of the SD1 car. The team assumed that there would be market growth with a future increase in European sales by 25 per cent. The scale and capacity of the plant would remain as the corporation had originally conceived. Instead of using the opportunity to revise the original projections, given the impact of the recent oil price rises or the difficulties being experienced by the SD1 project, the report backed up the corporate intentions. Indeed, the team relied on figures supplied by BL. As Dan Jones rightly observes, the Ryder Plan not only legitimated these very optimistic forecasts, but it increased the problems for management by centralizing decision making and creating one large 'cars division'. The Rover Company's experience during the SD1 of a series of divisional reorganizations was clear indication of how 'management was already dangerously overstretched'. Moreover, the Plan was emphasizing the benefits of scale economies following from increased market share yet, without specifying the way to achieve these economies through increased productivity.[20] The operation of the SD1 plant would illustrate this point in a graphic way.

In the context of the managerial upheaval surrounding the Ryder Inquiry, the severe disorientation of those remaining with the SD1 project and the increasing cost/time pressures on the pre-production phase from late 1975 until the opening in June 1976, was beset by additional problems which arose almost daily. Many of the problem appeared as the deep inconsistencies between various aspects of the design process became explicit. The 'step-like' process had failed to identify and resolve these contradictions early on, with disastrous consequences for both the proving of the plant and its operation. In short, the difficulties facing those involved assumed crisis proportions.

The importance of pre-production to the design process can be illustrated by reference to past and present Rover/Land Rover practice. As Table 4.2 showed, for Rover production specialists, pre-production was a vital stage for them because of the way they usually received the product from the vehicle engineers largely unseen and needed to discover the details of the car and their implications for production. The main production planners who had used this gradual, iterative process of experiment and adjustment on the P6 and Range Rover intended to use this process and method again with the SD1 precisely because of the problems with the car prototypes and the uncertainties over the plant design.[21] Site visits to observe the pre-production operation associated with the 110 Land Rover model in 1983 reinforced the importance which both management and workers attributed to this activity. The stage is a critical one as all involved discover the implications of the previous work of others in the design process and adjust methods, tactics and expectations accordingly. Records from the Rover Company and interviews with those concerned indicate that these adjustments, even disputes, were regarded as necessary and commonplace. The so-called engineering and product 'mods' (modifications) associated with the P6 project were part of the rhythm of Rover's version of the design process.[22]

In the SD1 pre-production phase this rhythm was violently interrupted and its customary practices were unable to operate. The replacement of leading production engineers and managers by the new 'Leyland Cars' divisional leadership, who were dismayed at the SD1's delay and the specialist car background of the Rover engineers at the beginning of pre-production, raised major problems. Rover product and production engineers were already struggling to embrace the wide range of problems we have already identified. The way that senior production engineers were left with responsibilities for ongoing P6 and Land Rover production as well as their SD1 duties was inevitable, given the nature of the step-like design process involved. They had not been freed of current commitments to work solely on the SD1 in a separate multi-specialist project team. It is the considered opinion of those who observed this process at first hand that the 'difficulties overwhelmed them'.[23]

The impact on the pre-production phase was immense. Not only were workers and their representatives bewildered at the changes of the past year, but the alterations in managers and specialists threatened a number of key relationships.[24] First, there was a major shift in approach and technique involved. The words of a skilled pre-production worker were indicative of a resentment of the new management which was to grow henceforth. 'A [senior production planner] and B [his number two] were engineers, real car builders, and we had worked with them on the P6. We had great respect for them. We talked the same language. C [A's replacement] was a mass production addict'.[25] Similarly, the removal of the company industrial relations director to another part of the corporation took away the co-architect of the major social innovation which had run in parallel to the product and production aspects of the SD1 design process, the Protected Earnings Plan. Whereas the union had regarded him as 'very academic, with great experience of negotiations. Honest. Straightforward. He came clean on the changes', by contrast they felt, 'the management in the cars division were distant and indistinct'.[26] Moreover, the managers brought in to oversee the pre-production immediately clashed with the skilled workers over their radically different approach. A senior shop steward described the difference thus:

> they [A and B] did actually take skilled people off the [P6] track and put them into a purpose built area to go through the pre-production stage. So we thought we were going in the right direction. [After the new management arrived] their only concern was to push the cars through.[27]

The expectations of both Rover management and workers regarding the SD1 pre-production centred on their conventional proving and testing activities. In the language of both groups, once the snags had been eliminated from the prototype car, the flow line of the 'building process' was to be progressively developed, starting from a ten-work station line. The 'hour function' is worked out and then broken down into smaller and smaller cycles. The specifications and fit of the car are gradually 'proved' in the three month (ninety days) period before the plant officially opens.[28] Two weeks prior to opening (Day 1), 'body show' rehearsals of the complete new line are held in the new facility. In the SD1 pre-production, the pressures and conflicts involved meant that these expectations were not realized.

The main obstacles involved the characteristics of the car, the disputes which arose out of the new management–worker relations and the breakdown of component supply lines on which this part of the design process depended.[29] The need to resolve the basic engineering problems in the SD1 car meant that pre-production could not begin smoothly. As one worker put it, 'we should have been refining, not working out basics as we were'.[30] The acceptance by management of plastic components and the monocoque body shell, for example, led the experienced Rover workers to extend their disdain for what appeared to them to be a markedly inferior product which threatened to devalue the skills associated with their trades and their self-respect as craftsmen.[31] But it was the collapse of previously hard-won agreements and accepted standards under the formidable pressure to meet the opening deadline which angered Rover workers the most. Those who had struggled to bring about the programme of reforms contained in the Protected Earnings Plan agreement were incensed at the contravention of the central clauses relating to the training of new workers (see below, 'Work Organization') or the provision for 'check studies' of official work and time measurement procedures. Their sense of injustice was intensified when, in order to try and meet the June target date for opening, union representatives had unofficially acccepted the need to, as one shop steward put it, 'throw away the rule book' so that the number of pre-launch vehicles could be completed.[32]

The example of the Rover industrial engineers illustrates the way preproduction was disrupted by the coming together of a variety of pressures embedded within the SD1 design process. The lateness of the issue of process specifications to the industrial engineers had already made their job difficult. When the process sheets were issued to the industrial engineers, in their first provisional colour and estimated task times, the shock was acute. They were forced to 'firm up' the times from a very under-developed form. Moreover, the IE Department was being stretched at the same time by the on-going task of converting existing piece-work arrangements to measured day-work between 1971 and 1975, associated with the PEP. They were doing so without the benefit of a complete corporate IE function, so that in 1973 they were working without a central IE manual (the eventual manual of 1978 is notable for the way it extols the notion of close collaboration between production and industrial engineers at a series of points).[33] The industrial engineering staff also felt isolated and excluded from the design process in so far as their responsibility for the detailed organization of work was concerned. The IE function was demoralized by the successful union opposition to time studies on preproduction and related assessment. An IE section leader recalled how:

on twelve different occasions we went on to the shop floor only to be ordered off by the management and we had stood about enough of this. Our union representatives had gone in, of which I was one, and no way could we get back in. Each time we were ordered off.[34]

The workers objected both on grounds of custom and that under these 'rushed' conditions they had no opportunity to mount 'check studies' on the IE's assessment as the PEP agreement allowed. The attempt by the IEs to time pre-production workers more directly led therefore to a series of stoppages and authority contests over the pre-production lines from 29 October to 13 November, when £3 million worth of output was lost.[35] The attempt by divisional managment to bring in contract IE staff from outside produced a dispute between the in-house work study department and the company. Even allowing for the relatively empirical style of Rover's IE department, the job cycle times remained loose and incomplete well into the plant's early operation.

Not only was pre-production further disrupted by breakdowns in component supply from outside the company, but the launch of the new car and facility was delayed for the same reason. The Leyland toolmakers' strike of April 1976 over pay differentials prevented the necessary tools being installed and put the launch back by four weeks. It appeared to the experienced Rover workers that the problems of supply breakdown which beset the P6 plant had still not been solved in spite of their many protests.[36] As the pressure intensified on the recently appointed management to meet a revised launch date, existing agreements were once again set aside, yet in such a way as to set up divisions among different sections of the work-force. The inducement of a raffle for a new SD1 offered to pre-production workers led to walkouts by P6 assemblers who felt they should be included.[37] The pre-production phase thus came to a close with 'loose' cycle times and task profiles which suggested major problems for the start-up of the new plant, a demoralized remnant of Rover management now working under only recently appointed superiors with little experience of speciality production approaches, and a work-force which was itself disorientated by the upheavals of 1975–6, in an atmosphere poisoned by suspicion.

Work organization
As the previous section has shown, the pre-production phase of the commissioning stage had many implications for both the general character of work organization as well as its detailed features. Whilst pre-production was the meeting-point for the product and production elements of the SD1 design process, where the assembly line and work cycles were run in an experimental way, there were two further contributory aspects of work organization which must be accounted for outside of pre-production: labour recruitment and job design.

The means of recruiting the shop floor workers for the new plant had an important bearing on the operation of the SD1 plant. The process was accompanied by an increase in inter-union conflict and a marked change in the character of the Rover work-force. It is necessary to recall that, although the Solihull joint union committee had welcomed the announcement of the increased need for labour during the establishment of the Special Projects Committee in the Autumn of 1973, they were also concerned about the méthod of recruitment and the introduction of new workers. Prior to the Protected Earnings Plan agreements, the traditional methods had relied heavily on local networks and both official and unofficial mechanisms. Work careers were long. Between 1971 and 1973 there were 220 officially recorded retirements, with an average career span of almost twenty-seven years.[38] Even in the early 1970s, after the influx of new labour to man the P6 line, 50 per cent of the Rover work-force still lived within the borough of Solihull or the immediate area. Kin-based recruitment networks reinforced the stability of the labour-force. An advertisement in 1972 is a good example of the company's use of family connections; it read, 'The Rover Company Ltd. Applications for Apprenticeship. Applications are invited from relatives of company employees who wish to be considered for apprenticeships commencing in August/September 1972'.[39] This gave the existing work-force its own character. A P6 paint worker described how 'there were husband and wife teams and sons, and they used to come to work arm in arm . . . You used to see families sitting together in the canteen'.[40]

Both personnel officers and union officials were concerned at the subjective basis of these practices, and in particular were anxious to officially regulate the means of recruitment and the method of induction in order to prevent abuse; hence the emphasis in the PEP agreements on systematic training provision.[41]

However, under the combined pressures generated during pre-production, management, after enjoying little success in attracting new workers, reverted to a version of the traditional practices. The task of supplying candidates for the plant was given to the largest union involved, the Transport and General Workers' Union. The senior shop steward who organized the recruitment drive described it thus: 'management wanted numbers, but they were unable to recruit skilled workers or car workers and so asked us to do the job. I ran the recruitment office in Broad Street and passed workers on to personnel'.[42]

But, given the dependent position of management and the friction between workers owing to the tensions within the pre-production phase, the recruitment process had three significant outcomes for the new plant. First, the TGWU was accused by the AUEW of discriminating against its members when recruiting workers in January of 1976. The disputes over the relevant 'spheres of influence' on the SD1 track continued intermittently through the opening and on to September 1977.[43] An AUEW official declared on 15 January 1976 that he believed that 'the company is reacting to pressure from the Transport union'. His charge is made all the more credible by the testimony of a TGWU steward who recalled the way they had not unnaturally used the opportunity to consolidate their position. He stated how:

the personnel department in this factory was at Transport House [Broad Street]. That's a fact. We had an arrangement whereby this factory was sewn up tight, lock, stock and barrel, and all the production lines, trim shop, paint shops and everything else. The company were desperate to recruit but they were limited in the choice of people that they could recruit because we sent them the applicants. We didn't say that any applicant that they interviewed had got to start—numbers of them were turned down—but they didn't have the opportunity of opening it up to anybody.[44]

Second, the lateness of the commissioning stage meant that management, with the large production volumes in mind, asked for more candidates than the TGWU office could handle. A senior manager stated in April 1976 that 'we are going to need thousands of new workers, rather than hundreds'. The result was that, given the delay over starting, many P6 workers left the company so that a large proportion of the plant's early work-force was 'green'. In other words, by 1977 it was clear that 300 of the 800 SD1 trackworkers were not only new to the company, but had never worked in a car factory of any kind before.[45] The threats which such 'green' labour posed to existing work arrangements and consciousness were quickly realized by the Rover unions. The problems which the hurried method of acceptance raised for future manning levels were as yet not fully appreciated. The third consequence of the haste which distinguished this phase was that the agreed 'training with rehabilitation' for either ex-P6 or new entrants to the company broke down and 'was never fully fulfilled'. Instead, the more experienced P6 workers found themselves given the task of training the newcomers; union resentment mounted.[46]

The third outside adviser brought in to assist the Rover management during the commissioning stage (following the Liaison Engineer and the OD specialist) was from the central industrial relations department. His experience with regard to the job improvement aspects of the SD1 project exemplifies the increasing problems which developed during commissioning, and which impelled management action, to the detriment of either the original corporate intentions for the SD1 or even the specialist concerns of the departments involved at divisional or company level. The question of the timing of interventions in the design process also arises.

Experience with a firm of management consultants led to the recruitment of a 'Job Improvement Adviser' by BL's central industrial relations department to help prosecute the series of job improvement experiments which followed the 1973 corporate industrial relations review (outlined above). The support given to 'participation' schemes by the Ryder Report appeared to reinforce the experiments.[47] The first task of this job improvement adviser was to assist the Rover management in the development of the intended job improvement aspects of the SD1 project which had been laid down in the concept and translation stages. The limitations of the central IR department's approach and the antipathy of production engineers to such alternative methods of working have already been noted.[48] Besides the Job Improvement Adviser being 'staggered' at the poor communications in the corporation, which resulted in his virtual isolation from almost every group associated with the SD1 project outside his own department, the resistance of production engineers to job improvement was unequivocal. In contrast to the impression given in the press that the SD1 was a breakthrough in participation, for example ('It is the first time that workers have been involved in all stages of planning'), the opposite was true. Before he became directly involved in the SD1, the adviser found that:

> The resistance was the crucial element . . . you would scupper what was going on [re: job improvement] by production engineering being sceptical about the whole process or wanting to know the return they would get before they went into it, or by production planners who would be sceptical in terms of the additional equipment that would be required.

The outright rejection of Volvo's model of group assembly was traced to the inability of conventional production engineering to even entertain the idea of the totally new component flows required.[49]

Yet, by the time the Adviser became involved in the SD1 project in June 1974, convictions held regarding production methods or the relative merits of the various experiments in new line arrangements (he had met with Chrysler and Ford engineers) were no longer directly relevant. He found that 'the problem was essentially that the project was disorganised', but above all, his room for manoeuvre was severely limited. As he explained, by late 1974, given the disorganization, 'the SD1's costs having gone through the roof' and the decisions made by the corporate finance in the light of BL's insolvency meant that his task was impossible. His main concern became the need to demonstrate that he had at least attempted some experiments. As he put it,

> I had missed the conceptual period. The boat had been missed totally because you couldn't actually make any changes: you had no time to do any 'run up' projects. The money was going out of control . . . that totally restricted what you could possibly do. One of my schemes was to run an experimental production line on the [existing] P6 which was the 2500 [car] down one side of the P6 shop . . . testing out and familiarising the shopfloor with the practices. But I was not allowed to purchase any more equipment: no more tooling. I didn't have a budget, so what could you do?[50]

He quickly realized that, as we have noted, the production engineers had already decided that the SD1 was to be 'a standard production line'.

The Job Improvement Adviser was reduced therefore, in his own words, to carrying out a series of minor experiments. He attempted a sequence of Holbar analyses on the work structure of supervisors on the Solihull site, given that it was widely recognized that their jobs had become increasingly ill-defined. A number of abortive attempts were made to establish staff consultation groups related to the envisaged form of work in the new plant. His experience as a participant in the commissioning stage of the SD1 led him to conclude that, rather than management controlling the design process, 'the wave of SD1 came over us and completely engulfed people'.[51]

II Operation

The operation of the new SD1 assembly plant from its opening on 30 June 1976 has been the subject of widespread comment both locally and within the car industry. The work of Chris Walder, an industrial journalist, apart, most attention has focused in a shallow way on the array of problems which developed. A far more coherent and sustainable interpretation of the six-year operating life of the productive unit can be built upon an understanding of the total SD1 design process. Without doubt, the plant evolved as a technical and social entity in its own right, as the account of the act of closure by Ahsan indicates, but the daily operation of the tracks came to embody almost every one of the relationships and conflicts which the design process had generated.[52] The schedule of crises, disputes and difficulties which any reconstruction of the plant's life soon uncovers is formidable. It is instructive to re-examine the operation of the plant in the light of the total SD1 project and from a processual perspective; this is particularly important when otherwise exemplary studies of designing, such as Abernathy or Miller and Rice, omit consideration of the final operating system.

The product
The 'start-up' of the Solihull facility is a clear example of the way in which the traditional and the new continued to collide and to fail to combine within the SD1 project. Part of the conventional Rover production management's recipe matched with the practices of the production engineers. Just as the process specialists regarded pre-production and the early running of the plant as a gradual learning and refining process so the plant management viewed the first six months as a period of adjustment. The latter group were used to waiting until the plant had run for two years while they learnt what the pattern of seasonal sales variations would look like. The early running of the Range Rover in 1970 is a case in point. Both the surviving Rover production managers and the workers who had been transferred from the P6 line had been tuned to such practices both from the P6's introduction in 1963 and through the modifications made in 1964.[53]

The approach of the recently introduced but now dominant managers from the Austin Morris areas of the corporation was quite different. As with pre-production, their major concern was to reach the high-volume output figures set at the concept stage, a concern which had now become a keen anxiety following the problems and delays during commissioning. Notions of slowly eliminating operating defects from car or plant, in the Rover manner, in order to establish the 'quality' and 'refinement' characteristics of the vehicles were absent. The early demand for the car was high, this being the first new Rover saloon for thirteen years. Five months after the launch, orders worth £40 million had been placed. A six-month waiting list developed and a black market for the SD1 appeared by July 1976.[54] The need to satisfy this early demand was strengthened by the announcement that the Leyland Cars division intended to enter the European market in the following March.

As management devoted great energy to meeting these output requirements, the unresolved difficulties related to the detailed engineering of the vehicle and production, left over from commissioning, remained. In complete contrast to the customary Rover approach, minor defects in the cars produced were not rectified in the plant but left to the dealers to handle. The previous method had, according to the plant management, 'meant delays with production workers spending valuable time on rectification'.[55] Apart from the negative effect on the long-time Rover owners who purchased the car, the new management's approach confirmed the worst fears of the 500 Rover car workers who had transferred from the P6 line. On 22 November 1976 a spot check showed that only 6 per cent of the output sampled was fit for immediate sale. An internal memo by the industrial engineers complained of the pressure on inexperienced managers trying to increase production as the financial threat of a major under-use of productive capacity loomed. The memo recorded how, 'we are pushing the car through the system . . . simply to give us good off-line figures, only to create a huge bottleneck [of unrectified cars] at the end of the system.'

On 25 November, fourteen track workers sent a letter to the Managing Director of Leyland Cars expressing their anxiety at the low quality of the finished £5,000 car.[56] In the following October the problems persisted, leading the plant shop stewards to 'press the Prime Minister to hold a public inquiry into the running of the £95 million Solihull plant'. They wished 'the government to get a team of experts to start a new system inside the factory so that production figures and quality can be improved'.[57] Those who worked in the facility agree on the scale and intensity of the problem. The testimony of a paint rectifier is indicative of management's anxiety and the shop floor response:

> We all complained. The figures [to be produced] were too high. You couldn't get quality with the 55 [units] per hour being asked for. OK for a mini, but not for the quality finish a Rover needed. Early on, paint defects appeared on the bonnet and roof. A clear problem. Yet they never stopped the track to find out what was wrong. As a result, 400 cars were put outside with the major paint defects.[58]

The concerns of the SD1 shop floor workers were well founded, and indeed, they pointed to the contradiction which had been at the centre of the SD1 project from its inception. In contrast to the crude, popular image of the 1970s militant car worker, the Rover labour-force was highlighting the ambitiousness of trying to produce a luxury car but in large volume; by using their knowledge from the P6 experience they drew attention to the danger in the production management's approach. As a senior corporate

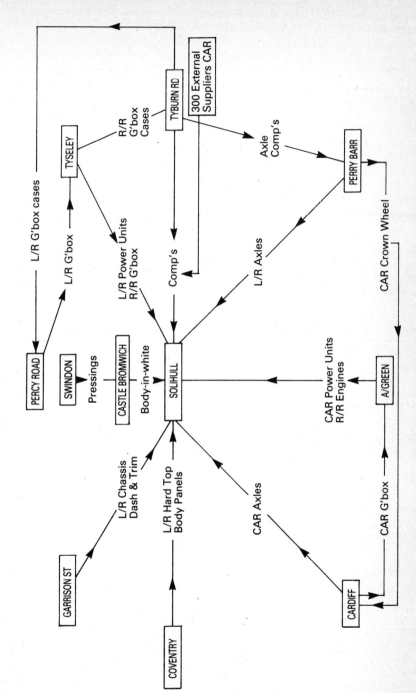

(L/R: Land Rover R/R: Range Rover)

Figure 5.1 Main inter-plant linkages in the Rover company.

sales and marketing officer had declared at the launch of the plant, 'Rover's name for quality is probably the best in Leyland Cars, and it is vital that we do nothing to jeopardise it. . . . What we need now is a steady supply of cars with guaranteed quality'.[59]

Unfortunately for the SD1 operation, the internal problems related to all three main elements of the productive unit during the concept, translation and commissioning phases meant that the odds against achieving the luxury/volume target would always be considerable. The external difficulties which confronted the plant from 1976 onwards served only to lengthen those odds.

Production facility
The external difficulties which confronted the techincal functioning of the SD1 plant were formidable: most arose from the malfunction of the larger fabrication cycle of which the Solihull facility was a part. The breakdown of component and material supplies together with the distinctive configuration of Rover plants were therefore major obstacles to the SD1 unit achieving its intended output.

The original decision of the corporation to retain the use of existing car body production facilities at Castle Bromwich rather than build an integrated SD1 production complex at Solihull meant that not only was the plant defying contemporary plant design norms, but it was also vulnerable to any breakdown of inter-site linkages.[60] The configuration of Rover plants which the SD1 plant inherited is shown in Figure 5.1. Table 5.1 indicates the geographical spread of the twelve main categories of components supplied to the Solihull plant. On 16 November 1976 the plant was nearly 20 per cent below the early production targets, owing to difficulties at the Castle Bromwich body plant. In January of the next year, body shell production from Castle Bromwhich was 80 per cent below target, with the result that the SD1 was only producing just under 400 units per week instead of its planned, 1,400.[61] In addition, the quality of the bodies supplied was inconsistent. An SD1 manager explained how:

> it was felt that there was a very good facility at Castle Bromwich, part of the old Pressed Steel Fisher Company, which traditionally had the responsibility for building bodies and therefore the site at Solihull could be given over to the assembly and painting and finishing; the bodies would be produced elsewhere because the resources were there, so use them. It was believed at that stage to be a logical transfer. [However] one of the major problems was the fact that frequently there were stoppages on the plant through failure of bodies to come through. What's more, when they did come, it was a case of somebody needing a hammer to quite literally bash them into place so they would fit, because the pressings were not absolutely correct . . . you found it again a source of anger and sheer frustration among the work-force.[62]

Management and work-force were equally irritated by the breakdown of material and component supply. The lack of reliable supplies had been a recurrent cause of concern during the whole P6 operation, and was a

Table 5.1 SD1 main component sources

1. Llanelli Radiators: radiators
2. SU Carburettors: carburettors
3. West Yorkshire Foundries: cylinder head and engine block
4. Rearsby Components: pressings and pressed assemblies
5. Swindon Body Plant: pressings and sub-assemblies
6. Oxford Radiators: air temperature control unit
7. Pengam: 77mm gearbox
8. Acocks Green: V8 engine
9. Bordesley Green: petrol tank
10. Castle Bromwich Body Plant: body-in-white assembly
11. Llanelli Pressings: seat frames and plastic items
12. Radford: rear axle

common problem within the industry. Component supplies, given the lack of action by Rover management to secure predictable flows from outside during the 1960s, also fell prey to a succession of pay disputes which occurred in the contracted electrical and engineering companies during 1975–77. In January 1977 internal component supplies from the Tyseley and Percy Road plants failed, while in October and November a five-week lay-off resulted at Solihull from the shut-down of the Radford rear axle production. By 18 November the company recorded shortages of components from: Lucas, GKN, AC Delco, Smiths Industries, George Angus, Rists Wires and Cables, Burman, Desoutter, J. Burns, E. Rose and Smith Clayton.[63] The 1977 Lucas toolmakers' strike was especially damaging. On 30 January 1978 one-third of the previous week's SD1 output was built without instruments. Three senior managers were forced to visit 'every firm which supplies Rover with parts—pleading for more prompt delivery'. The problems with those companies which supplied 'stopper' parts (major internal components for the vehicle) made for considerable rectification work, since 'the whole car had to be stripped down to re-introduce a stopper part'.[64]

If consideration of the problems connected with work organization in the SD1 facility are set aside for the moment, the combined impact of the malfunction of the fabrication cycle and the unresolved defects in the car and its design process meant that by 1977 and 1978, output targets were not met. At the plant opening, Leyland Cars announced a target of 50,000 units a year 'at least', consistent with the original concept of 'satisfying domestic demand' and selling the car throughout Europe. In the first months the high demand for the 3500 model led to an 'overtime boom' and into 1977 management looked to raising the current capacity from 1,200 to 2,000 per week. However, from April to October 1977, production ran at between 600 and 700 a week. It was observed in April how 'Leyland had hoped to be turning out more than 1,000 cars a week by now, but after all its production problems eventually settled for what is obviously considered a more realistic figure'.[65]

In December 1977 the introduction of the 2300 and 2600 variants of the main 3500 model raised passing hopes of running two assembly lines at the 1200 unit level. Yet, as the national sales figures show, the SD1 failed to increase its market share from the broadly stable levels of the P6, in the face of 'the increasingly capricious behaviour of consumers', post-1976. In 1975 and 1976, as the P6 was run down and the SD1 started up, Rover saloons took only 1.3 and 0.8 per cent of the British market, building up to 1.3 per cent in 1977 and 2.0 per cent in 1978.[66] Analyses in 1975 of the British car industry had shown that 'major penalties arise from excessive overheads and an inability to depreciate capital costs over competitive vehicle volumes'. The inability of production to reach 50 per cent of the plant capacity from 1967 to 1978 meant that these penalties applied to the SD1 *a fortiori*.[67]

The impact of the technical difficulties associated with the product and the Solihull plant on the work-force was doubly unfortunate for the project. A struggle to reach output targets, which many experienced workers considered inappropriate, meant that many workers resented the constant pressure to increase production at all costs. The pressure was exacerbated by the breakdown of supply lines. Workers who had complained in May 1969 on the P6 how, 'we seem to run out of components far too soon and too often. Surely better planning could offset this?' and how they had been laid off on sixty-five occasions in the past fourteen months due to supply breakdown, were dispirited at the failure to cure what seemed to be a continuing problem.[68] In November 1977 a senior Engineering Workers' Union official complained publicly of the consequent loss of wages while a TGWU shop steward spoke of the 'complete frustration among the men. It is chaos here'. The peculiarities of the detailed form of work organization in the SD1 plant became more intelligible when approached with an appreciation of the limitations imposed by the long-term tensions within the design process and the pressures generated by poor product quality and disappointing production levels.

Work organization
As in the case of the SD1 car and the production facility, the public image of the nature of work organization was quite at odds with reality. Reports, especially in the press, centred on the supposed introduction of 'the "group system" pioneered by Volvo', 'experiments to find means of getting more reliable output', the merging of the work of production and inspection, and how the plant was 'as well designed environmentally as possible'. The announcement in January 1977 that the plant had won the 'Factory of the Year Award', citing its 'superb working conditions' would seem to support the last point.[69] However, as has already been shown, the actions of production engineers and the previous unfolding of the SD1 design process already made the chances of the other quoted features coming to fruition quite remote. The production problems encountered between 1976 and 1978 made any resurrection of such ideas equally implausible.

None the less the essentially traditional arrangement of a straight assembly line with separate, sequential work-stations did develop its own distinctive features and attendant culture. These are explained by the continuation of themes and relationships from the preceding phases of the design process and their interplay within the turbulent environment of the SD1 plant. Before examining the details of work organization, an appreciation of the condition and motivations of the management and labour involved is required.

After the major conflict between the Rover Company and the new corporate leadership during the conception stage, and the sequence of restructuring which accompanied the translation and commissioning stages culminating in the Ryder reorganization in 1975, the lack of stability and continuity in the Solihull site management was apparent. It did not miss the notice of one motor industry expert at the opening of the plant, how there was 'one jarring note—because of the savage changes in top management during Leyland's last troubled years there will be almost no survivors from the original Rover team who first conceived the new car and factory'.[70]

The sense of disorientation of those who remained, combined with the inexperience of those brought in to manage the operation, meant that they were not well placed to meet the formidable difficulties which the new plant presented. Whilst Rover workers of long standing had little empathy with the newly appointed management, the standing of these recent entrants was further reduced by the turnover of plant management down to 1978. No manager apparently lasted beyond one year. Managerial control of production and labour especially was further weakened by the imperatives of 'cars at all cost', in the words of one SD1 foreman, whereby official procedures were set aside as managers tried desperately to meet production targets. Many of the informal understandings between management and union which grew up during the P6 operation were lost.[71]

The effect of the new yet unstable management of the SD1 facility on the plant supervisors was equally disruptive. The failure of the job improvement adviser to reform the work content of the supervisor, which was generally agreed to be slipping in the early 1970s, has already been noted. Yet it was the transition from Rover's long-held paternal style to the approach of the new management introduced during the SD1 project which undermined the confidence of certain supervisors. As one recalled,

> whilst you had a lot of respect for them [the Rover managers] it helped because everybody was interested in each other and their particular jobs. That started to die out when British Leyland really started to take over and the pride in the job went and it was just the numbers game, and if something was wrong with the car, well, dammit. ... The pressure was then continually on from management, where you got little or no backing, where you were expected to accept anything and the unions were that powerful and management that weak that we didn't know whether we were coming or going.[72]

The work stoppages resulting from component supply breakdown and hence the apparent lack of management control over production did not

help the supervisors' position. The OD consultant on a return visit to the
SD1 plant found the supervision 'fatalistic' and 'self-emasculating' in the
face of the plant's problems. Workers respect for the SD1 foremen was
further lowered by the practice, in common with other car factories, of
appointing ex-shop stewards to supervisory positions,[73] leading to the
inevitable suspicions of favouritism and partiality.

An example taken from the rectification lines (see figure 4.5) illustrates
two aspects of the character of supervision in the new plant. First, the
increase in scale of the SD1 operations and the problems associated with
production flow left ex-P6 workers bewildered at the lack of coherence
and contemptuous of the failings of management to remedy them.
Second, and most importantly, the shift from piece-work to measured day-
work, had of course placed great emphasis on the abilities of management
and foremen. Under the PEP it was the clear responsbility of management
to provide adequate materials and working conditions. An ex-P6 rectifier
sums up his reaction to the new plant thus:

> in the latter days [of P6], if you can imagine a small [rectification] bay
> producing with 38 painters on the end of the final lines, we had about
> 800 cars per week out—two foremen. These were the old Rover
> managers. We went to the SD1 and the new Leyland era and I ended up
> with 160 painters, 18 foremen producing less cars, in the 'modernest
> factory in Europe'! . . . On the old piece work system, the pool system,
> we had to get for instance 400 cars off between 38 men to get, say, £16 a
> week. The foremen stood back and the group then shoved cars on,
> shoved cars off. My main argument with the managers if the track
> stopped or if there were gaps in the track, it was actually the shop
> stewards on the shop floor that got production out to get the bonus up.
> Now from the situation we went into with measured day work was, I
> said to my foreman, after I'd worked with him for years, 'It's all yours
> now'. And so I sat back and got paid, rain or shine.[74]

Meanwhile, contrary to popular belief, the unions at Solihull were also
faced with a collection of problems posed by the new plant which
weakened their collective strength. It should be remembered that it was
only during the later operation of the P6 plant that a company-wide, joint
union body had emerged following the establishment of a comprehensive
union organization of the P6 plant. The recent growth of an official union
structure on the P6, though more soundly based than previous arrangements, was still reliant on the recognition and understandings generated
with the industrial relations management dating from 1969 and through
the PEP.[75] Indeed, the twenty-seven sections of what became the final
agreement of the PEP (published in January 1975) are indicative of the late
creation of a collective bargaining system in Rover by its need to cover and
define so many basic elements of formal procedures in the agreement. The
propensity for unilateral work group action remained during the P6's final
years from 1970 to 1976 in spite of the new institutional arrangements.[76]

However, as Rover management was replaced by Leyland Cars nomi-
nees, as the agreements within the PEP broke down in the run in to the

opening of the SD1 plant and as the number of green workers involved increased, so the problems mounted for the unions. As we noted during the translation and commissioning stages, the unions involved, especially the TGWU who were most directly concerned, had monitored the development of the car and the plant through both official channels and by using informal methods. Mindful of the volatile first years of the P6 tracks, the senior stewards planned their own shop floor organization 'to match the management zones'. Senior stewards' positions were allocated to the main areas of the SD1 facility, namely the track, final line, 'grey areas' (body marriage) and the paint shop. Other stewards were to be elected in the 'zones' within these areas (for example, there were six zones on the track, each one covering around a dozen of the seventy work stations).[77]

The crises and haste of pre-production, together with the erratic production of the first year meant that, with weak management and the PEP agreements and structures quickly falling into disuse, a version of the problems seen on the earlier P6 recurred in the SD1 plant. The new labour intake was a major destabilizing factor. At the simplest level, their inexperience of car plants made for difficulties. In the first months, new workers were continually getting lost in the huge (1 million sq. ft.) assembly hall, so that badges with a worker's name and section were issued. Sharp differences arose between the existing approach of the union officials and the almost 40 per cent of the work-force who were new to Rover. An ex-P6 steward of the Transport Union put the high incidence of small-scale arguments and disputes during the early years from 1976 to 1978 down to their 'inexperience'. He summed up their general character as 'everyone wanting to prove themselves; how tough they were in a dispute over cold bacon rolls'.[78] The attitudes of the new workers did not match the political consciousness of the ex-P6 stewards who had built their union organization during the widespread industrial conflict of the early 1970s. Involvement in the Saltley picketing during the 1973 coal dispute was followed by local campaigns against the Housing Finance Act and its raising of rents. Yet, in the SD1 plant, many of the new workers had not shared in these experiences, nor had they acquired the same convictions. Although such workers were noted for their spontaneous disputes around task-related issues this did not apply to wider political issues. In January 1977, for example, while the shop stewards adopted a policy of seeking pay rises outside the government's 'social contract', the work-force voted against a twenty-four-hour strike across BL in protest over the contract. The friction between the union leadership and the new sections is indicated by the views of an ex-P6 steward who pointed to their instrumentality thus:

we always did have that lump of labour that were there and all their interest was Saturdays and Sundays hours' overtime and doing the least they possibly could in their own individual interests [whereas he felt that he and his colleagues were] far more conscientious and involved and far more worried about what was happening in the car industry than some of the managers.[79]

After the inter-union disputes over recruitment and the erosion of the previous agreements and procedures, the well-known physical and social fragmentation of car work found expression in a growing sectionalist mentality. Not only was there a separation of interests between direct and indirect workers, between Rover workers and the SD1 intake, but the common tensions between areas of the assembly process appeared. The internal transport drivers were in a good position to observe the phenomenon: they noted on the one hand the suspicion of the track workers towards the paint shop crews 'hidden' in the adjacent paint plant, whereas, conversely, the paint workers were proud of their 'highly interdependent' work, where, 'the paint area was autonomous from final assembly and all else. It was our own world. We did our own thing'.[80] Sectionalization within the SD1 operation mirrored the problems, throughout the 1970s, in establishing a union 'co-ordinating body to cover all the Leyland car plants'.[81]

Informed by the condition of the plants, management and work-force, and hence their capacity to handle the contradictions of the SD1 design process as they unravelled during the new plant's operation, the form of work organization becomes more intelligible. An overview of work organization in the plant followed by an inspection of its detailed operation reveals that, as with the SD1 car and production facility, the organization of work represents a largely incremental innovation with few vestiges of the radical experiments it was intended to contain.

The scale of the 23-acre assembly facility and its three, 1,400 ft. long assembly lines (see figure 4.5) was certainly a major departure for the Rover Company. The innovative features of the paint plant have already been shown to lie within the three-floor arrangement of the paint process and its use of the electrodip process for the first time by the company. To those who operated the paint plant, the major difference was the introduction of semi-automatic underbody mastic application, 'surface' and final coats. Tinsmith repair, inspection and wet and dry sanding all remained manual tasks.[82] The monocoque car bodies were removed from the paint shop across a bridge to the assembly hall on a flat-bed roller conveyor. The bodies were then allocated to the assembly lines, where the main components were added (see Figure 4.5). Inspection points were to be sited at every tenth work station. The raised 'mezzanine' track (elevated 8 ft. above the ground) allowed under-car work and free movement of components from the main storage areas at the sides of the building. When the bodies reached the end of the assembly lines they were lifted by conveyor and turned 90 degrees, ready to be lowered on to the engine, transmission and axle assemblies which had been separately assembled. Final trim work (seating, etc.) was completed before the car moved through the rolling test bed, valeting bay and final inspection area.[83]

Although there were clear changes which affected certain occupations in the transition from P6 to SD1, the general character of work remained remarkably similar. The loss of the skilled manual paint sprayers, some undersealers and the replacement of the trim shop by buying-in parts was accepted by the trade unions at the beginning of the Special Projects

Committee: they set the loss against the overall increase in numbers to be employed on the SD1 and an apparent guarantee of future employment it represented. There were 2,400 direct workers, 450 indirects and 350 staff. Meanwhile, the division of labour and the general arrangements of tasks remained faithful to assembly line norms. As on P6, the progressive assembly operation relied on work group-based stations with up to twelve in a group. Broadly speaking, the assemblers' tasks were different only in so far as the detailed pattern of the body and its components were new.[84]

The much-vaunted experiments on job improvements and task re-designs, with one exception, never materialized. The plant convenor described the work in these terms, therefore, in August 1976: 'There is nothing different about this production line compared with any other line in the country. ... There is the same relentless pressure to keep up production', and it was noted by observers how, after two months of production, 'modified group assembly has still not been put into opera-tion'.[85]

An abortive attempt to conduct a small-scale experiment in job redesign on the front suspension sub-assembly section two months later confirmed that the mundanity of progressive assembly persisted. Union officials felt that what had appeared to be a possibility during the translation and commissioning stages, given the public statements of management and the loose arrangement of the lines during pre-production, was now out of the question as plant management struggled to meet output targets with no time for the radical alterations in working which the launch publicity contained.[86] Local commentators on the industry went back to SD1 project production engineers to seek an explanation. One senior engineer defended his ex-department's actions by pointing out how the line had been designed so that individual work stations could be split into a number of groups where workers could interchange jobs. 'So', he continued, 'if the present management want to run the factory in a different way, it is up to them'. Spokesmen for the division in 1976 then sought to insist that 'group production' was never envisaged, and rather that 'the chief concern was to make the factory as well designed environmentally as possible'. As they obliquely admitted, the problems of manufacturing a new car with a raw labour-force were formidable enough without the 'luxury' of experimenting with new production methods.[87]

An inspection of the basic induction, training, skill and task-related elements of line work in the SD1 plant, and how they emerged, will indi-cate how it was impossible for the original intentions for job improvement to survive. The way in which management continued the recruitment of workers in such large numbers in the first six months (e.g. 300 workers were introduced in the two weeks preceding 12 October 1976) had dire consequences for working methods in the plant. Management action in this respect was impelled by the need to raise output, clear the growing stock of cars awaiting rectification (there were 3,000 incomplete cars in November 1977) and 'staff up in anticipation of night shift working'. However, the ability of the plant to cope with such floods of workers, given the current difficulties in production, had the following results.[88] First, those already on the track were overwhelmed. A paint sprayer found it curious how they 'were crying out for labour on the SD1 in the summer of 1976. They said they needed sprayers, but when I arrived on the (paint) decks at first they had too many'. An industrial engineer who had been with the Rover Company for nearly thirty years was incredulous at the combination of green labour in such numbers and the additional problems they raised, apart from those related to the product. The work-flow broke down:

> When the SD1 started coming out it was a complete and utter shambles, cars going anywhere and everywhere. There was no flow of vehicles whatsoever; it was just an utter maze of chaos, and I'm not exaggerating. I had one manager who came to me on final lines and wanted to put in 50 more operators, to which I said 'Absolutely ridiculous'. And it was that bad, the situation, that even the shop stewards were saying 'No way can we accept more operators'. They flooded it, absolutely flooded it.[89]

The second outcome of such 'flooding' was that, as in pre-production, the formal training sequences which the unions had placed such store by when creating the PEP, never appeared. The previous inability to establish sound provisional job cycle times meant that large numbers of in-experienced workers had somehow to be trained and allocated to tasks at each work station. As a supposedly temporary measure, up to fifteen to twenty workers were grouped around each station to learn the job. The intention was to redeploy them on the other two assembly lines as they came into operation. Experienced Rover workers found that, in order to prevent this potentially serious threat to both their skills and their earning levels, the best option was to instruct the new entrants and to co-ordinate their induction themselves. Shop stewards, for example, requested that the process sheets from the production engineering and methods build phase be placed on the walls at the side of the track. As a result of management pressure for output and the induction of such numbers, training was reduced to *ad hoc* instruction overseen by supervisors within each zone. One supervisor on the assembly line found that,

> most of the time it was a case of saying to the guy, 'You'll have to go with that chap for an hour and then after that hour you'll be on your own because that chap is only doing it on a favour, he's helping me out by showing you while he's doing his own job'. It was as bad as that.

In the language of the SD1 shop floor, numerous 'domestic' (informal) agreements were made between workers and foremen over pay in order that some instruction could be given.[90] The third main outcome, there-fore, was that task assignments became distorted as workers struggled to cope within the heavily populated work stations and assembly operations were re-allocated amongst the group. Not only was the knowledge and dexterity of P6 work disappearing and safety being threatened, but as the station numbers and practices became commonly accepted, so problems were stored up for the future when management would try to tighten up on task profiles and manning levels.

The result of the entry of such green labour in the circumstances outlined above was that the character of work in the SD1 plant emerged not from the intended job improvement ideas, but from the customary, daily negotiations between workers and management on the shop floor. As union officials pointed out, under a measured day-work system the negotiations centred not on the rate for any particular job, since people now worked within five main grades, established on a plant-wide basis. Instead, attention under the PEP had shifted to the gradings of jobs, and especially the establishment of cycle times and conditions of work which critically affected workers' ability to meet the performance criteria on which measured day-work was based.[91] Freed from the responsibility of maintaining the conditions necessary for production to take place as under piece-work, and within the formally agreed principle of mutuality, workers met the high uncertainties and volatility of the SD1 production by attempting to shape their work through negotiation on the shop floor.[92]

So, while official reports spoke of three-and-a-half minute cycle times for the assembly line in June 1976, the experience of the IEs and shop stewards in the plant highlighted the way task times were continually changing, given their loose character in both pre-production and early operation. The fact that a dozen shop stewards had received basic training in industrial engineering as part of the PEP agreement meant that the traditional disagreements between workers and the plant IEs were augmented by competing specialist knowledge being added to the workers' side. The view of an IE section leader summarizes the importance of the work group as the locale for shaping the key task elements of time and method. In his words, rather than go via the foreman, 'we used to sell direct to the operator. Our argument was that it was strictly between the industrial engineer and the operator'.[93] The movement of workers between tasks, the manning of overtime assignments or the promotion of people to better-paid tasks (progression) were all bargained over according to the principle of mutuality.[94]

An indication of the limits of such shop floor negotiation in reshaping the tasks within the SD1 plant and its distinctive problems is given by the operation of such informal practices as 'backing' and the location of rectification work. At one extreme the unpredictable nature of SD1 production meant that workers' ability to reorganize their work was welcomed by management. An ex-'snagger' explained that, with the continuous problems with car body supplies and their quality, 'variations in working were vital'. Since 'a bad body means bad fittings and a poor pressing meant a poor fit' for components, 'lads did their own improvements: they worked out their own alternatives, experimented and ordered [screws and fixtures] from the stores. They rarely got credit from work study'. Time to conduct such exercises (or of course to use the opportunity simply to rest) was created by the common practice within the industry of working back ('backing') up the line and completing one's task ahead of the work cycle. A BL spokesman therefore defended the SD1 plant against the charge of a councillor who complained that fairy lights were appearing on the side rails of the mezzanine in November 1976, by referring to the acceptable practice of backing. He explained how 'the men have been doing these things in their own time, having done their work in less than the time allocated'.[95]

At the other extreme, the capacity to mount such informal redesigns of assembly working could not be co-ordinated on a larger scale, and especially not in the face of the SD1's production problems. The attempt by line shop stewards to establish the principle of rectification work being performed by each work group on the line (taken, ironically, from suggestions made by the Special Projects Committee) rather than in a separate area of the plant failed for two reasons. First, given the pressing need for major rectification work, the rectifiers from P6 were able to exert their influence to thwart such a move, and second, the uneven ability of work groups to accommodate rectification work meant that widespread support was not forthcoming.[96]

It is possible to use the preceding analysis of work organization to offer a deeper understanding of the volatile operation of the SD1 plant in contrast to prevailing accounts.[97] Most commentators note the high density of disputes in the plant, yet go little further than stating the outcomes and the immediate circumstances. While the walkout of 270 paint shop operators over 100° temperatures in July 1976 was widely noted, no account was taken of the long-term problems with working conditions in the company and the way worker expectations had been raised concerning the 'most modern factory in Europe' during the design process.[98] The experience of the P6 work-force in relation to the SD1 project has hitherto been generally unexplored and their many, to use their phrase, 'responsible motivations' have gone unrecorded. Clearly, the accumulation of grievances, and the addition of a sizeable influx of green labour, helps to explain some of the more spontaneous disputes. However, the major dispute over proposed night-shift working in September 1977 illustrates the combination of impulses involved. The way it was reported that workers apparently 'dismissed night working as unsound, disruptive to family life and a hazard to health' made good copy but misses the combination of issues involved. The Rover unions in particular were not merely reactive. Rather, it was their long-held conviction that the car would not sell in the numbers which the corporation forecast, backed up by their own monitoring of demand through delivery driver networks, which led them to oppose the scheme. In view of the SD1 experience and the way so many of the disputes can be related to the unfolding of the design process, it is plausible to suggest that the design process should be added to the model of multiple causation of conflict presented by Hyman.[99]

Without question, the rejection by the Solihull unions of the chance to join the new participation scheme covering the whole corporation, and the specific refusal to sign an agreement with the new Chief Executive in April 1978, was the result of their experience of the SD1 project.[100] However, in spite of a new plant management brought specially from the Triumph Speke works in 1977 and the radical rewriting of corporate strategy for the cars division by a new headquarters staff, the SD1 operation was unable to resolve its immense problems. In view of the large capital outlay made on the anticipation of such a major expansion in sales during the concept stage, the failure of the SD1 to improve on the Rover Company's traditional market share meant that overhead costs remained at crippling levels. As the Chairman of BL told the House of Commons Industry and Trade Committee on 4 March 1981, the Rover operation was simply unprofitable.[101] Given the capital cost of the project and the extent of the disparity between the envisaged sales and output of the SD1 and their real levels, there was little that the well-publicized corporate plan (of decentralized decision making, a 'product led' development and the unequivocal pursuit of the 'right to manage') could do to overcome such a basic financial contradiction.[102] The SD1 therefore fell prey to the policy of retrenchment which was central to the new corporate plan of 1979. With Rover body-in-white supplies switched from Castle Bromwich to the Oxford, Cowley plant in 1979 and Land Rover already a separate division within BL, the decision was announced on 12 May 1981 that the SD1 plant would close and production be switched to Cowley in March 1982.[103]

Conclusion

The SD1 project has proved a rich source of insights into industrial change in general and into innovation in the British auto industry in particular, but there are a number of features of the SD1 case which deserve highlighting. The attempt to understand a major episode in the life of the British motor industry which occurred in the 1960s and 1970s demonstrates the analytical potential of using the historical dimension. This involved setting the project within the immediate historical circumstances of the two decades in question, but also identifying the units of time appropriate to understanding specific features of the SD1 venture. The degree of innovation which the SD1 project involved could only be assessed by reference to Rover's history. The Rover business strategy evolved over the whole century and passed through a series of transforming events which were critical to explaining the relationship of Rover and British Leyland and its embodiment in the SD1 project. The differing rates of change between the Rover product, production process and mode of work organization meant the company was almost unique within the British car sector, and hence the degree of change which the corporate policy towards the SD1 implied, becomes clear.

The behaviour of Rover personnel during the project could not have been understood by reference solely to their immediate context. Their actions were governed by hidden, deeply embedded rules, some of which were laid down in the 1920s and which each generation of Rover personnel interpreted in the light of their own experience. The past did not determine the present; rather, past practices and events shaped and conditioned future actions. Nor does the history of the Rover Company confirm the view of those who see only immanent laws of industrial change in operation. The Rover Company operated in a market economy of a mature capitalist society which determined large areas of the behaviour of the business. Yet the way that relationship between the enterprise and the wider economy was experienced through time also owed a great deal to chance and accident, which should not be overlooked. It was apparent, for example, that in the crisis of the 1920s and 1930s, Rover could very easily have been taken over by Singer, or even have disappeared due to bankruptcy. But the discretion exercised by key actors and the highly subjective choices involved meant that Rover emerged as a viable specialist producer which continued to thwart the seemingly ineluctable long-term growth of large company domination of the car sector. Moreover, the scale of the upheaval which the 1970s represented for the car industry only becomes intelligible when set against the sector's long-term inability to develop corporate organization until the late 1960s.

Second, the comparative mode of enquiry yields great benefits. In spite of the much lauded 'world car' and the concern with the increasingly international nature of the auto industry in the 1960s and 1970s, the explanation of the British industry's character rests on first identifying its distinctiveness *vis-à-vis* other national car industries. The variety of productive units within BL, or across the sector, were distinctively British. It was the differences between the factor endowment, 'market characteristics', the relationship between industry and the state, company form, and the features of the labour-force which differentiated the British auto industry from other countries throughout the twentieth century.

In terms of the market, the contrasting development of product, production and work organization between Britain and the United States is readily explained. The growth in America of a mass consumer demand with a relatively uniform taste in the period 1900–20 led the early auto companies there to concentrate on a 'dominant design' of product, and to produce it in sufficiently large numbers via highly integrated, routinized work cycles, which in turn enabled a small number of companies to obtain the benefits of scale economies and corporate form. In Britain the converse was true. The market for cars remained socially fragmented for the first fifty years of this century: differences in social status and requirements made variety of product a virtue. Dominant design and standardization of the production process and organization of work were therefore slow to emerge. Similar differences emerged between the design hierarchies of the British and European auto producers. As a result, the shock of the arrival of the newly matured Japanese and Far Eastern manufacturers for the British car sector in the 1970s was far more intense than the earlier impact received from the emergence of the 'best practice' methods of the Americans.

The third main pillar of our research framework, the sector, also stands out as a key context for innovation. Those accounts of car work which omit consideration of the sector are therefore deeply flawed. The sector facilitates an understanding of innovation in a number of ways. The founding experience of the British auto industry, for example, with its reliance on craft coachwork techniques and localized engineering practices (e.g. the Coventry gang system) had profound implications for the development of production and bargaining forms. It also became evident from both interview and secondary evidence that the car industry is characterized by shared languages, constructs, 'recipes' and forms of knowledge. These may be 'taken for granted' and seldom articulated, but none the less they provide important reference for the action of individuals or collectivities at every level of the organizations involved. The design process is a case in point.

The fourth aspect of the research framework related to the enterprise. The example of the Rover Company and British Leyland confronts those theorists who conceive of structure in enterprises in the singular and as homogenous through time or across the levels of the organization. It became clear that the Rover Company alone possessed a collection of possible structures, a repertoire which was built up over its seventy-year existence. Not all its structures were brought into play at once. Instead, some basic structures, such as the set of relationships and capacities grouped around product design, were activated highly infrequently, with in some cases gaps of a dozen years between their activation. Other structures, such as the configuration of the relationships between production management and the work-force, were more continuous in their existence, yet receptive to the movement of the business cycle and the pulsations of the product market. The problems for a newly-formed corporation was therefore immense, not in merely co-ordinating a collection of companies but in coming to terms with the possible structures within them.

At the level of the enterprise, strategic innovation can be defined as major alterations in the portfolio of productive units and/or changes in their relative positions along the continuum of fluidity–specificity scale. Our extension of Abernathy's reasoning leads us to view the productive unit as composed of not just product and production process, but to include work organization. The study of British Leyland confirms that strategic innovation occurs by highly complex processes which involve all three areas. Moreover, projects of the scale of the SD1 may contain a combination of strategic, radical and incremental innovation involving marked differences in the way that change was perceived at the company, corporate or sector levels. As the SD1 project shows, the official design process was surrounded by many parallel processes moving along often quite separate trajectories. While the product design was being translated into a method of assembly, for example, between 1972 and 1976, the bargaining process over the employment contract which would hold in the new plant took place in relative isolation from 1969 to 1975. Corporate political conflicts around a new project are instances of other processes involved. Clearly, the four basic stages of the design process model (concept, translation, commissioning and operation) used in Chapters 4 and 5 do not offer by themselves a comprehensive overview of design and innovation. Rather, the usefulness of the device is in the way it can be used to begin to understand projects such as the SD1 and the degree of complexity involved; from the four main stages it was then possible to discover the abortive sub-phases, the problem-solving episodes which went through many iterations and the complete breakdown of key sequences within the 'stepped' process. The SD1 experience certainly demonstrates that the prevailing images of designing in the literature on the British auto industry require updating and thorough revision.[104]

The great stress which strategic innovation and its related processes place on the learning capacities of the enterprise would, from the experiences of Rover and BL, suggest that the view of Gregory is broadly correct. At least, from the point of view of the British car industry, major projects of strategic innovation such as the SD1 are rare, and there are therefore few organizations or people with experience of how to mount them; such 'major leaps' have a low success rate. It is less surprising, then, that companies such as BL should look elsewhere in the 1980s, and especially abroad, to acquire the knowledge and capacity to mount such operations. This is the case with the replacement model for the SD1, code-named the XX.[105]

There are a number of findings from studying the SD1 which require further emphasis. In the broadest sense, most studies of industrial change, often retardation, in Britain have typically focused on specialist areas of concern: for example, the examination of Britain's industrial relations 'system' or the relationship of science and industry. Few have drawn attention to the design process and the design and innovation capacity of organizations. Yet studies of the most successful corporations (in market terms) in the American economy show that the ability to mobilize resources and achieve the economies of co-ordination necessary for strategic innovation is a vital tool for survival. This ability has become even more salient as Japanese 'best practice' requires that major innovations across productive units should occur with increasing cyclical speed, and that all functions within an enterprise should consider designing a legitimate part of their activity.[106]

The design process is also of great value for the study of industry, even if the majority of social scientists give it little attention. In periods of industrial conflict, industrial relations experts have found that many relationships and previously submerged social patterns come to light. The same is true, by analogy, of the design process and its enormous risks. The range of BL's capacities, practices, values and modes of behaviour which the study of the SD1 project opened up, is highly illuminating and could be applied in similar contexts elsewhere. In contrast to recent emphasis in the labour process debate, it is the limitations of managerial knowledge and control in relation to innovation and the total design process which stand out from the SD1 experience. The continuing difficulty in commodifying space and time, or the dissipation of the Rover design capacity as a result of the fragmentation connected with the managerial division of labour are two important examples. The more recent development of the concept of 'productionizing' by Austin-Rover represents a clear attempt to resolve those problems associated with both the SD1 and earlier AD088 projects.[107]

As was shown in Chapters 4 and 5, the design process can be a change process with large degrees of uncertainty. The competing priorities and perception of those involved stand out. In such a process of change the 'design space' is not occupied solely and unilaterally by management; indeed, the process becomes an opportunity for interested groups to achieve a number of ends. These may include the chance to define status, to reshape power relations, or selectively to interpret major corporate policy intentions; unintended consequences abound. As Siedler notes, after studying the Ford Motor Company (renowned for its mechanistic planning procedures), 'the development of a new car is an infinite succession of compromises, a process of evolving priorities'.[108] Existing accounts of the auto industry, while examining many of the features of an enterprise which are relevant to the design process, ignore its detailed operation.

The SD1 project also shows that innovation is not the sole preserve of a single individual or group. In fact the design process may become fractured and fragmented by the operation of contest, struggle and conflict between the range of people who seek to use it; these contests are arguably as important to the labour process as those which occur only on the shop floor. Nor should the role of labour be mistakenly seen as reactive and negative, an image which is shown to be quite inappropriate, given the activity of the Rover work-force. The identification of the full pattern of involvement in design and innovation should involve, therefore, an awareness of the cultures which co-exist within the enterprise and their means of reproduction. The need to examine the mediating factors involved which derive from the sector or the wider society, or the way in which the SD1's image bore only slight resemblance to reality, make the design process especially relevant to industrial change. The changes forecast for product markets, and their implications for future forms of production, put together with the findings of our research, leads us to one further conclusion. As the design process increasingly becomes the object of managerial scrutiny, so should it command the attention of academic research.

Notes

1. Cf. E. J. Miller and A. R. Rice, *Systems of Organization: The Control of Task and Sentient Boundaries*, 1967, pp. 146–57.
2. Interview I with BL liaison engineer, p. 6.
3. Interview with Rover facility engineer, TI 792.
4. See Chapter 4, Note 67.
5. Interview II, with ex-snagger worker on P6 and SD1, p. 3.
6. In loc. cit., p. 4; interview with liaison engineer I, pp. 14 ff.
7. Interview with SD1 product engineer, pp. 11–13.
8. S. King and P. Turner, 'Rover at Seventy', *Motor*, 26 June 1974, pp. xxxii.
9. 'Notes for Consideration re Presentation on Rover Triumph to Don Ryder Team: Divisional Personnel and Staff Planning Aspects', 31 December 1974, Rover Archive.
10. 'Summary of Rover Triumph Top Management', in loc. cit.
11. *British Leyland: the Next Decade. An Abridged Version of a Report Presented to the Secretary of State for Industry by a Team of Inquiry led by Sir Don Ryder*, HMSO, 1975, p. 44.
12. Interview with SD1 product engineer, p. 16.
13. Interview with senior Rover IR officer, p. 12.
14. British Leyland's Industrial Relations Policy 1973 Onwards, 31 July 1973, Section 6, 'Problems of Managment', *passim*.

15. Interview with senior Rover IR officer, p. 12.
16. Interview with Rover job improvement adviser, TI 790,.
17. Interview with senior Rover product engineer, p. 12.
18. Interview III with liaison engineer, p. 3.
19. Interview with SD1 OD (Organization Development) consultant, pp. 2–4.
20. *British Leyland: the Next Decade*, pp. 2 and 4; *Birmingham Post* and *Mail News* Archive, Rover Section, 28 Colmore Circus, Birmingham (hereafter BMNA), 30 August 1974; M. Edwardes, *Back from the Brink: An Apocalyptic Experience*, 1983, p. 34; D. Jones, *Maturity and Crisis in the European Car Industry: Structural Change and Public Policy*, 1983, pp. 33 and 47.
21. Interview with senior production engineer, pp. 2–5.
22. Rover Company Directors' Minutes (hereafter RCDMins), Rover Archive, 1961, p. 154; 1963, pp. 347, 353 and 365.
23. Interview with Rover job improvement adviser, TI 231 and 256, senior Rover production engineer, p. 16 and corporate job improvement adviser, pp. 16–18.
24. Interview with senior P6 and SD1 shop steward II, p. 4. Stewards are TGWU unless otherwise stated.
25. In loc. cit., p. 3.
26. Interview with ex-snagger worker on P6 and SD1, III, p. 3.
27. Interview with senior P6 and SD1 assembly shop steward, I, TI 443–50.
28. Interviews with: senior P6 and SD1 shop steward, II, p. 3 and III, p. 1 and Rover facility engineer, TI 725 and 828.
29. Design, translation and commissioning of the SD1 plant was carried out under contract by a specialist paint technology company. Interview with senior contract manager in the paint technology contractors, p. 470. See Contract for SD1 Paint Plant at Rover Factory Solihull, 11 May 1973, between Rover Triumph British Leyland UK and X Engineering Company Limited, pp. 1–271.
30. Interview with ex-snagger worker on P6 and SD1, III, p. 3.
31. Op. cit., p. 1.
32. Interview with senior shop steward for Land Rover and P6 operations II, p. 22.
33. See BL Central Training Services, IE Manual, A1, 3.11 and *passim*. See also BL, 'Personnel Policies and Planning. Manual of Personnel Aspects of Project Development', January 1978, Ref. Code 100–00, p. 4 and *passim*.
34. Interview with Rover IE section leader, pp. 19 and 22.
35. BMNA, 29 October, 10 and 13 November 1975.
36. In loc. cit., 7 April 1976. Interview with senior Rover IR officer, pp. 13, 73–4.
37. BMNA, 16 June and 1 July 1976.
38. R. Whipp and P. A. Clark, 'A Car Plant for the '80s', Work Organization and the British Car Industry, Work Organization Research Centre, Aston University, October 1984, pp. 110–12.
39. *Rover News*, Rover Archive, January 1972, p. 7.
40. Interview with P6 and SD1 paint rectification worker, p. 6. See also interviews with SD1 stacker truck driver, p. 2 and ex-Rover production manager, p. 2.
41. Interview with ex-Rover personnel manager, pp. 26 and 30. For the best summary, see Memorandum of Agreement, British Leyland Cars, A Collective Agreement for a Protected Earnings Plan, Rover Plants, January 1975, Rover Archive, Section B.4, 'Training and Re-Training'.
42. Interview with senior P6 and SD1 shop steward II, p. 4. Cf. RCDMins, 27 June 1963 and 24 June 1968.

43. BMNA, 15 January 1976.
44. Interview with senior shop steward for Land Rover and P6 operation.
45. In loc. cit., and BMNA, 9 September 1977 and 29 April 1976.
46. Interview with senior P6 and SD1 shop steward III, pp. 1 and 4.
47. See Chap. 4, Section III, 'The translation stage'; British Leyland: the Next Decade, pp. 8 and 37–40.
48. See Chap. 4, in loc. cit.
49. BMNA, 30 June 1976; interview with Rover job improvement adviser, TI 105 ff., 124, 142 and 158.
50. Op. cit., TI 112, 305, 460 and 325–40.
51. Op. cit., TI 479, 500, 560, 585 and 660–704.
52. C. Walder, 'Decline and fall of the Rover empire', Birmingham Evening Mail, 8–10 June 1981; R. Ahsan, 'Solihull: Death of a Car Factory', New Left Review, 129, 1981, pp. 67–75.
53. Interview with ex-Rover production director, p. 2; RCDMins, 3 September 1970.
54. BMNA, 1 July and 4 August 1976.
55. In loc. cit., 24 June 1977.
56. In loc. cit., 22 November 1976.
57. In loc. cit., 22 October 1977 and 25 November 1976.
58. Interview with paint sprayer, SD1 paint plant, p. 2.
59. BL Mirror, Special Edition, 30 June 1976, p. 13.
60. G. Bloomfield, The World Automotive Industry, 1978, p. 35.
61. BMNA, 16 November 1976 and 19 January 1977.
62. Interview with Rover manager, p. 9. See also interview with senior shop steward for Land Rover and P6 operation.
63. See Chapter 3 Section V, p. 6: intended and unintended transformations; British Leyland: the Next Decade, p. 28; G. Clack, Industrial Relations in a British Car Factory, 1967, p. 14; BMNA, 8 and 18 November 1977. Cf. 'Investing for a successful future—engine manufacturing at Land Rover', in Automotive Manufacturing Update '81, No. 13, 1981, pp. 101–9.
64. BMNA, 30 January 1978; interviews with senior Rover IR officer, p. 10 and ex-snagger on P6 and SD1 III, p. 2.
65. BMNA, 30 June 1976; 27 April, 8 September and 28 October 1977.
66. In loc. cit., 2 December 1977; K. N. Bhaskar, The Future of the UK Motor Industry, 1979, p. 169; S. Sinclair, The World Car: The Future of the Automobile Industry, 1983, p. 10.
67. The Future of the British Car Industry: Report of the Central Policy Review Staff, 1975, pp. 75 and 94; K. N. Bhaskar, The Future of the World Motor Industry, 1980, pp. 48, 53 and 76; BL's Industrial Relations Policy, 1973, p. 19.
68. Whipp and Clark, 'A Car Plant for the '80s', Chap. 3, p. 104. An external consultant's report in 1970 found the following production record:

	1966–67	1967–68	1968–69	1969–70
Actual production as % of targets	86	76	65	76

69. BMNA, 6 September 1975, 26 August 1976 and 21 January 1977. The award was made by the Business and Industry Panel for the Environment.
70. J. Jackson, motoring correspondent of the Sunday Times, as quoted in BMNA, 27 June 1976.
71. Interviews with: foreman on SD1 No. 1 main assembly track, TI 145; SD1 OD consultant, p. 15; paint rectification shop steward, p. 12 and SD1 track worker (cross members), p. 2. BMNA, 13 March 1979.

72. Interview with IE section leader, p. 15.
73. Interviews with: SD1 OD consultant, p. 18; SD1 paint sprayer, p. 2. For a careful account of the foreman's job, see 'A Report on the Methods of Vehicle Sub Assembly at East Works', Solihull, No. 50001, Appendix 12, September 1976. The SD1 plant was known on site as the East Works. The managerial hierarchy in the P6 and SD1 plants went from the Plant Director responsible for the Solihull site down to the manufacturing managers of Land Rover, Range Rover, P6 and SD1: under each manager came the superintendent, foremen and junior foremen.
74. Interview with ex-P6 and SD1 paint rectifier, p. 10. On the SD1 assembly line there was one foreman to seventy workers, with two shop stewards.
75. See Chap. 3, Section V, 'P6: intended and unintended transformations'.
76. See Note 41, A Collective Agreement for a Protected Earnings Plan. The twenty-seven sections include: Trade Union Functions, Use of Work Standards, Effective Employee Resourcing, New Recruits and Sickness Benefit Scheme.
77. Interviews with senior P6 and SD1 shop stewards, II, p. 3 and final line shop steward, p. 1.
78. Interview with ex-P6 rectification steward, p. 1.
79. Whipp and Clark, 'A Car Plant for the '80s', p. 123; BMNA, 29 January and 15 April 1977; interview with rectification steward, pp. 3 and 11. See Ahsan, 'Death of a Car Factory', pp. 67, 70, 72 and 75.
80. Interviews with internal transport driver, p. 1 and paint sprayer, p. 2.
81. BMNA, 12 July 1977. The BL Unions also wanted the sixty manual pay bargaining units covering thirty-seven plants to be covered by an annual wage agreement negotiated on a common date. Cf. Ahsan, op. cit., p. 71.
82. Project Solihull (ND BL News Services 1976?) 'The Paint Plant'; interview with SD1 paint sprayer shop steward, pp. 1 and 2.
83. Project Solihull, 'assembling the cars'.
84. Interview with senior P6 and SD1 shop steward, I, pp. 4 ff.
85. BMNA, 26 August 1976; interview with SD1 industrial engineer, p. 21.
86. A Report on the Methods of Vehicle Sub Assembly, Summary of Recommendations, p. 8; interview with SD1 final assembly foreman TI, 455. Cf. Ahsan, op. cit., p. 69.
87. BMNA, 26 August 1976.
88. In loc. cit., 12 October 1976 and 18 November 1977.
89. Interviews with SD1 paint sprayer, p. 1 and SD1 IE section leader, pp. 18 and 25.
90. Interviews with SD1 supervisor, TI 118–44 and OD consultant, p. 8 and SD1 paint rectification shop steward, p. 17, who described his experience thus: 'I went into work one morning [on the P6] and found that overnight they'd just sent the people over on to the brand new car [track] . . . So there was no real training, we trained our own people. There was no sort of place where we all went away to be trained in the new paint or the new car; we actually went over there and found out by our mistakes—trial and error.'
91. The grades and rates per hour were as follows: Grade A, £1.5425; B, £1.4890; C, £1.4358; D, £1.3825; E, £1.3290 (A Collective Agreement for a Protected Earnings Plan, p. 34). The main occupations found in each grade on the SD1 were: A, auto-electrician, pattern makers, maintenance; B, paint sprayers, floaters, rectifiers; C, assembly track workers, engine dress, trim shop; D, labourers, storekeepers; E, cleaners.
92. A Collective Agreement for a Protected Earnings Plan, pp. 41, 47 and 48. Section 1.h of Appendix 5, entitled 'Industrial Engineering' states, 'When-

ever there is a change in the production schedule or production requirements, tasks may have to be re-assigned and work re-allocated. Such changes
will be explained to the employees and mutually agreed.'

93. Interviews with senior P6 and SD1 assembly shop steward, TI 230; IE section
leader, pp. 19 20 and 24. Cf. BL Training Services IE Manual, A1.6110, p. 2.

94. Interview with senior shop steward for Land Rover and P6, p. 21. BMNA, 16
January 1978.

95. Interviews with SD1 foreman, TI 124; senior P6 and SD1 assembly shop
steward, TI 327; ex-snagger worker on P6 and SD1, II *passim*. BMNA, 16
November 1976. I am indebted to Paul Willis of the Centre for Contemporary
Cultural Studies, Birmingham University, for the chance to listen to his interviews with SD1 workers and their parallel accounts of such informal practices. On the ability to 'flimpse' (fiddle) task arrangements, see interview with
SD1 paint rectification shop steward, p. 18.

96. Interviews with ex-P6 and SD1 senior shop steward II, p. 4 and Rover facility
engineers, TI 118 and 474.

97. G. Robson, *The Rover Story*, Chap. 12, pp. 149–59; K. N. Bhaskar, *The Future
of the UK Motor Industry*, 1979, pp. 87–8.

98. BMNA, 7 and 8 July 1976 and 28 June 1977.

99. In loc. cit., 8, 9 and 17 September 1977. Interviews with senior P6 and SD1
shop steward, III, p. 3 and SD1 final assembly steward, p. 2. Note the use of
car delivery drivers' knowledge of the monthly sales levels of the SD1 by the
plant work-force. The night shift dispute also produced an unusual alliance
between the TGWU and the IE department when they drew up a 'continental'
working system alternative based on a seven-day week (twelve hours a day
for three days) with slip relief. The continental system meant that Saturday
working, which BL's component supply pattern could not accommodate. R.
Hyman, *Strikes*, 1972, pp. 120 and *passim*.

100. BMNA, 31 August and 21 September 1977, and 26 April 1978.

101. Interviews with: senior Rover production engineer, p. 18; senior Land Rover
and P6 shop steward, 27–8 and 32, and P6 and SD1 assembly shop steward,
TI 386, pp. 421–84; Edwardes, *Back from the Brink*, pp. 60, 62, 64, 87 and
184; Jones, *Maturity and Crisis*, p. 48; Edwardes to *The House of Commons
Industry and Trade Committee, Finance for BL*, 1981, p. 79.

102. Walder, 'Decline and Fall of the Rover Empire', *Birmingham Evening Mail*,
10 June 1981. In 1976 the SD1 took 0.5 per cent of the British market; in its
first full year of production, 1977, 1 per cent (14,200). Its peak was reached in
1978 with 2 per cent (31,500). The figures for 1979 and 1980 were 1.75 per
cent and 1.6 per cent respectively. See Note 101.

103. Walder, in loc. cit.

104. See R. Whipp and P. A. Clark, *A Car Plant for the '80s*, Chap. 3, Section IV.

105. S. Gregory, 'Large Technological Projects', mimeo., Aston University, 1983;
'Project xx Work Shared', *The Engineer*, 20 January 1978; E. Fiddy, J. G.
Bright and R. Hurrion, 'See—Why: Interactive Simulation on the Screen',
Automotive Manufacturing Update '81, No. 13, 1981, pp. 168–71.

106. We are grateful to W. Abernathy for this finding, based on his experience in
Japan in 1981–2.

107. Interview with senior AD088 project member, p. 9.

108. E. Seidler, *Let's Call it Fiesta*, Lausanne, 1976, as quoted in S. Sinclair, *The
World Car: The Future of the Automobile Industry*, 1983, p. 10.

PART III

6 Conclusions

Introduction

Four key themes are highlighted in this final chapter:

— a summary of the refinements and revisions made to the innovation perspective of Abernathy;
— an examination of the typicality of the SD1 case study and the implications for comparisons of that case with other major change programmes in the automobile industry;
— the implications of that analysis for the evolvement and application of computer-based design technologies such as those being introduced by General Motors;
— the defining features of the orientation taken in this study of automobile industry.

The four themes are designed to highlight the specificity of particular car industries and to demonstrate the generality of our analyses.

The previous three chapters have provided a detailed and contextualized analysis of strategic innovation in a European car firm. That reconstruction was designed to provide a comparison to the seminal analysis of the American industry by Abernathy[1] in his detailed, longitudinal analysis of innovation, with particular reference to the case of the Ford Motor Company. In this final chapter we return to themes introduced in Chapters 1 and 2 to emphasize the ways in which Abernathy's focus has been taken as that point of departure.

It will be recalled that Abernathy contends that the American auto industry achieved a design hierarchy which permitted the corporate leaders to pursue policies of high-volume production in which annual styling changes could be superimposed on mass produced components whose unit costs were progressively reduced by narrowly focused technological innovation in the production process. Abernathy recognized that these features and practices represented an implicit corporate strategy, yet did not examine the tractability of those strategies. Instead, it was suggested that the strategies could be redirected to cope with the technological ferment[2] which arises from the impacts of micro-electronics on the design and production of cars. The central problem which Abernathy neglected is that of strategic implementation. How does a major car firm adjust the multiplicity of internal and external interdependencies it is involved in? This question can be sharpened by examining strategic implementation outside the American context. We have taken the case of British Leyland to demonstrate the size and scope of the problem of corporate adjustment.

This final chapter summarizes the refinements and extensions which are necessary for an adequate understanding of the problems of innovation in the manner initiated by Abernathy. The summary is then briefly applied to a speculative analysis of the problems of the British-owned automobile industry as compared with other international firms. Attention is then given to the intention by General Motors to use the new computer-based design technologies to obtain a competitive advantage over their international competitors—especially the Japanese. Certain features of that programme are examined, especially the assumptions about corporate cultures and the potential for innovation. Finally, a short section summarizes the core themes of our analysis.

I Abernathy's interpretation: elaborations

Prior to Abernathy's various studies of the automobile industry, the dominant tendency was to treat innovation as a dramatic process of creative reconstruction which tried to satisfy the uncertain demands of the American consumer. Abernathy's interpretations sought to replace this drama by identifying the precise forms and degrees of innovativeness in the American automobile industry and to critique the orthodox conception of best practice held by both corporate leaders and by the highly influencial 'voice' of the business schools, the media and the specialist journalists.

Abernathy apart, previous analyses had tended to treat strategic and radical innovations as separate and exceptional features. That orthodoxy had a number of advantages, and most obviously in the giving of a defined and delimited focus to certain problems. However, the segmental approach to innovation seriously understates the extent to which strategic innovations operate across a configuration of three major facets: the product, the processes and facilities, and the work organization at all levels. Also, these general features operate uniquely in any given corporate culture.

The distinctive contribution of Abernathy was to show that in American automobile firms there was a narrow yet distinctive variety of managerial strategies. It seems that there is an 'American System of Organizing'[3] in which the pace and locations of innovation in the product and in the processes of manufacture are synthesized and matched very closely to the dominant pattern of the North American markets. The market has been pliable for the major corporations and also these corporations were able—until the 1970s—to supply the styling and imagery which the North American consumer preferred. There can be little doubt that the media of film, television and radio choreographed an environment in which the American car was a central adjunct to every social activity—courting, travel, crime, vacations, location of homes and entertainment.[4] Equally, the symbiotic relationship between Motor City, American culture, and high standards of living provided a self-enclosed world. Reflection on the events of the past two decades shows quite clearly that American 'best practice' is not necessarily appropriate for the Japanese and European contexts. Rather, the diffusion of that best practice requires considerable revision and re-invention by the adopters.[5]

Following Abernathy, we have argued that innovation should be seen as a central part of the normal rhythm of activities required from an automobile firm which intends to survive. Corporate cultures and structures must possess a repertoire which can simultaneously cope with

1. the ongoing routinized production of cars for the known and existing markets;
2. envisaging and designing new cars some five to ten years ahead of their actual requirement by the public;
3. routinely and continuously modifying existing cars and their modes of production and selling on the basis of learning from experience and from the consumers' experiences as users;[6]
4. translating new concepts of the car, its modes of assembly and work organization;
5. commissioning and operating new forms of production whilst also phasing out previous forms.

These five areas were implied in Abernathy's analysis. Because of their practical consequences for corporate adjustment, the five aspects of the repertoire required detailed attention beyond that which Abernathy's uncompleted investigation of innovation had achieved.

One basic problem facing any corporate culture is to develop the multiple structures and cultures for obtaining efficiency in the ongoing operating systems whilst simultaneously developing a design capacity in the more future-orientated segments. Another facet of that basic problem is to achieve major strategic innovations across the three key dimensions of the product, the facilities and the work organization. Abernathy provided the best initial framework for examining innovation in the automobile industry, yet it was clear to him that this perspective requires extension and revision. We have concentrated on the organizational aspects in an attempt to extend and refine the initial framework.

Innovation is an organizational process—a capacity—which has to embrace and connect together numerous elements. For the purposes of exposition, our account focuses on the triangle of product, process/facilities and work organization. Most notably, the extension of Abernathy has situated the design capacity in its total contexts and has shown that innovation both requires its own special form of work organization and also is capable of producing new forms of work organization. It is in the area of work organization that the major extensions are required.

Work organization refers to all levels of the corporation, especially to the rich variety of corporate cultures which are required within the successful corporation. An essential feature is that there is a repertoire of structures and cultures. The theatrical analogy of a repertoire is useful. Most established theatrical companies create a repertoire by rehearsing the next production at the same time as they are giving an existing performance of a quite different play. Similarly, corporations have to live in a plurality of different time frames.

The American car firms adopt a highly segmented and specialized approach to innovation and design. Our interpretation, which draws on the analysis of knowledge technologies,[7] confirms and elaborates

Abernathy's claim that there are structural rigidities. His hypothesis would be that the institutionalized approaches to innovation are so routinized that any future adaptations would simply be refinements rather than radical alterations. Comparing the routineness of the social technologies is revealing, especially in what is known about the problems faced in the 1970s by the European operations of General Motors,[8] where it was some ten years before the adaptive process of adjusting to the emerging features of the European market and society were successfully encoded into a new form of top-level work organization.

The situation for the work organization of the SD1 case has to be examined within the European context. The differences from innovation in North America are marked. These differences may in part be explained by three features. First, the European context contained market characteristics which subdivided a population which was similar in size to North America into many regional and class-derived variants. These variants impeded the mass marketing and mass production skills of the large American multinationals, whilst inhibiting European firms in their search for international markets.[9] European car firms rarely possessed the capability of both developing the design hierarchies appropriate to their home markets and also gaining a significant market share in North America. The story of the small, successful Swedish firm, Volvo, is exceptional and instructive, particularly in comparison with British Leyland.[10] Until the marked growth of the European market in the 1960s and the incorporation of Britain in the 1970s, the American corporations were not as successful as their image would have implied. The American multinationals, alleged to be the masters of best practice in car design and manufacture, did not achieve 25 per cent of the European market until after 1985.[11]

Second, there seems to be a distinctive British approach to work organization in the automobile industry.[12] The SD1 project may be regarded as a very recognizable feature of what is typical in the British context. The case study of the SD1 suggests that the less formal British approach is at its most vulnerable when innovation accompanies the creation of a new corporate identity. This is because its segmentalism—which is similar to that found in American corporations—rests on informal, oral practices of communication whose construction and subsequent decoding require long periods of initiation for new executives. In particular, the fragmentation within the managerial division of labour[13] creates immense barriers to the free flows of important information. Moreover, these practices can inhibit the operation of an overall architecture of objectives which would give coherence to the bounded rationality of all the many sub-groups.[14] The SD1 project is a classic case.

Third, the effectiveness of the SD1 design processes has been questioned. This is the most contentious facet, because the narratives constructed by the critics[15] do not include significant suggestions of how alternatives might have been managed. If one asks the famous 'what if …?' question, then it becomes clear that the critics of British Leyland have failed to make sensible comparisons. For instance, if BL had faced the adjustment problems experienced by the European division of GM, then they would have been able to draw on all the resources of the corporation with its considerable wealth of human capital. Studies of GM in Europe show that their problems of adjustment were considerable.[16] Thus BL requires similar time scales and recognition of the enormous transformation involved in the conception of what is corporate knowledge.[17]

Abernathy's account of the Ford approach provides an excellent and revealing comparison to that of Rover and BL. However, in order to unravel and analyse the fate of Rover and BL it is necessary to make a more extensive treatment of

— the contexts involved;
— the fit between corporate decision making and the intended shift in its design hierarchy.

This was undertaken in Chapters 3, 4 and 5. These chapters provide the basis for further revisions to the Abernathy perspective.

Abernathy rightly goes straight to the core problem: what is the corporate strategy for innovation? The reconstruction of Ford's strategy provided important insights into otherwise hidden basic recipes and strategic formulae which informed decision making over several decades. The implication to be drawn from Abernathy[18] is that there was a corporate strategy which was controlled and steered from the top level.

Such an interpretation requires revision. First, from the perspectives of the top decision makers, the opportunities and threats are much more complex than Abernathy suggests. Abernathy unwittingly contributes to the image of the auto industry as monolithic and omniscient. Thus, even when the environment seems stable and there is a dominant design such as the roadster, there is still an external pressure and a mixture of internal drives towards discovering new competitive edges towards competitors. The Abernathy interpretation gives too little attention to the daily and seasonal problems of the market-place and the uncertainties which that generates. Second, Abernathy was insufficiently comparative. He correctly identified certain rigidities in the Ford approach to innovation, yet failed to discern that rigidities are common. What is distinctive about American car firms is the form which rigidities acquire over time. Abernathy successfully demonstrated that corporate cultures must achieve a design hierarchy appropriate to their context, and showed how the acquisition of this design hierarchy is also based on certain rigidities in forms of work organization. However, he did not fully explore how the differences in contexts between America and Europe imply different forms of work organization and different strategies of innovation. For example, the organizational systems or repertoires of Rover were very different to those found in Ford and GM, whilst also being equally rigid and equally difficult to alter when circumstances and intentions required an alteration.

Third, Abernathy seemed to assume that if a rigidity could be detected, then entire social systems could be re-scripted.[19] Our analysis suggests that the 'reforming' of large corporations might be suitably likened to the 'awakening of a giant'.[20] Abernathy correctly notes that a new script can be written down, yet he wrongly presumes that interpreting the new script is simply a matter of routine corporate training. The SD1 study shows that little can be achieved until the new script is learned systematically and then performed coherently. Abernathy's neglect of the human, social and organizational dimensions creates an analytical void in the understanding of the processes by which strategic and radical innovation is accomplished. Fourth, Abernathy portrays the corporation as detached from the surrounding regional economy and societal structure. The crucial facts of the regional context and infrastructure which permitted Ford to start as an assembler (cf. Rover) at the beginning of the twentieth century are omitted.

Fifth, Abernathy treats the corporation as a unitary, centralized entity in which conflicts and competition within the managerial division of labour were so minor that certain strategic recipes could be freely superimposed by the top leadership. Even if this is the correct interpretation of events in American car firms, there is a requirement to undertake further explanation and a deeper analysis. Otherwise, the interpretation seems to create a disembodied set of rules which can be openly applied in every setting. Because Abernathy concentrated on the American 'winners' of the competitive processes of the first seven decades of the twentieth century, he invokes an omniscience which, as Peters and Waterman demonstrate, is largely unjustified.

Sixth, Abernathy neglects the relationship between capital, management and labour. In Chapters 4 and 5 we have demonstrated that this set of relationships has a significant impact on the choices of new methods of working and in their implementation. Our interpretation has been grounded in recognition that innovation is an integral component in industrial relations.[21]

In addition to the revisions Abernathy suggested in the previous six points, it is important to extend his treatment of the relationship between design and innovation. We have suggested that design and innovation should be seen as required capacities in large enterprises.

There are two major ways in which design can be handled: either through the subcontracting out of design experience to a collection of specialist agencies so that design is undertaken through proxy, or through the establishment of an internal design capability. The case study of Rover illustrates each possibility. In the early days the designing was done by proxy, initially with a fair degree of success. Also, Rover's early attempts to establish an internal capability through P. A. Poppe's department were associated with considerable difficulties. In the four decades after 1932 the internal design teams handled the car design whilst leaving certain crucial facets of the design of the process to the large, experienced suppliers of basic equipment such as bodies, dies, assembly line equipment and paint plants. After 1972, British Leyland attempted to create its own total design capability, yet found by the early 1980s that they were having to subcontract key parts of the process to German and to Japanese firms. By the mid-1980s, BL's capability to handle in-house design and development had been reduced to a minimum level. On the other hand, in the same period there had been a sharp growth in the number of independent consulting agencies, each of which specialized in a particular sub-set of product design and in some cases in the overall process of strategic innovation.

Design and innovation are distinctive activities which are normally regarded as elements in the specialized competences within the managerial division of labour. Similarly, the activities of Research and Development were huge areas of growth in total numbers and in new in-house specialisms during the 1960s and 1970s. Since then, many corporations have reassessed their in-house specialists and have concluded that external agencies are a superior source of advice. This conclusion is largely based on the simple fact that external agencies specialize in *new problems* which require the learning of new analytical skills. The external agency experiences the new problems in a variety of settings and therefore has the best opportunity to shape the problems and to design novel, appropriate solutions. In an era typified by technological ferment in the product as well as in the production process, and therefore by implication in design, these agencies have a competitive advantage over in-house specialisms. However, as Kanter[22] observes, the successful incorporation of external advice requires considerable adjustment to the internal managerial division of labour.

II History, culture and design hierarchies

This section examines the generalizability of the SD1 study and uses the refinements to the Abernathy perspective to separate out those features which are least typical of the auto industry. This process of separation also provides a basis for a speculative exploration of the extent to which the SD1 project was an opening move in the shifting of the corporate repertoires of British Leyland to help create a new design hierarchy.

The logic of Abernathy's theory requires the recognition that both national contexts and their long-term features provide key inputs to the most apprporiate design hierarchies. These two features significantly determine the learning trajectories which any corporation is likely to be able to follow. Therefore, if the appropriateness of a learned design hierarchy becomes lessened, for whatever reason, then enormous transformations are required. Abernathy confirmed Rosenberg's[23] claim that innovation must be examined with reference to the many specific interdependencies of a firm's relationships to suppliers, to dealers, to financial sources and even to institutions of higher education. Abernathy implicitly questioned the universal relevance of the American experience. In the later writings this implicit theme was made explicit in the comparisons between American, European and Japanese practices.

We have sought to demonstrate the practical and theoretical relevance of a comparative and historical approach by showing that the design hierarchies operating in the European contexts were distinct from those found in North America. It is therefore useful to start with a comparison from within the European context. One very illuminating comparison to the SD1 already exists: the case of the Swedish car firm, Volvo. In the same period (1965–85) they introduced enormous innovations in their facilities and work organization, initially at Kalmar, and then used that plant as a key learning experience for design and operation of later plants.[24]

The famous Kalmar plant was both a radical departure in the technology of car assembly and in work organization, whilst also retaining the basic principles of flowline production. In the discussion of Kalmar, too little attention has been given by social scientists to the ways in which the new plant retained best practice policies of production control. The plant was designed and conceived by production engineers to introduce teamwork within a relatively tight framework of time constraints. However, it must be conceded that the interpretation of the flowline for the production of speciality cars was a radical departure for the industry and one which created a second, alternative template for best practice work organization.

The new technology of on-line data control was used to provide the work group with the ability to rectify its own faults.[25] Jonsson[26] shows that the design of the Kalmar plant was the direct outcome of changes in ideology amongst its production engineers and corporate leadership during the 1960s. In other words, the antecedents of change were on the corporate agenda well before the actual changes.

To what extent were the innovations in Volvo attributable to historical and cultural features? Volvo was founded just after the mid-1920s as the protected offspring of another leading Swedish company in the electronics industry.[27] It seems highly probable that Volvo institutionalized both a high degree of science-led engineering expertise as well as many American concepts of how to survive in the automobile industry. The directors of Volvo clearly acknowledge the importance of their visits to America in the formative period 1928–33, and highlight the positive assistance received from American firms. Because of the small home market, it was only possible for a Swedish firm to survive by also developing a strong export market. This was recognized by the directors in their calculations of market size and in choosing the break-even point. It was they who sought out niches in the European and North American markets, thereby implicitly placing Volvo on a design hierarchy which had to incorporate extra-European facets. The rigours of the Swedish climate were paralleled in North America and so car sales were well suited to both markets. Also, labour relations in Sweden were historically dissimilar to those of Britain,[28] such that there were more opportunities for capital and management to take initiatives in work organization and new technology.

Volvo entered the 1970s with a series of imaginative shifts in their design of the car, particularly in its safety features and its suitability for North American climatic variations. Volvo introduced the major design innovation of the post-war era when they designed the assembly line at Kalmar[29] around a palletized system and small group assembly. Since then Volvo have adopted a highly pragmatic approach to total design, being prepared to modify and adapt principles to the specific contexts of the market and the region.[30] Yet, it is quite clear that the Volvo approach to innovation and work organization was strongly based in the same cost conscious attitudes to the commodification of time and space as may be found in Ford and in General Motors or in the leading Japanese firms. The difference is that the internal management specialists developed a distinct skill in the effective design of alternative forms of work organization.

Compared to Volvo, the approach taken on the SD1 project may seem prosaic, even pedestrian. Yet those involved in its creation would argue that the design hierarchy which they implicitly followed for the SD1 and for the factory and its work organization were well suited to the British market and regional contexts. That claim requires some brief amplification. The Solihull factory was innovative in certain respects, especially in the provision of pleasant working conditions and in the creation of safety features. Also, the lines were designed with a capability for having teamwork and for having rectification areas where those teams of workers could repair their own defective workmanship. These team-based forms of work organization had been practised in the region,[31] but neither the employers nor the trade unions were sympathetic to the use of teamwork as a means of intensifying the labour process.

In contrast to Volvo, the design teams for the SD1 factory were more skilled at mechanical innovations than at electronic and electrical innovations. Equally important, the equipment suppliers were unsympathetic to the Kalmar technology. The opposition of SD1 engineers was not dissimilar to that found in much of Europe and in North America at that time, and still found today. Their opposition was based on the argument that the Kalmar technology was unlikely to be found to be appropriate outside Sweden and hence they were unwilling to shift to a technology which was incompatible with the established recipes and which had no obvious relative advantage in cost terms.

The SD1 design engineers had to build buffer stocks into the factory in order to be prepared for the interruptions to supplies which were arising from the suppliers in the region. They knew that it was unlikely that the Solihull site could have been used to build a two-storey factory, even one as elegant as the Kalmar plant.

The SD1 management did not possess the corporate training capacities which Volvo had developed. The principle source of problems for the SD1 was related to the market for speciality cars. The SD1 was never able to compete effectively in the European market where BMW were so successful, nor was it able to penetrate the North American market. The SD1 project was constantly disrupted by uncertainties and indecision in the corporate leadership of BL and the financial collapse of the mid-1970s.

The generalizability of the SD1 case study can now be established. It is sensible to start by taking the least typical features of the SD1. Strategic innovation is most often undertaken by altering only one or two of the three key areas represented by product/process and work organization. Thus, in the Volvo case at Kalmar, the product remained relatively stable whilst radical changes were introduced in facilities and in work organization. Furthermore, enormous alterations of the scope anticipated in the SD1 case are usually preceded by long periods in which corporate managements work through new concepts and explore new modes of operating on a small scale. The example of Volvo illustrates this small-scale experimental approach to radical change. Also, it is clear from Abernathy's reconstruction of the Ford moving assembly line that its introduction was preceded by the development of managerial skills and learning from previous, smaller innovations. Also, the success of the Japanese auto industry has been attributed to their practices of extensive discussion prior to major changes. Comparison of the SD1 case with Volvo and with other international experiences shows that the case study presents in heightened form the high density of routine constraints and demands which innovation involves.

The SD1 project may be regarded as the first step by BL in the development of an international competence. The SD1 programme was the largest financial investment in the British context for forty years. Later projects have included the famous Metro,[32] successor to the never-profitable Mini, and the more recent Maestro and Montego. Most recently, BL has engaged in joint ventures with Honda in the production of a mid-range Rover. Each of these successive projects has been accompanied by public claims that they represent a 'leap' forward in technology and in work organization. The claims made about the Metro are very similar to those made in the early 1970s with respect to the launching of the SD1 concept.

Therefore, it is relevant to explore the degree to which BL has actually managed to develop a design capacity as a total process which is genuinely competitive in the international market. In 1985 it was apparent that BL had neither built up the financial foundation to engage in new strategic innovations, nor had its small market share (under 20 per cent of the British market) provided the basis for developing strong overseas sales. The BL presence in Europe and in North America remains at a fragile level. Can there be a future for small firms like BL, Volvo and BMW?

By the mid-1980s the number of operative car firms in North America had actually increased, whilst in Europe few firms made a substantial profit. In North America the entry of Japanese firms explained the expansion. By this time the search for the world car still seemed as far off as it had in 1970, and analysts like Dan Jones were sceptical about the concept. Also, there was some basis for believing that the optimum size of a car firm might be considerably less than previous estimates. Jones, for example, suggested that for many components there were optimum production runs of around 400,000 and less, compared with nearer to a million in the 1970s. These findings would appear to be good news for small speciality firms like Volvo.

Compared to its European competitors, BL is now very small, only slightly larger than BMW, the speciality car producer. Each holds around 4 per cent of the European market. That market is very unprofitable because of surplus capacity, ferocious competition and the penetration of Japanese imports which hold about 12 per cent. The five largest suppliers (Fiat,

Renault, Ford, General Motors and Volkswagen) have very similar shares and have just under 65 per cent between them.

III Design, new technology and the GM approach

In Chapter 2 the evolving role of technology was approached within the framework suggested by Bell and Kaplinsky.[33] They contended that technology would tend to unfold along three dimensions, each of which was initially autonomous, yet all of which possessed the potential to be inter-linked at the final stage which is now approaching. The automobile industry provides strong support for their perspective which neatly extends Abernathy's model of the life cycle for technological innovation in productive units into the managerial process and hierarchy. Kaplinsky contends that the new information technology will have major impacts on the processes of design, translation and commissioning.

Leading car firms are already gaining competence in the new technologies. This means that novel internal and external relationships will have to be developed. Firms will need to acquire and to institutionalize cognitive skills in software writing as well as in the effective use of the new office-centred technologies. Some of these new requirements can be internalized, possibly by purchasing companies with an established track record. Probably the greatest change for Western companies will be in their relationships to suppliers of components. These relationships must change because the car builder will be dependent upon the research and development skills of the supplier as the means for making full use of computer based design.

Overall, the new technologies will greatly alter the existing division of labour within management by downgrading certain quasi-craft mental skills and upgrading new imaginative skills. If the experiences of other industries (e.g. petrochemicals) provide a guideline, then it is probable that numbers in managerial jobs will be sharply pruned. Also, there are likely to be changes in the internal division of labour amongst managers and the technocrats. For example in the Anglo-Saxon firms where there are strongly-held views about professional expertise and segmentation, there are already clear signs of transformation. There is every indication that corporate leaders are seeking to re-shape the composition of managerial skills and to alter existing, sometimes implicit, lines of demarcation.

The innovations in technology are having impacts in at least four areas of the design and innovation activities of car firms. One future area of application will be the provision of terminals and visual display units at the dealerships, so that customers will have the opportunity to select a package of features for their car (e.g. colour, trim and radio) which can be transmitted instantly to the assembly lines of the chosen manufacturer. The customized car could then be delivered in ten to fourteen days. This form of technological innovation will be the most difficult and the longest to install, yet its implications are enormous. The extension of consumer choice will require refinements in the handling of information at the assembly stage of the car and in the linking of that stage to the previous stages of painting. Only a part of the additional requirements can be incorporated into the new technology. There will be a significant increase in the kinds of cognitive skills required of operators when each car may have to be treated both as part of a large batch and also as a unique product. The second area of application is in the storing of basic scientific information about the composition of all the raw materials and all the components. This information is now used in conjunction with the changing prices of raw materials.

The third area concerns basic data on manufacturing. This includes the capacities of the equipment, the times taken, and the costs. Computer aided manufacturing (CAM) has been heavily developed in the past decade. North American firms have developed data based systems which permit them to estimate a probable future situation. It is already routinely possible to use the data banks on human performance at all stages in car manufacture to have instant comparisons of the different organizational and cost consequences of competing methods of manufacture. Clearly, there is a requirement for reliable data, and this problem has been a focus of attention for all the major car firms which have replaced direct time study methods by various synthetic systems. The North America, French, Swedish and German producers gained this capacity in the early 1970s.

Finally, there has been an enormous explosion in the simulation of the characteristics of the car, including its performance in accidents. Computer based designing improves the previous methods by reducing the length of time needed to test a new idea, whilst simultaneously increasing the chance to explore a wider range of alternative ideas. The length of the designing stage can be reduced in time, possibly by as much as one-quarter. Further, because it is possible to simulate future manufacturing conditions, it is possible to replace the 'rule of thumb' approach to commissioning a new car and a new plant by a more pre-structured approach.

Each of these four developments is exemplified in the existing practices and future intentions of General Motors,[34] who have made a series of moves which, it is claimed, will give them a technology-led advantage over their rivals, especially over the Japanese firms which now hold around one-quarter of the North American market.

A good starting-point for examining these moves is the recent purchase by GM of companies whose skills can be partially ingested into GM. The most prominent purchases are of the third largest software house in the United States (EDS) and the purchase of a specialist electronics firm operating in the defence industry (Hughes Corporation). In each case, the objective of the purchase is selectively to internalize new skills rather than to diversify, although there will be some degree of diversification. Thus, in the case of the software firm, the intention is that their core skills will provide the essential 'scaffolding' of new programmes to exploit the new technology both in design and on the shop floor. Similarly, it is expected that the electronics firm will provide expertise which is complementary to that already held by GM.

GM has also engaged in a joint venture with Toyota by which the

Japanese firm will supply small cars through GM for the American market. GM executives are reported to regard this strategy as a means of maintaining their corporate image in the small car sector whilst simultaneously permitting GM to focus its resources on the new technology for design rather than developing a small car.

In the North American market, GM has massively reorganized its operations to create two large, virtually autonomous divisions, one each for large cars and for small cars. These enormous organizational transformations will be accompanied by a $7 billion investment in the new computer based technologies for design and for manufacturing. This innovation will involve reorganizing the tasks and the structure of work for some 1,200 design experts, of whom 500 hold doctorates. These design experts will spearhead the new design concepts through all stages from the designing to the commissioning and operating of new systems. In this way, GM's leadership seeks to remove segmentation between management and experts. The new design teams will be able to simulate all aspects of future innovation, including work organization and manning. GM claims these changes in technology will reduce the design cycle by six months and the costs of design by a quarter. GM's approach combines the use of technology with a clear vision of the new managerial forms of work organization in which teamwork will take precedence.

The extent of the claims made by GM dwarf those made at the commencement of the SD1 programme. There are two contrasting interpretations of their likelihood of success. The optimists point to GM's steady and calm approach to organizational innovation in the 1970s. Kanter, for example, emphasizes that GM have already acquired a corporate culture appropriate for executing the new programme.[35] Further support arises from Lawrence and Dyer, who emphasize the capacity of major American corporations to adapt to changes in the external environment.[36] In addition, both Wall Street experts and former pessimists about Motor City such as Abernathy all conclude that design is the Achilles' heel of the Japanese industry. Clearly, they do not fear a European invasion! Against this wave of mid-1980s optimism one has to juxtapose the basic thesis about international competition which was introduced at the start of Chapter 2, where attention was given to the retardation debate. The debate has been conventionally about the long-term decline of Britain. However, exponents of the long-term, institutional approach to world history cite the continuing shifts of the new centres of international economy.[37] According to this interpretation, the underlying trends in the automobile industry could be much less favourable for the American industry.

The assessment of these contrasting projections of the future for the American industry and for the GM strategy will hinge on the differences between Ford's institutionalized approach to innovation as revealed by Abernathy and the rather more flexible approach of GM. Also, GM approaches this new situation with enormous financial and organizational capacities. They have an established and extensive programme of corporate training which will play a central role. In that respect, GM approach this major turning-point from a very different point of departure to that which faced the SD1 project.

IV Design and innovation: the total process

What are the principal conclusions which may be drawn from the synthesis of perspectives introduced in Chapter 2 and from their application to the SD1 case study? This section summarizes the main themes of the book, draws attention to the political learning which innovation entails and discusses the role which academic analyses can play in relation to the problem of innovation in the automobile industry.

In Chapter 1 the purpose of the book was established. The aim of the book is to contribute to an emerging perspective which seeks to examine specific enterprises comparatively and longitudinally within the context of international competition in the automobile sector. Our contribution focuses on the capacity of car firms to innovate as a total process. The four core dimensions in this new perspective were identified in Chapter 2 as: the historical, the comparative, the sector and the enterprise. We argued that Abernathy's studies of innovation in the American context provided the single most fruitful point of departure from which to develop these four core dimensions. However, as Abernathy recognized, it was also necessary to incorporate further refinements and extensions.

The comparative dimension of Abernathy required considerable sharpening to develop the implicit evolutionary model which was nesting in his use of the concept of design hierarchy. In order to achieve that clarification of the concept of design hierarchy we chose a striking comparison to Ford by selecting the portfolio of productive units belonging to Rover, a British speciality car manufacturer.

The longitudinal dimension of Abernathy was examined to demonstrate that the design hierarchies which are available to a specific corporation are strongly influenced by the corporate leadership's choice of markets. British car firms neglected Europe, largely failed in North America and preferred the British/'Empire' markets. This was a strategic choice which may be contrasted with that of Volvo, whose leadership chose to learn about the niches in the European market and in North America. The choice of markets is highly consequential because over time it shapes the range of trajectories of evolvement which are open to a specific corporation. The trajectories available to British firms in the British/'Empire' markets became less rewarding and viable to long-run survival than those of continental Europe and of North America. However, even the two wealthy American multinationals found the British and continental European markets very awkward to decode and to dominate. Yet, their presence in the mass production sectors of Europe certainly affected pan-European developments, and still continues to do so (e.g. the Fiat and Ford relationship).

We prised open Abernathy's implicitly longitudinal analysis by introducing the approach of historians to the analysis of a problem (e.g. innovation) 'in time'. We chose the structure–event–structure pespective and the analytically structured narrative pioneered by the Annales School. The enterprise was conceptualized as containing a repertoire of processes which had to be activated in the anticipation of future problems. Processes of innovation were central to our concept of the repertoire. This synthesized perspective was applied to Rover (in Chapter 3) and to the SD1 programme (Chapters 4 and 5). However, the notion of 'event' as a singular, short period of transformation is too dramatic. Rather, what occurs is a pivotal change in a core set of internal relationships which, in due course, trigger further series of changes until the repertoire is reconstituted. The actual directions taken after the initial triggering may be neither as intended nor as anticipated. Also, the members of the enterprise will differ in their capacity to cope with the period of the 'event'. Members of Rover succeeded in the period 1932–4 and after when the new leadership shifted the market choices into the speciality sector. However, it is also possible for an 'event' to precipitate schismatic tendencies, as occurred at Rover in the years after the introduction of the P6 range in the 1960s.

It is agreed that innovation should be understood and practised within a long time perspective. We have argued that the life-cycle perspective should be used with great care. The adoption of a singular birth-to-maturity linear schema can be very deceptive both for those in the auto industry and for analysts of innovation, because there are great problems of interpreting the directions of change, especially in separating turning-points from the normal seasonal variations in customer purchasing. For those working in the auto industry there is a continuous and uncertain process of disaggregating the rhythmic seasonal variations from the deeply hidden secular transformations. For example, Chapter 3 illustrated how, in the 1920s, the corporate leadership of Rover experienced great difficulties in characterizing the changing location of competitive advantage in the British market. The confusion which they experienced parallels the slow response in the 1970s of North American companies when they were faced by the preference of a section of the market for small European and Japanese cars.

When looking back on these periods of corporate uncertainty it is simple to reflect on what might have been. However, the use of counterfactual thinking must always acknowledge that there are periods of great indeterminacy in all sectors of industry. Also, there certainly are chance factors in operation which transform intentions into unintended outcomes.

It was conjectured (in Chapter 2) that corporations would develop highly specific, local forms of cognitive knowledge and skills which would be shaped by the consequences of their choice of markets. Later, in the case study, it became very clear that corporate knowledge is so highly specific and so politically embedded that even nearby productive units in the same firm may find considerable difficulty in translating abstract corporate policies into specific projects.

The auto sector contains a connected array of varied corporations which are increasingly interdependent. Rosenberg's contention, that any focal corporation is embedded in a complex array of interdependencies, proved very helpful. For example, in Britain the capacity of the SD1 design engineers to draw on the Kalmar concept was significantly constrained by the normative frameworks of entrepreneurs in the supply industry.

Design and innovation have been extensively written about in the prescriptive literature, but that literature has often neglected what can be learned from descriptive studies of innovation. One serious defect of the prescriptive literature is the implicit assumption that design and innovation are the sole prerogative of the corporate leadership. The SD1 study reveals the plurality of competing and interdependent sets of employees who are involved. There are multiple and complex relationships. Chapters 3, 4 and 5 have documented the ways in which non-managerial groups are indirectly and directly involved in design and in the implementation of strategies of innovation.

The future of the automobile industry is one of the areas which the new perspective attempts to unravel. This book suggests that there are two appropriate contributions which can be made by academics. The most obvious contribution is in prising open the recipes of the future held by those working in the industry. Those recipes reflect and characterize established practices in the industry. Another contribution is in the development of sophisticated planning and scenario writing. It is in this type of exercise that the perspective on design as a total process can make a very considerable contribution. Neither of these contributions corresponds to the preferred role of the academic in offering law-like scholarly advice.

The recipes used by those working in the industry are the human capital of knowledge on which both the industry and specific firms rely in their everyday actions. The recipes are typically known to competent adults and yet are part of the unspoken, taken-for-granted normative framework which are so difficult to examine reflectively. Until recently the significance of the everyday languages used by organizational members was regarded as unimportant. However, one enduring contribution of Peters and Waterman[38] has been to show how much these langauges are both a strength and a weakness. Languages contain the implicit, specific details by which broad corporate policies can be decoded and transformed into routine actions. Abernathy contributed to the languages of executives in the car industry by demonstrating the importance of the sector life cycle perspective and by showing that recognition must be given to the indeterminacy within which all human actions operate.

Indeterminacy about the future affects the ways in which academics can contribute. The academic advice given to those working in the British auto industry illustrates the problem. In the 1960s and 1970s, when the sector life-cycle model seemed secure, it was then possible for economists to refer to the maturity of the sector and to argue that the British-owned industry was far below the minimum size needed to survive. However, in the 1980s the technological ferment of the past decade, coupled with the publicity surrounding the Japanese methods of production,[39] has introduced a more optimistic tenor into academic contribution to policy analysis. Jones rightly emphasized that the increasing technological ferment is leading to the replacement of established methods of car assembly and is also changing the methods of production used in the component supply industry.[40] These changes are having extensive impacts on all firms in the industry. Jones contends that the changes provide new opportunities for survival because they are accompanied by a reduction in the minimum economic batch size necessary for survival. Therefore, Jones suggests that this 'turning-point' provides the British-owned BL with the opportunity to 'leap-frog' over existing technologies into the new.

Such optimism requires some qualification. There can be little doubt that British Leyland is seeking to come to terms with its own small size and diverse product range, whilst also facing the technological ferment. Also, the commercial linkage between BL and Honda is a major development. Yet, the danger of the economists' prognostications is that they ignore the problems of structural transformation which form the centre-piece of Chapters 3, 4 and 5. It is simply not the case that adaptation to change occurs automatically or by decree. Furthermore, BL is not alone in making adjustments. All the twenty or so surviving car firms are also making their own adjustments to the new situation.

It is at this point that the comparative and historical perspective should be reintroduced. The contemporary manoeuvres of BL should be compared with the parallel shifts of corporate objectives by all the other car firms. Moreover, it is important to examine the degree to which the recent pronoucements of BL with regard to its own future are more soundly based than those which were made in the early 1970s. For this reason the claims about the success of the post-SD1 adjustments need to be seen in the context of the continuing requirement of BL for external funding to cover the design costs of new models. In the case of BL, the grasping of the new opportunities means that the existing body of corporate knowledge has to be 'creatively destroyed' and constructively replaced. It is just this aspect which GM is addressing with such intensity. One wonders, therefore, whether BL can mount the organizational programme of adjustment which the technological ferment presents.

The design process is a matter of strategic innovation, and strategic innovation with large degrees of uncertainty and indeterminacy. There are multiple opportunities to shift directions. In such a process the 'design space' is not occupied solely and unilaterally by management; indeed, the process becomes an opportunity for many interested groups to achieve a variety of ends. These may include the chance to advance their status, to re-shape power relations, or selectively to interpret major corporate policy intentions. Unintended consequences abound and accumulate. The very operation of context, struggle and conflict amongst those with access to the design process may fracture and fragment that process. It is just as likely that intra-management contests will cause fracturing as any which are generated from the frontier of control between management and labour. Indeed, labour may play, as was the case in the SD1 project, an important constructive role, both indirectly by filling the gaps not covered in designing, and in sharing in the politicking.

Design as a total process cannot be isolated within the enterprise. There are mediating forces which arise from the market-place, from the state, from regional factors and from the actions of competitors. To study the design process is to begin the complex task of understanding innovation.

Notes

1. W. J. Abernathy, *The Productivity Dilemma: Roadblock to Innovation in the Automobile Industry*, Baltimore, 1978.
2. W. J. Abernathy and K. B. Clark, *Industrial Renaissance: Producing a Competitive Future for America*, Boston, 1983.
3. P. A. Clark, *Anglo-American Patterns of Commercial and Industrial Innovation*, 1986 (forthcoming).
4. C. Brookeman, *American Culture and Society since the 1930s*, 1985.
5. Clark, op. cit.
6. N. Rosenberg, 'Learning by Using', in his *Inside the Blackbox: Technology and Economics*, 1982.
7. C. Perrow, *Organizational Analysis*, 1970.
8. G. K. Pralahad and Y. L. Doz, 'Managing Managers: The Work of Top Management', in J. G. Hunt, D-M. Hosking, C. A. Schrieshiem and R. Stewart, *Leaders and Managers: International Perspectives on Managerial Behaviour and Leadership*, 1984, pp. 336–74.
9. W. Lewchuk, 'The British Motor Industry, 1896–1982. The Roots of Decline', mimeo., Harvard University, 1983.
10. G. Nicol, *Volvo: Great Car Series*, 1975.
11. Specific details can be found in 'Europe's carmakers splutter on subsidies', *The Economist*, 12 January 1985, pp. 59–60. The background analysis is to be found in S. Sinclair, *The World Car: The Future of the Automobile Industry*, 1983.
12. Clark, op. cit.
13. J. Child, M. Fores, I. Glover and P. Lawrence, 'A Price to Pay? Professionalization and Work Organization in Britain and West Germany', *Sociology*, **17**, 1, 1983, pp. 63–78.
14. J. G. March and H. A. Simon, *Organizations*, New York, 1958.
15. The journalist signalled the forthcoming closure of the SD1 plant in a closely argued series of articles. See G. Jones, C. Walder and N. Freedman, 'The Road to Ruin' in three parts appearing on 8, 9 and 10 June 1981 under the headlines: 'Decline and Fall of the Rover Empire', 'Anarchy Reigns—Courtesy of the Bosses' and 'Rot that Wrecked the Dream Machine'.
16. Pralahad and Doz, op. cit.
17. M. Earl, *The Economic Imagination*, 1985.
18. Abernathy, 1978, op. cit.
19. Abernathy and Clark, op. cit.
20. A. M. Pettigrew, *The Awakening Giant: Continuity and Change in Imperial Chemical Industries*, 1985.
21. T. J. Peters and R. H. Waterman, *In Search of Excellence: Lessons from America's Best Run Companies*, 1982; R. Whipp, 'Management, Design and Industrial Relations in the British Auto Industry' *Industrial Relations Journal*, 1986.
22. R. M. Kanter, *The Change Masters: Corporate Entrepreneurs at Work*, 1983. See also P. A. Technology (P. A. Technology, 1985), pp. 1–7 and *passim*.
23. The concept of interdependence is dealt with in N. Rosenberg, 'Technological

Change in the Machine Tool Industry, 1840–1910', in his *Perspectives on Technology*, 1976.

24. B. Jonsson, 'Corporate Strategy for People at Work—the Volvo Experience', mimeo., AB Volvo, 1981; S. Aguren et al., *Volvo Kalmar Revisited: Ten Years of Experience*, Stockholm, 1984.

25. See the discussion in J. R. Galbraith, *Organization Design*, 1977.

26. Jonsson, op. cit.

27. Nicol, op. cit.

28. G. Ingham, *Strikes and Industrial Conflict: Britain and Scandinavia*, 1974.

29. Jonsson, op. cit.

30. See Auguren et al., op. cit.

31. See A. L. Friedman, *Industry and Labour: Class Struggle at Work and Monopoly Capitalism*, 1977; S. Melman, *Decision Making and Productivity*, 1958.

32. P. Willman and G. Winch, *Innovation and Management Control: Labour Relations at BL Cars*, 1985.

33. R. Kaplinsky, *Automation: The Technology and Society*, 1984.

34. Sinclair, op. cit., p. 73.

35. Kanter, op. cit.

36. P. R. Lawrence and D. Dyer, *Renewing American Industry*, 1982.

37. F. Braudel, *The Perspective of the World*, 1984.

38. Peters and Waterman, op. cit.

39. R. J. Schonberger, *Japanese Manufacturing Techniques: Nine Hidden Lessons in Simplicity*, 1982.

40. D. T. Jones, *Maturity and Crisis in the European Car Industry: Structural Change and Public Policy*, 1981.

Index

220   Index